Romans at War

ROMANS AT WAR

The Roman Military in the Republic and Empire

Simon Elliott

CASEMATE
Oxford & Philadelphia

Published in Great Britain and the United States of America in 2020 by
CASEMATE PUBLISHERS
The Old Music Hall, 106–108 Cowley Road., Oxford, OX4 1JE, UK
and
1950 Lawrence Road, Havertown, PA 19083, USA

© Casemate Publishers

Hardcover Edition: ISBN 978-1-61200-885-1
Digital Edition: ISBN 978-1-61200-886-8

A CIP record for this book is available from the British Library

Printed and bound in Malta by Melita Press

For a complete list of Casemate titles, please contact:

CASEMATE PUBLISHERS (UK)
Telephone (01865) 241249
Email: casemate-uk@casematepublishers.co.uk
www.casematepublishers.co.uk

CASEMATE PUBLISHERS (US)
Telephone (610) 853-9131
Fax (610) 853-9146
Email: casemate@casematepublishers.com
www.casematepublishers.com

All images are from author's collection, unless stated otherwise.
Some of the material in this book previously appeared in the Casemate Short History series, *Julius Caesar: Rome's Greatest Warlord* (2019) and *Roman Legionaries: Soldiers of Empire* (2018)

Front cover: Late Roman legionaries or *auxilia palatina* preparing to receive an attack. Many recruits in the later Roman military formations were their former German and Gothic opponents. (Graham Sumner)

Back cover: Roman *equites* at the charge. (Graham Sumner)

Contents

The *cursus honorum*

The *cursus honorum* was the set career path for aristocratic Roman men of the senatorial class. During the last two centuries of the Roman Republic, this was generally as follows:

- Military service.

- *Quaestor*, the lowest ranked magistrate – minimum age 30 years old.

- *Aedile* or tribune, a mid-ranking magistrate, for example those responsible for public buildings/ festivals – minimum age 37 years old.

- Praetor, a senior elected magistrate – minimum age 40 years old.

- Consulship, one of the two senior magistrates in Rome. Once at this level the noble could be considered for a Provincial Governorship – minimum age 43 years old.

they came from Italy. They enjoyed the widest range of protections and privileges as defined by the Roman state, and as such could travel the breadth of the Empire pursuing their personal and professional ambitions. Roman women had a limited type of citizenship and were not allowed to vote or stand for public or civil office. Freemen born outside of Italy in the imperial provinces were called *peregrini* (literally 'one from abroad') until Caracalla's AD 212 *constitutio Antoniniana* (edict of Antonius) that made all freemen of the Empire citizens. As such, in the 1st and 2nd centuries AD *peregrini* made up the vast majority of the Empire's inhabitants. Further down the social ladder one then had freedmen, former slaves who had been manumitted by their masters either through earning enough money to buy their freedom or for good service. Once free these former slaves often remained with the wider family of their former owner, the *pater familias* (head of family), frequently taking their name in some way. Providing the correct process of manumission was followed, freedmen could become citizens/*peregrini*, though with fewer civic rights than a freeman including not being

able to stand for the vast number of public offices. Their children were freemen. Many freedmen became highly successful, and given they were not allowed to stand for public office found other ways to celebrate their lives. A common example was the provision of monumentalised funerary monuments, a well-known example being that of the baker Marcus Vergilius Eurysaces in Rome. Meanwhile, at the bottom of society were slaves.

In terms of chronology, this book covers three specific phases of the Roman military establishment. The first is that of the Roman Republic, this dating from the overthrow of the Etrusco-Roman King Tarquin the Proud in 509 BC through to the accession of Augustus as the first emperor. This is dated to 27 BC when, as Octavian, the Senate first acknowledged him as emperor. From that time, we talk of the Principate phase of Empire. This lasted until AD 284 with the accession of Diocletian and the end of the 'Crisis of the 3rd Century'. After this time, we talk of the Dominate Empire instead. The reasoning behind the differential naming of the early and later Roman Empire is fully detailed in Chapter 3. Broadly, the book concludes chronologically with

Senatorial provinces, early 1st century AD

- Hispanica Baetica in southern Spain

- Gallia Narbonensis in southern France

- Corsica et Sardinia

- Africa Proconsularis in North Africa

- Cyrenaica et Creta

- Epirus

- Macedonia

- Achaia

- Asia in western Anatolia

- Bithynia et Pontus

(*opposite*)
Principate auxiliary *equites* wearing sports helmets used when displaying their prowess in exhibitions of their skills. (Graham Sumner)

the fall of the Empire in the west in AD 476 with the abdication of Romulus Augustulus.

Finally, much of this work focuses on the Roman military of the Principate Empire. At this time the Empire was divided into provinces and an understanding of these is important. The word itself provides interesting insight into the Roman attitude to its Empire, the Latin *provincia* referencing land 'for conquering'. There were actually two kinds of province in the Principate Roman Empire. These were senatorial provinces left to the Senate to administer, whose governors were officially called proconsuls and remained in post for a year, and imperial provinces retained under the supervision of the emperor. The emperor personally chose the governors for these, they often being styled *legati Augusti pro praetor* to officially mark them out as deputies of the emperor. Senatorial provinces tended to be those deep within the Empire where less trouble was expected.

In this work I will specifically use proconsul to reference the governor of these senatorial provinces, and governor to reference this position in an imperial province.

Roman military spearheads found by Museum of London Archaeology when excavating the Bloomberg London building on the Walbrook in London. Given the location is close to the site of the Governor's Palace, they could be associated with his guard troops.

Timeline

This timeline of key events in the Roman Republic and Empire provides a framework for this study of the Roman military. Given many of the examples during the Principate phase of Empire are set in Britain, the timeline particularly focuses on events there.

Date	Event
579 BC	Accession of Servius Tullius
534 BC	Accession of Tarquin the Proud as king in Rome
509 BC	Overthrow of Tarquin the Proud, Roman Republic begins
494 BC	First Secession of the Plebs
390 BC	Battle of Allia, sack of Rome
280 BC	Beginning of the Pyrrhic War in Italy
264 BC	Beginning of the First Punic War
218 BC	Beginning of the Second Punic War, battle of the Trebia
217 BC	Battle of Lake Trasimene
216 BC	Battle of Cannae
214 BC	Beginning of First Macedonian War
202 BC	Battle of Zama
200 BC	Beginning of Second Macedonian War
197 BC	Battle of Cynoscephalai
192 BC	Beginning of Roman–Seleucid War
190 BC	Battle of Magnesia
172 BC	Beginning of Third Macedonian War
168 BC	Battle of Pydna
150 BC	Beginning of Fourth Macedonian War

(*opposite*)
Badly damaged Etruscan helmet, the price of standing up to the might of Rome, even in the early Republican period.

149 BC	Beginning of Third Punic War
146 BC	Sackings of Carthage and Corinth
113 BC	Beginning of the Cimbrian War
107 BC	Marius elected consul for the first time
100 BC	Gaius Julius Caesar born
88 BC	Sulla's First Civil War
86 BC	Marius dies
83 BC	Sulla's Second Civil War
82 BC	Sulla becomes dictator, Caesar flees to Asia to join the military
78 BC	Sulla dies, Caesar returns to Rome
75 BC	Caesar captured by Cilician pirates while travelling to Rhodes
73 BC	Caesar appointed as one of the 15 pontiffs serving the *Pontifex Maximus*, returns to Rome
63 BC	Caesar elected *Pontifex Maximus*
62 BC	Caesar is a praetor, then proconsul in Hispania Ulterior
60 BC	First Triumvirate
59 BC	Caesar is consul
58 BC	Beginning of Caesar's Gallic Wars. He campaigns against the Helvetii and Suebi
57 BC	Caesar campaigns against the Belgae
56 BC	Conference of Lucca, campaign against the Veneti, battle of Morbihan
55 BC	Massacre of the Usipetes and Tencteri, Caesar's first incursion to Britain
54 BC	Caesar's second incursion to Britain
53 BC	Rebellion of the Eburones and Nervii tribes in Gaul. Death of Crassus at the battle of Carrhae against the Parthians
52 BC	Gallic revolt under Vercingetorix, siege of Alesia. End of the Gallic Wars
49 BC	Caesar crosses the Rubicon river with *legio XIII*. Spanish campaign against the *optimates*
48 BC	Battle of Pharsalus, death of Pompey in Egypt
47 BC	Alexandrian War, Caesar campaigns against Pharnaces II
46 BC	Battle of Thapsus, quadruple triumph in Rome
45 BC	Battle of Munda
44 BC	Caesar appointed dictator for life, assassinated on the Ides of March

42 BC	Battle of Philippi
31 BC	Battle of Actium
27 BC	Roman conquest of northern Spain begins. Octavian becomes Augustus. Beginning of the Principate Empire
AD 9	Varus's three legions, together with nine auxiliary units, destroyed in Teutoburg Forest, Germany by the Cherusci tribe and others led by Arminius
AD 40	Caligula's planned invasion of Britain aborted
AD 43	The third, and successful, Roman invasion of Britain under Emperor Claudius, with the legionaries, auxiliaries and naval *milites* commanded by Aulus Plautius. Province of Britannia established
AD 44	Future Emperor Vespasian successfully campaigns in the south-west of Britain, leading *legio II Augusta*
AD 47	Vespasian successfully concludes his campaign to conquer the south-west of Britain, returning to Rome with Plautius. The new governor Publius Ostorius Scapula campaigns in north Wales, also subduing the first revolt by Iceni tribe in the north of East Anglia

Roman legionary of the late 2nd century AD. Note a *hasta* has replaced the *pilum*. Figure painted by the author.

AD 48	The first revolt of the Brigantes tribe in northern Britain
AD 49	A *coloniae* for veterans founded at Colchester, with the *legio XX Valeria Victrix* moving to Gloucester. Scapula campaigns in Wales
AD 50	Construction begins of first forum in the newly founded city of London
AD 51	The leader of the British resistance to Roman rule, Caratacus, is captured by the Romans after being handed over by the Brigantian Queen, Cartimandua. The Silures tribe in southern Wales is pacified by Governor Didius Gallus
AD 52	Claudius dies, Nero becomes the emperor
AD 54	Quintus Veranius becomes the governor in Britain, dying in office. Rome intervenes in favour of Queen Cartimandua in a dispute over the leadership of the Brigantes
AD 57	Gaius Suetonius Paulinus becomes the governor of Britain
AD 58	The initial subjugation of the Druids in the far west, and the initial invasion of Anglesey by the governor Gaius Suetonius Paulinus. This campaign is cut short by the Boudiccan revolt
AD 59/ 60	The Boudiccan revolt takes place, featuring the destruction of Colchester, St Albans and London. The revolt is defeated by Paulinus, followed by the suicide of Boudicca
AD 60/61	Publius Petronius Turpilianus becomes the governor, followed by Marcus Trebellius Maximus
AD 61/ 63	First 'Great' Jewish Revolt
AD 66	Nero is overthrown, with Galba becoming the emperor
AD 68	The Year of Four Emperors. Vespasian is the ultimate victor and becomes emperor. In Britain Cartimandua, Queen of the Brigantes and ally of Rome, is overthrown by former husband Venutius. Marcus Vettius Bolanus is the new governor
AD 69	The *Classis Britannica* (regional navy in Britain) is named for the first time in the context of the Batavian Revolt of Civilis on the River Rhine
AD 70	Fall of Jerusalem to Titus
AD 71	Vespasian orders the new British governor Quintus Petilius Cerialis to campaign in the north of Britain. The Brigantes are defeated, with Venutius captured and killed
AD 74	Sextus Julius Frontinus is appointed as the new governor in Britain. Further campaigning in Wales follows, and Chester is founded
AD 77	Gnaeus Julius Agricola becomes the new governor in Britain. Wales and western Britain are finally conquered
AD 78	Agricola consolidates the Roman control of Brigantian territory, and then begins planning his campaign in the far north of the islands of Britain
AD 79	Agricola begins his campaign to subdue the whole of the north of Britain, including Scotland. Vespasian dies and is replaced by his son Titus
AD 80	Agricola continues his campaigning in Scotland
AD 81	The death of Titus who is succeeded by his younger brother Domitian

AD 82	Further campaigning by Agricola in Scotland
AD 83	Agricola brings the combined Caledonian tribes to battle at Mons Graupius in the Grampians, south of the Moray Firth (possibly even further north). After his victory the *Classis Britannica* circumnavigates northern Scotland. The conquest of Britain is declared 'complete', with construction then beginning of a monumental arch at Richborough in modern Kent to commemorate the event
AD 87	Roman troops are withdrawn from the far north of Britain because of pressures elsewhere in the Empire. The legionary fortress of Inchtuthill in Tayside is abandoned
AD 90	Lincoln becomes a *colonia*
AD 96	Domitian is assassinated, this event bringing to an end the Flavian dynasty. He is succeeded by Nerva. Gloucester becomes a *colonia*

Trajan, one of the great warrior emperors of the Principate Roman Empire. (Livius.org/Jona Lendering)

AD 98	The death of Nerva, who is succeeded by Trajan. In Britain, Publius Metilius Nepos is the new governor, followed by Titus Avidius Quietus
AD 100	Trajan orders the full withdrawal of Roman troops from Scotland, and then establishes a new frontier along the Solway Firth–Tyne line. All of the defences north of this line are abandoned by AD 105
AD 101	Beginning of Trajan's first Dacian campaign
AD 103	Lucius Neratius Marcellus is the new governor
AD 105	The beginning of Trajan's second Dacian campaign
AD 115	The beginning of Trajan's campaign against Parthia. Beginning of the Second Jewish Revolt. Marcus Atilius Bradua is the new governor in Britain
AD 117	The death of Trajan and succession of Hadrian. This coincides with major disturbances in the north of the province of Britannia
AD 122	Emperor Hadrian visits Britain, initiating the construction of Hadrian's Wall on the Solway Firth–Tyne line. Aulus Platorius Nepos is the new governor, arriving with the emperor and being tasked with the wall's construction
AD 132	The beginning of the Third 'bar Kokhba' Jewish Revolt
AD 138	The death of Hadrian and succession of Antoninus Pius. Quintus Lollius Urbicus is the new governor in Britain
AD 142	Military engagements north of Hadrian's Wall continue under Quintus Lollius Urbicus, on the orders of Antoninus Pius, in an attempt to subdue the tribes of northern Britain and southern Scotland, the latter region being conquered again. Construction then begins of the Antonine Wall along Clyde–Forth line as a new northern frontier
AD 145	Gnaeus Papirus Aelianus is the new governor in Britain
AD 155	Central St Albans is destroyed by a major fire
AD 157	Gnaeus Julius Verus is the new governor in Britain
AD 161	Emperor Antoninus Pius dies and is succeeded by Marcus Aurelius and Lucius Verus. Beginning of the Roman–Parthian War
AD 162	Marcus Statius Priscuss is the new governor of Britain, followed by Sextus Calpurnius Agricola. The Antonine Wall is evacuated, with the northern border once again moving south to the line of Hadrian's Wall
AD 166	Beginning of the Marcomannic Wars
AD 169	Death of Lucius Verus. More trouble in northern Britain
AD 174	Caerellius is the new governor in Britain
AD 175	5,500 Sarmatian cavalry are sent to Britain, perhaps because of a military emergency
AD 178	Ulpius Marcellus is the new governor in Britain
AD 180	Marcus Aurelius dies and is replaced by Commodus
AD 182	The tribes either side of Hadrian's Wall start raiding along and across the border, with Roman troops responding with counter-raids. Towns far to the south of the

wall begin constructing the first earth-and-timber defence circuits, indicating that tribal raiding penetrated far into the province

AD 184	Commodus receives his seventh acclamation as Imperator, taking the title Britannicus indicating some kind of military victory in the province
AD 185	Some 1,500 picked troops from Britain travel to Rome with a petition for the Emperor Commodus. They ask that he dismisses the Praetorian prefect Perennis. The new governor in Britain is future Emperor Publius Helvius Pertinax
AD 191/192	Decimus Clodius Albinus becomes the new governor in Britain
AD 193	The 'Year of the Five Emperors', with Septimius Severus emerging as the ultimate victor
AD 196	British governor Albinus usurps, invades Gaul and is proclaimed emperor by the legions from Britain and Spain
AD 197	Albinus is defeated by Severus at the closely fought battle of Lugdunum (modern Lyon) and is killed. Planning begins to divide the province of Britain into two, Britannia Superior and Britannia Inferior. Virius Lupus is the new governor in Britain
AD 197/198	Severus sends military commissioners to Britain aiming to quickly suppress the remaining supporters of Albinus. Roman troops rebuild parts of Hadrian's Wall (some of which may have actually been destroyed) and other parts of the northern defences that had been damaged by an increase in tribal raiding after Albinus had travelled to Gaul with his troops. Construction also starts at this time of the land walls of London. Severus begins his reforms of the military, while he himself campaigns in Parthia for two years
AD 202	Severus campaigns in North Africa. Gaius Valerius Pudens is the new governor in Britain
AD 205	Lucius Alfenus Senecio is the new governor in Britain
AD 207	News arrives in Rome from Britain (perhaps the letter from Senecio detailed by Herodian) asking Severus for urgent assistance in the form of the emperor himself or more troops. He responds with both
AD 208	Severus arrives in Britain with the imperial household and a huge army, planning a major campaign against the Maeatae and Caledonian tribal confederations north of Hadrian's Wall. St Alban is martyred
AD 209	The first Severan campaign in Scotland begins
AD 210	The second Severan campaign in Scotland begins, led by Caracalla as the emperor is too ill to actively participate. Genocide ordered by Severus
AD 211	Severus dies at York, with his sons Caracalla and Geta becoming joint emperors. The campaign in the north of Britain is suspended with the brothers returning to Rome. Caracalla murders Geta. Britain is later officially divided into two provinces, Britannia Superior and Britannia Inferior
AD 216	Marcus Antonius Gordianus is the new governor of Britannia Inferior
AD 222	Tiberius Julius Pollienus Auspex is the new governor of Britannia Superior
AD 223	Claudius Xenophon is the new governor of Britannia Inferior
AD 224	Ardashir I of Persia defeats his Parthian overlords over a two-year period, bringing

the Sassanid Persian Empire into being. Rome now has a fully symmetrical threat on her eastern border

AD 225	Maximus is the new governor of Britannia Inferior
AD 226	Calvisius Rufus becomes the new governor of Britannia Inferior, being followed by Valerius Crescens and then by Claudius Appelinus
AD 235	Assassination of Severus Alexander, ending the Severan dynasty and beginning the 'Crisis of the 3rd Century'. Maximinus Thrax becomes emperor
AD 237	Tuccianus becomes the new governor of Britannia Inferior
AD 238	Marcus Martiannius Pulcher becomes the new governor of Britannia Superior. Maecilius Fuscus becomes the new governor of Britannia Inferior, quickly followed by Egnatius Lucilianus
AD 242	Nonius Philippus becomes the new governor of Britannia Inferior
AD 244	Aemilianus becomes the new governor of Britannia Inferior
AD 249	The last potential mention of the *Classis Britannica*, on epigraphy in Arles commemorating Saturninus, ex-captain in the British Fleet
AD 250	Irish raiding takes place along the west coast, with Germanic raiding along the east coast
AD 253	Desticius Juba becomes the new governor of Britannia Superior
AD 260	The 'Gallic Empire' is declared by Postumus, this splitting Britain, Gaul and Spain away from the Empire for 14 years
AD 262	Octavius Sabinus becomes the new governor of Britannia Inferior
AD 268	Postumus is murdered by his own troops
AD 274	Emperor Aurelian defeats the 'Gallic Empire', with Britain, Gaul and Spain then rejoining the Empire.
AD 277	Vandals and Burgundian mercenaries are settled in Britain, with Victorinus defeating a British usurpation.
AD 284	Diocletian becomes the emperor, initiating the Diocletianic reforms of the military. The end of the 'Crisis of the 3rd Century' and beginning of the Dominate phase of Empire
AD 286	The usurpation of Carausius, which splits Britain and northern Gaul away from the Empire
AD 293	The western caesar Constantius Chlorus recaptures northern Gaul from Carausius who is then assassinated by Allectus, the latter then taking over control from his former master in Britain
AD 296	The fourth Roman invasion of Britain, with Constantius Chlorus invading to defeat Allectus, the western caesar then returning the two provinces to the Empire. Around this time Britain is declared a diocese as part of the Diocletianic Reformation, with the four provinces of Maxima Caesariensis, Britannia Prima, Flavia Caesariensis and Britannia Secunda
AD 297	The first use of the term Pict to describe the confederation of tribes in northern Scotland

AD 306	Constantius Chlorus campaigns in the north of Britain, then dies in York. His son Constantine is proclaimed emperor by the legionaries of *legio VI Victrix*
AD 312	Constantine becomes the sole emperor in the west after winning the battle of Milvian Bridge against Maxentius, with his military reforms beginning around this time
AD 314	Constantine and Licinius agree to end the persecution of Christians, while three British bishops attend the Council of Bishops at Arles
AD 324	Constantine becomes the sole emperor of the whole Empire
AD 325	The first mention of *comitatenses* field army troops
AD 337	Constantine prepares for war with Sassanid Persia but falls ill in Nicomedia and dies
AD 343	Emperor Constans makes a surprise winter crossing of the English Channel to Britain following the defeat of his brother Constantine II three years earlier, possibly in the context of a military emergency in the north of the diocese
AD 350	The military leader Magnentius (born in Britain) usurps power in Gaul, with the provinces in Britain and Spain quickly supporting him, and ultimately the whole of the Western Empire
AD 351	Magnentius is defeated by eastern Emperor Constantius II at the battle of Mursa Major, and then retreats to Gaul. Magnentius is defeated again at the battle of Mons Seleucus, after which he commits suicide. Constantius II sends Paul 'the chain' to Britain to purge the aristocracy after the revolt of Magnentius. The *vicarius* of the diocese, Martinus, commits suicide rather than face trial
AD 356	Emperor Julian builds a new fleet of 600 to 800 ships to transport grain from Britain to feed his Rhine army
AD 357	The battle of Strasbourg, where Julian defeats the Alamanni
AD 358	Alypius becomes the new *vicarius* of the diocese
AD 359	British bishops attend the Council of Rimini.
AD 367	Civilis becomes the new vicarius of the diocese. The 'Great Conspiracy' of Picts, Attecotti, Irish and Germanic raiders attacks Britain, overwhelming the frontier defences. Comes Theodosius arrives in Britain to suppress the revolt and restore order, with Magnus Maximus serving under him. The northern frontier is then rebuilt yet again
AD 378	The battle of Adrianople takes place where the eastern armies of Emperor Valens are defeated by the Gothic army of Fritigern. This is a defeat the Empire struggles to recover from
AD 383	Magnus Maximus (now the British military commander, and possibly the *vicarius* of the diocese) campaigns against Pictish and Irish raiders. He is proclaimed the emperor by his troops, then invading Gaul which declares its support for him, as does Spain
AD 387	Magnus Maximus invades Italy where he ousts Emperor Valentinian II
AD 388	Magnus Maximus is defeated and executed by Theodosius I, emperor in the east
AD 391	Theodosius I bans pagan worship, although the practice still continues in Britain

AD 395	Chrysanthus becomes the new *vicarius* of the diocese
AD 400	The western Empire *magister militum* Stilicho campaigns in Britain and defeats Pictish, Irish and Germanic raiders. He then withdraws many troops from the diocese to help defend Italy against the Goths, with Britain left dangerously exposed to further attack. Victorinus becomes the new *vicarius*
AD 402	The last import of base coins into Britain takes place
AD 405	Heavy Irish raiding on the south-western coast of Britain occurs, this being a possible date for the capture of St Patrick
AD 406	Vandals, Burgundians, Alans, Franks and Suevi overrun the *limes Germanicus* near Mainz and then invade Gaul
AD 407	In swift succession the military in Britain declare Marcus, then Gratian and finally Constantine III to be the emperor. The latter crosses to Gaul with the remaining *comitatenses* from Britain, setting up his capital at Arles. The diocese now only has the *limitanei* (border troops) to defend its frontiers
AD 409	The British aristocracy throw out their Roman administrators, with the diocese cut adrift from the remaining parts of the Western Empire
AD 410	Western Emperor Honorius allegedly tells the Britons to look to their own defences (note here the debate about the accuracy of this report)
AD 411	Constantine III is captured and executed on the orders of Honorius
AD 429	St Germanus visits Britain to debate with the Pelagian Christians there. Further conflict takes place with Pictish and Irish raiders
AD 430	The effective end of coin use in Britain
AD 451	The *magister militum* in the west, Flavius Aetius, defeats Attila the Hun at the battle of the Catalaunian Plains
AD 454	The Britons appeal to Aetius by letter in 'the groans of the Britons' request for military assistance, but no troops are available to help at this time
AD 476	The last western Emperor Romulus Augustulus is deposed by his *magister militum* Flavius Odaocer. The end of the Roman Empire in the west

(*opposite*)
The 'mad and bad' emperor
Commodus, dressed as
Hercules with whom
he had a major fixation.
Commodus' assassination
on New Year's Eve AD 192/
AD 193 ushered in the
'Year of the Five Emperors'
which saw Septimius
Severus the eventual victor.
(Livius.org/Jona Lendering)

Glossary

Aedile	A mid-ranking magistrate.
Aeneid	The epic Latin poem written by Virgil which tells the story of the Trojan leader Aeneas and his travels to Italy. His tale became one of the classic creation stories of the Romans.
Ala	A unit of organization for Roman cavalry.
Angon	An armour-piercing javelin.
Auxilia	Regular mounted and foot soldiers who supported the legionaries of the Roman Empire, and who later under the Dominate phase of Empire went on to equal (and in some cases surpass) them in martial prowess. They often operated independently.
Auxilia sagittarri	Specialist bow-armed *auxilia*.
Ballistarii	Artillery crew in late Roman armies.
Barritus	A Germanic battle cry.
Bebrae	A heavy throwing spear used by the Marcomanni.
Bireme	A war galley with two banks of oars. In the Roman Empire they became the principal warship, and were often called *liburnae*.
Buccellarii	The mercenary bodyguards of late Roman leaders.
Caligae	The classic Roman hobnailed sandal, a vital component of the Roman soldier's kit.
Castra Praetoria	The Praetorian Guard barracks in Rome.
Centurion	The key officer in the Roman legions and *auxilia* units, named after the century of troops they commanded.
Cives Romani	A Roman citizen who originated in Italy.
Civitas **capital**	A 'county town' capital of a region within a Roman province.
Cohortes urbanae	The urban cohorts were the equivalent of modern *gendarmerie* or armed police, created by Augustus to provide a policing function in major Roman cities and towns.
Coloniae	A Roman town for settled veteran soldiers.
Comitatenses	Units in the field armies of the late Roman Empire.
Comitatius praesentalis	A late Roman field army commanded by the emperor in person.
Consilium Principis	The senior advisory body giving counsel to a Roman emperor.
Consul	The title given to one of the two most senior magistrates in the Roman Republic, and later remaining a key title in the Principate and Dominate Empires.

Contos	Long cavalry lance.
'Crisis of the 3rd Century'	The latest phase of the Roman Principate Empire between the assassination of Severus Alexander in AD 235 and the accession of Diocletian in AD 284. This was a time of a great stress within the Empire when it was beset by enemy aggression across its wide frontiers, civil war, economic dislocation and plague.
Cuneus	Swine head formation used by Roman legionaries and *auxilia*.
Cura annonae	The official grain supply to the citizens of Rome.
Curial	The lowest class of aristocrats in Roman society.
Diocese	The largest geographical unit of organization in the Dominate Roman Empire.
Diocletianic Reformation	The wide-ranging reforms of the Dominate Empire by the emperor Diocletian.
Dominate	The later chronological phase of the Roman Empire, from the accession of Diocletian in AD 284 through to the fall of the Empire in the west in AD 476.
Dominus	Meaning Lord, the word that gave the Dominate phase of empire its name.
Emperor	The dictatorial ruler of the Roman Empire from 27 BC when the Senate first styled Octavian as Augustus.
Equestrian	The second highest class of aristocrats in Roman society.
Equites	Roman cavalry.
Equites Cataphractarii	Heavily armoured cataphract shock cavalry, with both man and horse wearing armour.
Equites clibanarii	Armoured shock cavalry.
Equites contariorum	Lance-armed shock cavalry.
Equites dalmatae	Javelin-armed skirmishing cavalry.
Equites illyriciani	Javelin-armed skirmishing cavalry.
Equites mauri	Javelin-armed skirmishing cavalry.
Equites sagittarii	Bow-armed skirmishing cavalry.
Equites scutarii	Guard cavalry.
Equites singulares Augusti	Imperial guard cavalry.
Evocatii Augusti	Re-enlisted Praetorian guardsmen.
Fabricae	State-owned manufactories making weapons and equipment for the Roman military.
Falx	A two-handed slashing weapon used by Bastarnae and Dacian warriors.
Fiscus	The Imperial treasury.

Foederates	Bands and units of Germanic and Gothic warriors fighting in late Roman armies.
Forum Romanum	The political centre of day-to-day life in Rome, both during the Republic and Empire.
Framea	Early German throwing spear.
Francisca	A heavy throwing axe used as a shock weapon by Frankish warriors.
Freeman	A man or woman who had never been a slave.
Freedman	A man or woman who was a manumitted slave.
Galley	A key form of maritime transport in the ancient world, the galley featured oars along its length to provide the power to propel the vessel through the water in addition to, or instead of, a sail.
Gladius Hispaniensis	The iconic infantry sword used by Roman legionaries from the mid-Republic through to the later Principate phase of Empire.
Governor	The senior military and legal official in charge of a Roman Imperial province. Appointed by the emperor.
Greave	A band of armour wrapped around the lower leg.
Hasta	A Roman spear.
Laeti	Entire communities of Germanic and Gothic warriors allowed to settle within the Empire
Lanciarii	A lighter type of legionary able to skirmish with javelins.
Lancea	Auxiliary foot spear.
Legate	A senior Roman military officer.
Legion	The formal name given to the large specific formations of Roman front line warriors.
Legionary	The name given to warriors who served in the legions.
Legionary fortress	The largest type of permanent Roman military base, designed to house an entire legion.
Liburnae	A name used to describe Roman *bireme* war galleys of the Empire.
Limitanei	Units of border troops in the late Roman army.
Litoris Saxonici per Britanniam	Count of the Saxon Shore.
Lorica hamata	A chainmail hauberk.
Lorica plumata	Cataphract armour covering both rider and horse.
Lorica segmentata	A cuirass made from bands and hoops of articulated iron armour.
Lorica squamata	A scalemail hauberk.
Magister equitum	The commander of mounted troops in a late Roman field army.

Magister militum	The overall commander of a late Roman field army.
Manicae	An iron arm guard used by Roman soldiers.
Manumission	The act of freeing a slave.
Marching camp	The temporary fortification built by Roman troops at the end of each marching day in enemy territory.
Martiobarbuli	Lead-weighted throwing dart.
Municipia	A Roman city or town of mercantile origin.
Navarchus	The commander of a squadron of ships in a Roman fleet.
Numeri	Temporary units of indigenous troops.
Optimates	The reactionary, pro-Senate political faction in late Republican Rome.
Patrician	Leading members of the Roman aristocracy, usually senators.
Peregrini	Freemen born outside of Italy in the Imperial provinces, until the reforms of Caracalla.
Pharetra	Quiver.
Pilum	Lead-weighted throwing javelin.
Plumbatae	Lead-weighted throwing dart.
Populares	The popular, radical political faction in late Republican Rome.
Praefectus alae	A Roman cavalry commander.
Praefectus castrorum	The camp prefect of a Roman legion, and its third in command.
Praefectus classis	A Roman fleet admiral of the Empire, always appointed by the emperor.
Praefectus vigilum	Commander of the *vigiles*.
Praetentura Italiae et Alpium	Fortifications built in northern Italy by Marcus Aurelius.
Praetor	A senior elected magistrate.
Primus Pilus	Senior legionary centurion.
Principate	The phase of the Roman Empire lasting from the Senate styling Octavian as Augustus in 27 BC through to the accession of Diocletian in AD 284.
Proconsul	The senior military and legal official in charge of a Roman Senatorial province. Appointed by the Senate, and in the Empire then approved by the emperor.
Procurator	The senior financial officer in a Roman province, appointed by the emperor.
Protectores	The close personal bodyguard and staff officers of late Roman emperors.
Province	A large geographical unit of organisation in the Roman Principate Empire, and a smaller unit in the Dominate.

Pseudocomitatenses	Units of *limitanei* brigaded into late Roman field armies.
Punic	A word used to describe Carthaginian armies and territory.
Roman Empire	This lasted from 27 BC when Octavian was first styled Augustus by the Senate through to the fall of the western Empire in AD 476, though it continued to exist in the east.
Roman Republic	This lasted from the overthrow of Tarquin the Proud in 709 BC through to 27 BC when Octavian was first styled Augustus by the Senate.
Scholae Palatinae	Mounted guardsman of the later Empire.
Scutum	The ubiquitous large rectangular body shield used by Roman legionaries from the mid-Republican period to the late Principate phase of Empire.
Seax	A form of long Saxon combat knife.
Senate House (*Curia*)	The Senate house where the senators gathered to debate legislation.
Senator	The most senior class of Roman aristocrat.
Skutatoi	Byzantine heavy infantry.
Spatha	A long sword, originally a Roman cavalry weapon but which later replaced the gladius as the primary sword of foot troops.
Spiculum	An armour-piercing javelin.
Subpraefectus	The deputy commander of a regional fleet in the Principate Empire.
Symmachiarii	Moorish javelin-armed skirmishers.
Testudo	A defensive formation of interlocking shields used by Roman legionaries.
Tribune	A mid-ranking magistrate.
Tribuni angusticlavii	Junior officers in a Roman legion.
Tribunus laticlavius	Second in command of a Roman legion.
Tribunus militum	Commander of a *vexillation* of Dominate Empire Imperial guard cavalry.
Trireme	A war galley with three banks of oars.
Vicarius	The senior official running a Roman diocese.
Vigiles urbani	Watchmen of Rome.
'Year of the Four Emperors'	The civil wars of AD 69 that ultimately saw Vespasian become emperor, initiating the Flavian dynasty.
'Year of the Five Emperors'	The civil wars of AD 193 that finally saw Septimius Severus become emperor, initiating the Severan dynasty.

(*opposite*)
The Arch of Septimius Severus in Lepcis Magna, Tripolitania in the province of Africa Proconsularis. Home town of the great warrior emperor. (Livius.org/Jona Lendering)

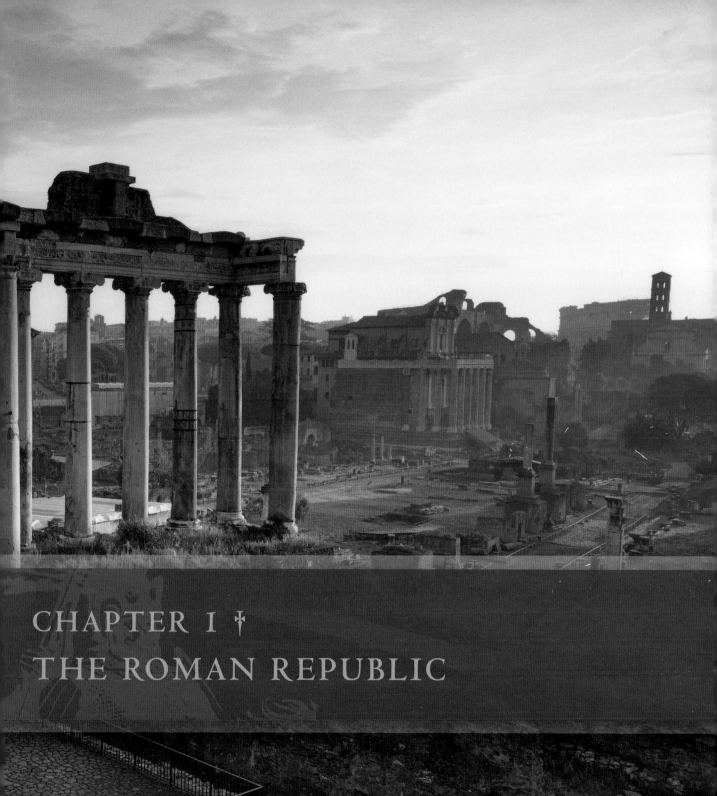

CHAPTER I †
THE ROMAN REPUBLIC

The Roman military machine is so well known to us today that it is easy for us to take its rise to dominance in the ancient world for granted. However, its origins were complex and have their roots deep within the Roman Republic, and even earlier. Therefore, to provide context for the subsequent chapters in this book which focus exclusively on the Roman military, I set out here a detailed background of early Rome prior to the onset of the Republic, and then provide a description of the early republican period as the power of Rome grew, first across the Italian peninsula and then throughout the Mediterranean. I then close the chapter by considering the late Republic as it spiraled to its demise through incessant civil war, this setting the scene for the onset of the Roman Empire detailed in Chapter 3.

Early Rome

Rome's rise to greatness was never guaranteed and was a painstaking process featuring many setbacks. These challenges were interspersed with long periods of consolidation. It was during the latter that Rome assimilated many of the ideas – both cultural and practical – of its opponents, an ability as detailed in the Introduction that helps explain the longevity of both the Republic and later Empire. This trend is particularly evident during the former.

The origins of Rome are shrouded in myth. The most familiar founding story is that concerning the twins Romulus and Remus. In the tale they were born in the Latin town of Alba Longa to the vestal virgin Rhea Silvia. She was the daughter of a former king, Numitor, who had been usurped and imprisoned by his brother Amulius. It was the latter who forced Rhea Silvia to become a vestal virgin after taking the crown. She conceived the twins when visited by Mars in a sacred grove dedicated to the god of war. Amulius ordered the twins killed and so their mother abandoned them on the banks of the River Tiber. There they were saved by the river god Tiberinus. The story then says the twins were suckled by a she-wolf in a cave later called the Lupercal. They were eventually

adopted by a shepherd called Faustulus, growing to manhood unaware of their aristocratic origins. However, their natural leadership qualities came to the fore and through a series of escapades they eventually became aware of their own identities, later helping restore their grandfather to his throne. They then decided to build their own settlement on the banks of the Tiber and chose the site that later became Rome. The twins then fell out over which of the seven hills there they should build the new town on, Romulus preferring the Palatine Hill and Remus the Aventine Hill. When Romulus claimed divine support for his choice, violence broke out and Romulus killed Remus. The former then founded Rome on the Palatine Hill, the date for this event set by Roman annalists as 21 April 753 BC.

This dramatic legend had to be reconciled with another great founding myth of Rome, however. This was set much earlier, in the context of the Trojan War. Here the Trojan refugee Aeneas escaped to Italy following the fall of Troy, landing near Anzio south of Rome with his followers after a series of adventures across the Mediterranean. After defeating local opposition his son Iulus, namesake of the later Julio-Claudian family, founded Alba Longa and established the line of kings which bridged the gap between the Trojan

(*previous pages*)
Forum Romanum in Rome, Italy during sunrise. (Getty Images)

(*opposite*)
Mythological scene on painted wall plaster from Pompeii. The warriors are equipped as Greek hoplites, as were the earliest First Class Roman soldiers.

The Second Temple of Hera, Paestum in Campania, Magna Graecia. Classical Greek culture had a big influence on the Etrusco-Romans.

Wars in the later 2nd millennium BC and Rome's ultimate founding. The Roman poet Virgil later merged both stories in his 1st-century BC epic the *Aeneid*, one of Rome's greatest literary works.

However, the original settlement was founded, its location was crucial to its subsequent rise to global dominance. It was one of a number built on hilltops on the left bank of the River Tiber in central Italy at its lowest crossing point. This river is one of two major waterways that rise in the central Apennine Mountains bisecting Italy. The Tiber flows south into the Tyrrhenian Sea, while the other is the River Arno which flows west into the same sea. The region between the two, from Pisa in the north to Ostia (the port of Rome) in the south, was called Etruria and was originally home to the Villanovan Iron Age culture that began around 900 BC.

This evolved by the early 7th century BC into the Etruscan culture, with the growing villages of rich Etruria coalescing into powerful city-states such as Caere, Veii and Tarquinii. Etruscan influence spread rapidly, largely through their seafaring skills, with a mercantile empire soon established in the western Mediterranean. Through this they soon came into contact with the Greek colonies in southern Italy and eastern Sicily, and the Phoenicians who were establishing the Punic Empire in North Africa. From the former they adopted the Greek hoplite phalanx as the principal formation of their better-armed troops, as fully detailed in Chapter 2. This gave them a distinctive edge as they looked south to the settlements above the eastern bank of the Tiber, including Rome, and the region to their south called Latium. Soon these were all under their control, with Rome being governed by an Etrusco-Roman king. The second of these, Servius Tullius (579 BC to 535 BC), was particularly important as he formalised the military systems of Rome for the first time,

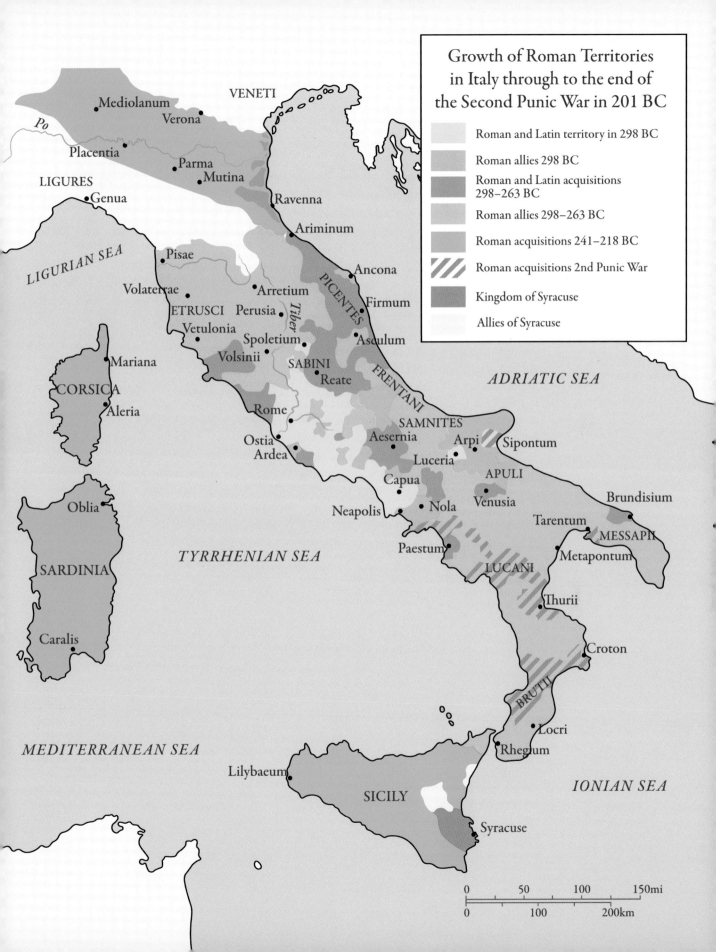

Growth of Roman Territories in Italy through to the end of the Second Punic War in 201 BC

- Roman and Latin territory in 298 BC
- Roman allies 298 BC
- Roman and Latin acquisitions 298–263 BC
- Roman allies 298–263 BC
- Roman acquisitions 241–218 BC
- Roman acquisitions 2nd Punic War
- Kingdom of Syracuse
- Allies of Syracuse

VENETI

Po

Mediolanum
Verona
Placentia
Parma
Mutina
LIGURES
Genua
Ravenna
Ariminum

LIGURIAN SEA

Pisae
Ancona
Volaterrae
Arretium
Firmum
ETRUSCI
Perusia
PICENTES
Tiber
Vetulonia
Spoletium
Asculum
Volsinii
SABINI
Reate
FRENTANI
ADRIATIC SEA

CORSICA
Mariana
Aleria

Rome
SAMNITES
Ostia
Aesernia
Arpi
Sipontum
Ardea
Luceria
Capua
APULI
Venusia
Brundisium
Neapolis
Nola
Tarentum
MESSAPII
Paestum
Metapontum
LUCANI

SARDINIA
Oblia

TYRRHENIAN SEA

Thurii

Caralis

Croton

BRUTII

Locri

MEDITERRANEAN SEA

Rhegium

Lilybaeum

IONIAN SEA

SICILY

Syracuse

0   50   100   150mi
0   100   200km

following Etruscan tradition by introducing the hoplite phalanx for the best Etrusco-Roman troops (again, see Chapter 2 for detail).

Etruscan power reached its height in the mid-6th century BC when they conquered much of Campania below Latium, including many of the Greek settlements of Magna Graecia. However, crucially they failed to capture the key city of Cumae there. This formed the centre of regional resistance to Etruscan rule, defeating the latter in battle in 524 BC. The event emboldened the other conquered settlements and those in Latium formed the Latin League that, together with the Greek settlements of Magna Graecia, began to drive the Etruscans back north into Etruria. Rome's first rise to regional dominance occurred at this time when it became the principal town of the league during the reign of Tarquin the Proud (534–509 BC). He was still nevertheless Etrusco-Roman, and in 509 BC the Roman aristocracy expelled him and the Republic was born. It was in the context of the latter event that we have the story of Horatio and his two companions holding the last bridge over the River Tiber from Etruscans returning to try to help Tarquin. As the legend goes, their sacrifice proved worthwhile, with Tarquin the last Roman king.

The Early Republic

After the fall of the monarchy the new Roman Republic came under the control of the great families of Rome, called the patricians based on the Latin word *pater* (father). It was only members of these great families that could hold religious or political office, particularly the Senate where the most important members of the nobility carried out legislation under the aegis of two annually elected consuls. The remaining citizens were known as plebeians who had no political authority, even though many were as wealthy, if not more so, than many of the patricians. Tensions between the two classes grew rapidly, particularly as the poorer residents provided the bulk of the army. In 494 BC matters came to a head when the plebeians went on strike. They gathered outside Rome and refused to move until they were granted representation, this

event later being called the First Secession of the Plebs. Against the odds, the dramatic move worked, and the plebeians were rewarded with their own assembly called the *Concillium Plebis* (council of the plebs). This body had a degree of oversight on the legislation proposed by the consuls and enacted by the Senate. Thus, while the government of the Roman Republic was by no means democratic (also excluding women from any public office), it was much more so than the preceding monarchy, and that became an important part of the Roman psyche.

During the early Republic, Roman foreign policy and military activity was often far from successful. Much of the 5th century BC was spent struggling against external threats from near and far. In the first instance Rome fought the Latin War with its erstwhile Latin League partners from 498–493 BC. Even though Rome was victorious in the main engagement, at the battle of Regallus in 496 BC, the town had to acknowledge her Latin neighbours as equals in the subsequent Cassian Treaty.

As Etruscan power waned, the Latin League then spent much of the next 50 years fending off repeated raiding in force by the various hill tribes of the Apennines, for example the Aequi, Umbri, Sabini and Volsci. These found themselves increasingly squeezed out of their own lands and onto the plains of Latium by the expansion of the Samnites to the south and east. By the mid-5th century BC these tribes, driving out all before them, burst into southern Italy and conquered Campania, Apulia and Lucania. The Latin towns led the fightback, with the Aequi defeated in 431 BC and the Volsci then driven back into the hills. The Latin League then consolidated their control over central-western Italy, with comparative peace descending on the region for a short time.

However, this was not to last as the Etruscans to the north remained a threat. They again drew the attention of Rome which, in 404 BC, began a long eight-year siege of the Etruscan city of Veii. This finally fell in 396 BC and proved to be the high point for Roman foreign policy in the first half of the 4th century BC. This was because their next opponents were the Senones Gauls from northern

(*opposite*)
Pyrrhus of Epirus, whose Hellenistic lancers, pikemen and elephants were a shock to the Roman military establishment.

Bay of Biscay

PYRENEES

Ebro

SPAIN

Tagus

Saguntum ⚔ 219

Balearic Islands

Guadalquivir

Baecula ⚔ 208

Ilipa ⚔ 206

Carthago Nova
⚔ 209

MEDITERRANEAN
SEA

NUMIDIA

Western Mediterranean During the Punic Wars

Carthaginian territory
about 270 BC

Roman territory
about 270 BC

→ Hannibal's route
270–219 BC

⚔ 219 Battle site with
approximate year (BC)

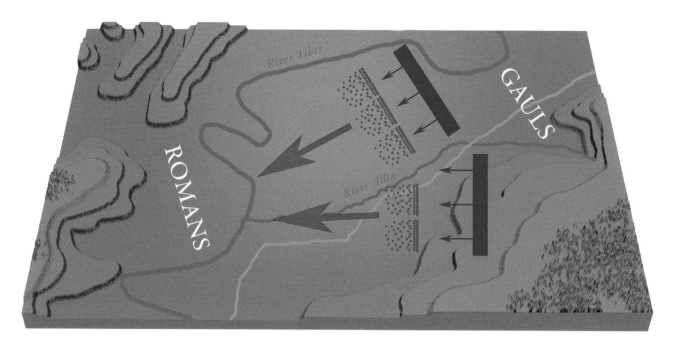

Open   **Contour**   **River**   **Road**   **Romans**   **Gauls**

Italy. Here Celts from central Europe had been settling in the Po Valley for some time, challenging the Etruscans who had established Bologne (later Roman *Bononia*) as their principal city there. The riches to the south proved too strong a draw and, after bursting through Etruria, a Gallic army under the chieftain Brennus found itself on the borders of Latium. Rome deployed its legions expecting a swift victory but was shocked when they were annihilated at the battle of Allia in 390 BC. This was only 17km to the north of Rome, which was promptly sacked. This traumatic event prompted the building of the first defensive circuit of the city in the form of the 11km-long Servian Walls.

In the midst of these events an appointment occurred in Rome that was to have a profound effect on the development of the Roman military system, leading to the appearance of the legionary for the first time. This was the appointment of Marcus Furius Camillus as consular tribune to command the army in 401 BC. A patrician with

extensive experience of campaigning against the Aequi and Volsci, he realised that Rome's incessant campaigning, which came to a head with the long siege of Veii, was proving financially unsustainable. He therefore raised taxation to a level where it could support the army on long campaigns and re-balanced the books of the Roman treasury. Then, with his Camillan Reforms of the military, he introduced the manipular system into the legions of Rome, with the legionary at its centre (see Chapter 3 for full detail). These developments rapidly superseded the earlier Tullian system.

The new system was quickly tested, once more against the Etruscans to the north. In the mid-4th century Rome and her Latin League partners fought a series of increasingly vicious wars against the Etrurian city states. A final assault in 351 BC broke Etruscan resistance. The Etruscans then lost Bologne to the Gauls in 350 BC. The absence of an opponent to the north now left the towns of Latium free to look inward once more, and a final struggle for dominance of the Latin League began. Rome emerged as the victor and now controlled all of western Italy from southern Etruria to northern Campania.

By now city-sized, its next opponents were the Samnites of Samnium, an Oscan-speaking people of south-central Italy used to fighting in the rough terrain of their homelands. Initially an ally of the Latin League against the Volsci, war broke out with Rome in 343 BC. This lasted for 50 years through the First, Second and Third Samnite Wars and included the famous Roman defeat at the Caudian Forks in 321 BC. This was a pass near Caudium, the capital of the Samnite Caudini tribe. Here, both Roman consuls led their combined armies into a trap where their whole force was captured, every man being forced to pass under a 'yoke' formed from three spears, two stuck in the ground and one placed horizontally over them. Rome never forgave the Samnites for this humiliation and within five

years the 'Caudine Peace' had broken down, with hostilities renewed. The Samnites were for the most part victorious, but typically the Romans refused to accept defeat and tenaciously fought back. The Samnites eventually sued for peace in 304 BC. This was again short lived, lasting only six years. The Samnites then launched a full out assault on Rome in 296 BC, gathering a coalition of allies including the Gauls, the remaining Etruscan city states and Umbrians, aiming to curb the growing of Rome once and for all. Again, they were initially successful, but ultimately lost the key battle at Sentinum in 295 BC when only the Gauls turned up to fight alongside them. This marked the end of Samnite resistance to Roman expansion southwards, and also of Etruscan independence. It was also a remarkable example of Roman grit, they never cowing to adversity and always coming back until victorious.

Rome now turned its attention to northern

Initial Roman and Carthaginian deployments at the battle of Cannae in 216 BC when Hannibal famously carried out a double envelopment of the Roman army, inflicting an enormous defeat. Typically however, the Romans refused to surrender in the Second Punic War and by 201 BC were victorious.
(Nigel Emsen)

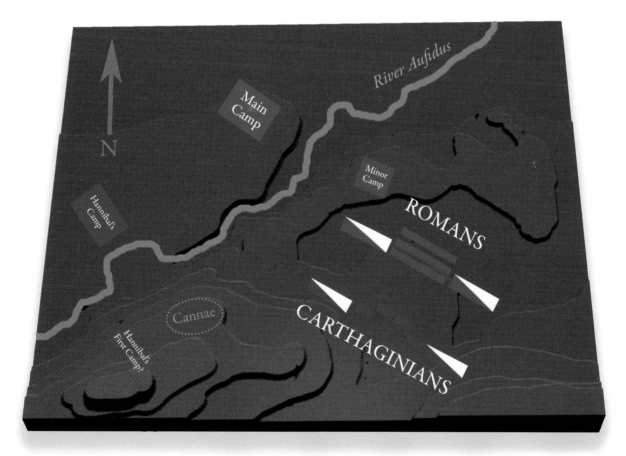

Open Ground   Contour   River   Carthaginians   Romans

Italy where the Gauls still dominated. In the early 280s BC a large-scale migration took place of the Gallic peoples of central Europe and northern Italy, caused by population pressure. Huge tribal groupings began to head eastwards and south. Soon the Senones tribe were once more on the borders of Etruria, now under Roman control. In 284 BC a Roman army, 13,000 strong, marched north to intercept them but was massacred at the battle of Arretium. The Romans responded with more grit, launching a massive counterstrike into the heart of Senonian territory in the Po Valley. After a brief struggle they evicted the whole tribe out of Italy. Another Gallic tribe, the Boii, then raided south but were fought to a standstill and sued for peace. This ended effective Gallic resistance in the north.

Rome now controlled most of the Italian peninsula excepting the Greek cities to the south, which became the next object of her attention. Rome tried to force them into an alliance but was quickly rebuffed. Taranto, the leading naval power on the peninsula, then appealed for help from Pyrrhus of Epirus on the western coast of the Balkans. The Epirot king, a relation of Alexander the Great, responded positively and in 280 BC crossed the Adriatic with an army 25,000 strong. These crack troops fought in the Hellenistic military tradition with pikemen, lance-armed shock cavalry and war elephants. A Roman army quickly marched south when word reached the city that Pyrrhus was gathering allies from Rome's enemies across Italy, of which by this time there were many, holding grudges against earlier defeats. A major battle ensued at Heraclea. This was the first time the Romans, with their maniples of legionaries, fought a Macedonian-style phalanx. It was to prove a bruising experience, with Pyrrhus winning narrowly. Two further battles occurred at Asculum in 279 BC – another narrow Epirot victory – and Beneventum in 275 BC, when the Romans were finally victorious. The war had been a close-run thing though and made a lasting impression on the Romans. One result was the evolution of the Camillan manipular system into a more streamlined form, this detailed in Chapter 2, known as the Polybian system after the 2nd-century Greek historian Polybius. It also marked the beginning of Roman interest in that most tantalizing of ancient warfare troop types, the war elephant.

Roman expansion continued and now began to take on an international flavour. By 272 BC Taranto had been captured, providing Rome with an effective maritime capability for the first time (see description in Chapter 3 about the evolution of Roman naval power). This caused an inevitable clash with Carthage, the regional superpower of the western Mediterranean, and the First Punic War broke out in 264 BC over control of the key Sicilian city of Messina. This lasted until 241 BC and included the battle of Agrigentum on the south coast of Sicily in 261 BC where the legions of Rome defeated the Carthaginians for the first time in a set piece battle. After this the conflict was largely naval (again see Chapter 2), with the Romans copying Carthaginian maritime technology and tactics and ending the war the victor. Carthage evacuated Sicily and paid a huge indemnity.

However, it was the Second Punic War that truly tested the power and resilience of Rome to breaking point. This broke out in 218 BC and lasted 17 years, with the Roman fleet at the outset cutting off the Carthaginian North African homeland from its colonies in Spain. The Carthaginian leader Hannibal responded with his audacious plan to invade Italy through southern Gaul and the Alps, defeating the legions of Rome and their allies three times at the Trebia in 218 BC, Lake Trasimene in 217 BC and Cannae in 216 BC. The last of these was a battle of titanic scale, with 50,000 Carthaginians facing 86,000 Romans. Hannibal here famously completed his famous double envelopment of the legions. A massacre followed, with 50,000 Romans being killed. Such losses would bring most opponents to their knees, but not Rome. Soon new legions were raised, including two of freed slaves. Even though most of southern Italy now defected to Hannibal, he failed to capture Rome itself, given his lack of a viable siege train, and was ultimately pinned down in southern Italy. Attempts to re-supply him from North Africa and Spain failed due to Roman naval power, and in 204 BC Rome went on the offensive.

This featured consul Publius Cornelius Scipio (later Africanus) landing a sizeable force of 25,000 in the Carthaginian heartland near Tunis. The legions, joined by Numidian allies including their famous light cavalry, had their revenge for Cannae in 202 BC when Scipio finally defeated Hannibal at Zama. Peace quickly followed, under the most onerous terms for the Carthaginians.

The Third Punic War broke out in 146 BC with Carthage backed into a corner by the escalating demands of Rome. This was a very one-sided affair, with Carthage itself destroyed and 50,000 of its citizens sold into slavery. The event marked the beginning of Rome's mastery of the western Mediterranean, with Sicily, Sardinia and Corsica, the Balearic Islands, Spain and North Africa gradually coming under direct Roman control.

Meanwhile, an additional outcome of the Second Punic War was that Roman attention also turned to the eastern Mediterranean and the remaining Hellenistic kingdoms there. Here, the Macedonian King Philip V had unwisely been caught trying to agree a treaty with Hannibal when the latter was still in Italy. Soon the First Macedonian War began, followed by three more that finally saw Macedonia become a Roman province in 146 BC. Rome was also victorious fighting the over-confident Seleucid monarch Antiochus III in the Seleucid–Rome War. These campaigns featured a number of enormous set-piece battles between legion and phalanx. The key ones were Cynoscephalai in 197 BC where Philip V was defeated during the Second Macedonian War, Magnesia in 190 BC when Antiochus III was defeated in western Anatolia, and Pydna in 168 BC when new Macedonian King Perseus was defeated in the Third Macedonian War. The final resistance to Roman hegemony in Greece came in 146 BC when the Achaean League in the northern and central Peloponnese declared war on Rome.

Land walls of Pompeii, showing the scars from slingshots and *ballistae* when Sulla stormed the town during the Social War.

The ensuing Achaean War was a short-lived affair, the Achaeans being totally defeated, and its leading city Corinth sacked and raised to the ground.

Rome was now the undoubted superpower in the Mediterranean, its legions triumphant across the region. One result of its spectacular success against the Hellenistic kingdoms was that fabulous amounts of loot and plunder now began making their way to Rome, enriching army commanders and troops alike. It should be remembered that when Alexander the Great finally defeated the Achaemenid Persian Empire in the later 4th century BC, the Macedonian conquerors inherited the vast wealth of this huge empire. Following the Wars of the Successors after Alexander's death, this was then spread out among the various successor states, particularly the Macedonian, Seleucid and Ptolemaic kingdoms of the eastern Mediterranean. This is what fell into Rome's lap, dwarfing the riches amassed after the defeat of Carthage. The aristocracy back in Rome could now see fortunes were to be made in the east through military conquest, which from this point proved an enormous draw. Soon, civil war loomed on the horizon.

The Later Republic

As the Republic matured Rome, victorious and rich, turned on itself. First, in 133 BC the tribune Tiberius Sempronius Gracchus proposed to distribute stretches of state-owned land in Italy, illegally occupied by the rich, to the poor. However, instead of following the usual practice of first consulting the Senate, he presented his idea directly to an assembly of the people. In so doing he deposed from office another tribune opposing the distribution, arguing that his reforms should be funded from the money that came from the riches now pouring into Rome from the eastern Mediterranean. His land bill passed but, when he tried to stand for election for another term, he was assassinated by a group of senators. This set the tone for all that followed in the next century.

In 123 BC Tiberius's brother Gaius was elected as a tribune, introducing a whole package of radical legislation. By far his most controversial reform was his regularisation of the *cura annonae* (grain supply) in Rome. Due to the city's rapid growth it was increasingly reliant on grain imports from Sicily, North Africa and Egypt. This meant that the price of grain could fluctuate wildly, influenced by factors as diverse as slave revolts, plagues of locusts or simply the size of the annual harvest each year. This fluctuation exposed the citizens of Rome to occasional food shortages when the price was too high or the amount of grain available too low. Gaius therefore stabilised the price of grain at a sustainable level and introduced a state subsidy to pay for it. To raise the funds for the subsidy he introduced a system of tax farming in Rome's newly conquered territories in the eastern Mediterranean where huge corporations publicly bid for the right to collect the taxes for a percentage of profit. Despite the system being open to huge levels of corruption, which in some cases beggared the new provinces, the people of Rome didn't care. They now had their cheap grain, with the system lasting into the late Republic. It also illustrated the Roman attitude to public administration, with only a small core of officials managing the Republic's vast territory by sub-contracting responsibility out to private business and individual *publicani* (administrators).

Gaius was now getting into his stride but realised he would need another term as tribune to complete his reforming ambitions. He didn't want to stand for election himself again but put forward his closest supporter Fulvius Flaccus to take his place. However, such was Gaius's popularity that he was re-elected anyway, alongside his friend. Their manifesto was even more radical than that for Gaius's first term of office. It included a plan to enfranchise all Italian citizens, and for a major Roman colony to be built on the site of Carthage, the Punic capital laid waste by Rome at the end of the Third Punic War. Gaius himself travelled to North Africa to see the latter founded. Both policies caused even more friction with the Senate and their supporters, and when Gaius and Flaccus failed to be re-elected in 121 BC they knew they were exposed to retribution. An attempt to drag them before the Senate failed when they refused to attend, Flaccus convincing Gaius that it was a trap, and so it proved. Bloodshed soon followed, with Gaius fleeing and eventually taking his own life with the help of a servant in a sacred grove. Some 250 of his supporters also died, fighting a rear-guard action to buy him time to escape, ironically on the same bridge held by Horatio and his companions 400 years earlier.

Next, towards the end of the century, a new figure rose to pre-eminence in Rome, one who would come to dominate Roman politics for the first decades of the 1st century BC. This was the highly successful statesman and soldier Gaius Marius, who eventually served as consul an unprecedented seven times. The context for his rise to the top was the next great external threat to the Republic, in the form of the sanguineous Cimbrian Wars.

The Cimbri were a Germanic people who originated from Jutland in modern Denmark. In the later 2nd century BC, they, along with neighbouring tribes such as the Teutons and Ambrones, migrated south into Gaul where they fought a series of wars with the Gallic tribes there. In 113 BC they invaded the lands of the Taurisci, a confederation of Gallic tribes in Noricum (modern Austria and part of Slovenia). These were Roman allies and the Senate decided to send an army to their aid. The Roman force was commanded by the consul Gnaeus Papirus Carbo who requested the Cimbri retreat. They did so but were deceived by the Romans who set an ambush for them. The Cimbri found out and attacked the Romans first, at the battle of Noreia. Carbo's treachery backfired spectacularly with the Romans suffering a huge defeat. They were only saved from complete annihilation by a storm, with Carbo lucky to escape.

This engagement marked the beginning of the Cimbrian War that lasted until 101 BC. The Cimbri could have attacked Italy at this point but chose instead to head west to Gaul where they invaded the new Roman province of Transalpine Gaul in 109 BC. A Roman army under Marcus Junius Silanus was sent to intercept, but yet again the legions were comprehensively defeated. Next, in 107 BC, the Romans were once more defeated, this time by the Gallic Tigurini tribe who were allies of the Cimbri. The name of this battle is unrecorded, but shortly afterwards the Romans again engaged the Tigurini, this time at the battle of Burdigala (modern Bordeaux). The result was the same, total defeat, with the consul Lucius Cassius Longinus Ravalla killed.

Much worse was to follow. In 105 BC the Romans resolved to settle matters with the Cimbri once and for all. The new consul Gnaeus Mallius Maximus gathered a huge force of 80,000 legionaries and allies. It was so large that part had to be commanded by Quintus Servilius Caepio, his fellow consul and the governor of Cisalpine Gaul in northern Italy. The two disliked each other intensely so they set off in two separate columns, both arriving at the River Rhône near modern Orange at the same time. Distrusting each other, they camped on opposite sides of the river. Caepio then attacked the nearby Cimbri and their Teuton and Ambrones allies on his own, trying to steal the glory, but his legions were soon crushed. Maximus and his troops saw all this from their camp and became demoralised. When engaged by the Germans they too were quickly broken. Many Romans tried to flee but were slaughtered. Altogether the Romans lost 60,000 men, the largest number since Cannae. Only Maximus, Caepio and a few horsemen escaped the engagement, later named the battle of Arausio, with the Rhône choked with dead legionaries for many days afterwards.

Panic now gripped Rome, with the phrase *terror cimbricus* being used to describe the mood of the people. Roman grit showed through again however, though this time in the form of the aforementioned great political and military leader Marius. He was born in 157 BC, though not to an aristocratic family. Through sheer hard work and ambition, he rose to become a *quaestor* in 123 BC, then tribune of the plebs in 119 BC and praetor in 115 BC. Though no great administrator, he proved to be a supreme soldier. His first command was in Spain where he earned fame by defeating a bandit uprising and then setting Rome's silver mining interests there on a firm footing. Then in 109 BC he travelled to Numidia to serve as the *legate* under the consul Quintus Metellus Numidicus. Here the Romans were engaged in the Jugurthine War

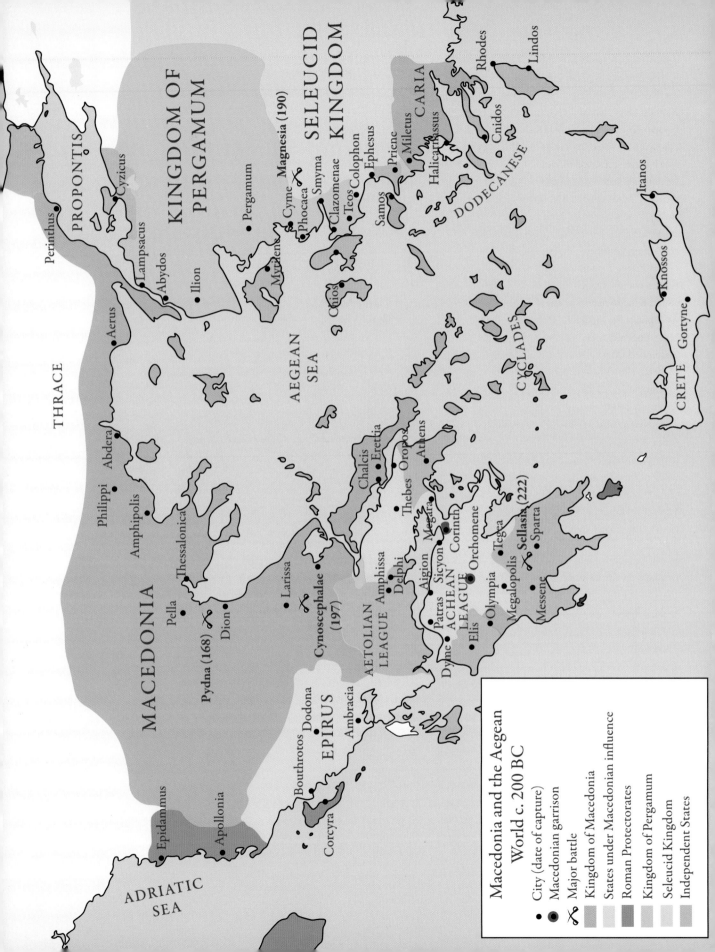

THRACE

PROPONTIS

KINGDOM OF PERGAMUM

SELEUCID KINGDOM

CARIA

Perinthus

Cyzicus

Lampsacus
Abydos

Ilion

Aerus

Pergamum

Magnesia (190)
Cyme
Phocaea   Smyrna
Clazomenae
Mytilene   Teos Colophon
Ephesus
Samos   Priene
Miletus
Halicarnassus
Cnidos

Rhodes
Lindos

DODECANESE

Chios

AEGEAN
SEA

CYCLADES

Itanos

Knossos

CRETE
Gortyne

ADRIATIC
SEA

Epidamnus
Apollonia

Corcyra

Bouthrotos Dodona
EPIRUS
Ambracia

MACEDONIA

Philippi
Abdera
Amphipolis
Thessalonica
Pella
Pydna (168)
Dion

Larissa

Cynoscephalae
(197)

AETOLIAN
LEAGUE   Amphissa
Delphi

Chalcis
Eretria

Oropos
Thebes   Athens
Megara
Aigion Sicyon Corinth
Patras   Orchomene
ACHEAN   Olympia   Tegea
Dyme LEAGUE   Megalopolis Sellasia (222)
Elis   Messene   Sparta

Macedonia and the Aegean
World c. 200 BC

• City (date of capture)
⊙ Macedonian garrison
⚔ Major battle

▨ Kingdom of Macedonia
▨ States under Macedonian influence
▨ Roman Protectorates
▨ Kingdom of Pergamum
▨ Seleucid Kingdom
▨ Independent States

against the rogue Numidian King Jugurtha. This had broken out in 112 BC and was proving difficult for Rome to conclude satisfactorily. Marius and Metellus soon fell out, especially when the latter's troops began supporting Marius's own claim to take over complete command of the legions there. Marius then returned to Rome in 107 BC to stand for consul, succeeding and then initiating a new series of reforms of the Roman military. He was then granted Numidia as his own province where he returned with fresh troops, officially taking control of the campaign from Metellus.

His first act there was to send his *quaestor* and future enemy Lucius Cornelius Sulla to nearby Mauretania to negotiate the kingdom withdrawing its support for Jugurtha. Then, with the help of its King Bocchus 1, Sulla captured Jugurtha and the war ended. Marius was wildly popular among the plebeian classes in Rome and despite Sulla's key role in Jugurtha's demise he was acclaimed the hero of the hour, being granted a triumph where Jugurtha was paraded through the streets of Rome, his royal robes and earrings being ripped off. Thrown into the Tullianum prison, he died there of starvation in 104 BC.

After the shattering defeat of the legions at the battle of Arausio, the Roman people now turned to Marius for salvation. He was elected consul once more in 104 BC, even though he was still in Numidia concluding matters there. Arriving back in Rome for his triumph, he took up his consulship immediately by entering the senate after the victory parade still wearing his triumphator's robes. This didn't impress the conservative Senate, but the people loved it.

Marius now gathered an army to counter any Cimbrian invasion, basing it in southern Gaul. There he waited, training new legions and being elected consul again in 103 BC and 102 BC. In the latter year he finally confronted the Cimbri's allies who had started to move south. At the battle of Aquae Sextiae in Aix-en-Provence he destroyed a combined force of Teutons and Ambrones, inflicting 90,000 casualties on the Germans and capturing 20,000 including the Teuton King Teutobod.

Marius was elected consul again in 101 BC and in that year was able to tackle the Cimbri head on. The enormous tribe had begun to move south and for the first time penetrated the Alpine passes, entering Cisalpine Gaul. The Roman force there of 20,000 troops withdrew behind the Po river, allowing the Cimbri to devastate the fertile countryside to its north. This gave Marius time to arrive with his legions from southern Gaul, his army now totalling 32,000 men, and he led the combined Roman force to an immense victory at the battle of Vercellae near to the confluence of the Po and Sesia rivers. Here his newly reformed legions proved to be superior to the Cimbri warriors, though credit was also given at the time to Sulla who led the Roman and allied cavalry that also played a key role in the battle. Defeat for the Cimbri was total, with them losing up to 160,000 men with 60,000 captured including a large number of camp followers. Soon the slave markets of Rome were overflowing.

Marius was once again the hero of the hour, though the successful conclusion of the Cimbrian War marked the beginning of the long enmity between Marius and Sulla as the latter felt that, certainly in the Jugerthine War, the consul hadn't given him the credit for his actions. Marius then further alienated himself with the patricians by granting full Roman citizenship to his allied Italian soldiers without asking permission from the Senate. This was to have unforeseen consequences and caused the next great crisis to face the Republic.

Marius's success had one unforeseen circumstance that in retrospect we can see actually hastened the collapse of the Republic. This was the appearance of a new phenomenon at the top of Roman society in the form of a new class of political leaders who were effectively independent warlords, each with their own armies. Admittedly, the term warlord might actually seem anachronistic given the structured nature of Roman society, but the term is very appropriate for the likes of Marius, Sulla, Gnaeus Pompey, Marcus Licinius Crassus, Gaius Julius Caesar, Marc Anthony and Gaius Octavian. Their appearance was facilitated by the military reforms of Marius himself in 107 BC at the height of the Cimbrian Wars, these fully detailed in Chapter 2. In short, he created a new kind of

BRITAIN

GERMANIA

GAUL

Alesia

CISALPINE
GAUL

ILLYRICUM

ATLANTIC
OCEAN

TRANSALPINE GAUL

Jan
49 BC

Dyrrhachium

Rome

Corfinium

Jan–Aug
48 BC

June
49 BC

Ilerda

Capua

Brundisium

HISPANIA
CITERIOR

SARDINIA

HISPANIA
ULTERIOR

Sept
45 BC

Jan
46 BC

SICILY

Munda

Syracuse

AFRICA

Thapsus

MEDITERRANEAN
SEA

MAURETANIA

NUMIDIA

Caesar's Movements in the Civil War, 49–45 BC

0   200   300   400   500   600

Roman provinces

Roman-controlled territory and client kingdoms

Direction of campaigning

Territorial borders

SARMATIA

BLACK SEA

PONTUS

ARMENIA

BITHYNIA

GALATIA

CAPPADOCIA

Byzantium

THRACE

ACEDONIA

ASIA

LYCAONIA

CILICIA

Antioch

Carrhae

PARTHIA

Aug 47 BC

SYRIA

Cyprus

arsalus

ACHAEA

JUDAEA

ARABIA

Oct 48 BC

Alexandria

Cyrene

KINGDOM OF THE PTOLEMIES

CYRENAICA

legion that included all of the specialists in its ranks needed to enable it to operate independent of long lines of supply. Such formations were therefore very mobile, allowing the new Roman warlords of the late Republic (often proconsuls governing new frontier provinces) to build private armies of multiple legions to conquer enemy territory and to fight each other. As part of his military reforms Marius also removed the property requirement to serve in the legions, opening their ranks to the lower end of Roman society. With little money of their own, such troops proved very loyal to their leaders. A particular driver here was the vast wealth of the former Hellenistic kingdoms in the eastern Mediterranean detailed above, forever drawing these warlords to the region, ever desirous of enriching themselves, their soldiers and their supporters back in Rome.

Also at this time, as the first warlords appeared, the political differences among the political classes in Rome began to overtly coalesce into two political 'parties' (the term used in the broadest sense). These were the reactionary pro-Senate *optimates* (translating as 'best ones') and the radical, reforming and populist *populares* (translating as 'favouring the people'). From this point onwards, the late republican warlords had to pick a side if they wanted political support, with Sulla soon the darling of the *optimates* and Marius the *populares*.

Such disagreements were set aside for a short period in the early 90s BC when Rome was rocked by a conflict that caught many by surprise. This was the Social War, a viscous affair when some of Rome's erstwhile Italian *socii* (allies) in the Apennines rose in revolt. Troops from the Italian legions, armed in the Roman fashion, had frequently fought alongside Rome's own legions. They had proved so valuable to Marius that, as detailed above, he had granted Roman citizenship to his Italian troops after the battle of Vercellae. However, this gave a newfound sense of power to the Italian political classes who now demanded a greater say in Roman foreign policy. After all, it was their soldiers who were fighting and dying alongside those of Rome. With trouble brewing, in 91 BC the tribune Marcus Livius Drusus proposed new legislation in Rome to try to avert a crisis

developing. This would have admitted all Italians to citizenship but provoked a huge backlash in the Senate, with Drusus soon assassinated. This was the last straw for the Italians and many now rose in revolt.

The specific Italian peoples who challenged Rome were the Marsi in the northern Apennines and the Samnites, once one of Rome's most feared enemies, to their south. The two formed their own confederation with its headquarters at the city of Corfinium, due east of Rome across the Apennines. To mark their new alliance, they renamed the town Italia and created their own Senate and army. It should be noted that many Italians, for example the Etrurians and Umbrians, didn't join the insurrection.

The rebels were initially successful, with the Marsi inflicting defeats on Roman armies in the north and the Samnites bursting onto Campanian coastal plain in the south. There, the rich cities along the Bay of Naples, for example Surrentum, Stabiae, Herculaneum and Nola, fell one by one. Pompeii was spared a siege given it supported the rebellion from early on, though paid the price for this later.

Marius was in charge of the Roman forces in the northern sector. Now 67, he was far less energetic than previously and viewed as slower on campaign by the *optimates* than his rival Sulla. The Senate accused him of staying in his military camp in the region for too long, though when he did emerge, he inflicted two defeats on the Marsi. He then waited to be appointed supreme commander of all the Roman forces in the field, but when this did not happen, he retired to Rome, taking no further part on the war.

The Senate realised this revolt needed to be brought to a halt as quickly as possible and decided to offer the rebels concessions, with the consul Lucius Julius Caesar helping to pass a law which granted Roman citizenship to any Italians who had not participated in the uprising. This may also have extended to those still fighting but who agreed to immediately put down their weapons. The move proved decisive and soon the rebellion began to falter. The Senate then appointed new military commanders tasked with bringing the war to a conclusion. Consul Gnaeus Pompeius Strabo was placed in charge of the three legions in the north, while Sulla was given command of those in the south. Victory followed victory for the Romans, and war was over by 89 BC.

To cement the peace newer laws were now passed favourable to the Italians. A key one organised the formal inclusion of all Italians south of the River Po into the Roman state as full citizens, such that from this time all of Italy south of this line was now a single Roman nation. All seemed set for a period of peace after the dramas of the Jugurthine, Cimbrian and Social Wars. However, this proved a false hope because, in 88 BC, a full civil war broke out. The protagonists were none other than Rome's two leading warlords, Marius and Sulla.

Sulla's First Civil War lasted from 88 BC to 87 BC and occurred in the context of the First Mithridatic War, Rome's first conflict with Mithridates VI of Pontus. This began in 89 BC, with Sulla being given command of the army in his capacity as one of the two consuls. This was a plum command for the ambitious warlord as he knew there was fabulous wealth to be gained by conquering Mithridates' empire in Anatolia, around the Black Sea and in Greece. Some of this territory comprised Roman provinces seized by the Pontic king, so there was also glory to be had restoring Roman rule. However, Marius also wanted the post. Having encountered Mithridates on an earlier tour to the east, when he had warned the king not the fight with Rome, he thought himself to be the expert on the region. Relations between Sulla and Marius, already poor, became increasingly strained and in 88 BC conflict broke out.

The flashpoint occurred when one of the tribunes of the plebs, Sulpicius, suggested that the votes of the recently enfranchised Italians be evenly split among the existing Roman voting tribes. The Senate blocked the move, so he turned to Marius for support, then putting forward a long list of proposals to the popular assembly designed to bypass the Senate. One of his suggestions was to take command of the army away from Sulla, the *optimates'* champion. This was a real threat to the consul, and he played for time by retiring to examine the heavens for omens. This was one of his rights as a consul and meant that all public business in Rome had to cease until Sulla had completed his task. Sulpicius now overreacted, bringing his *populares* supporters onto the streets of the capital. Violence between the *optimates* and *populares* ensued, with Sulla having to flee and seek shelter with Marius. The latter saw his opportunity and made a number of demands of the consul who agreed to allow public business to return to normal. In short order he was stripped of his command, with Marius now put in charge of the army to fight Mithridates.

Sulla knew his days would be numbered if he stayed in Rome, so he fled. He headed south, reaching an army of six veteran legions at Nola in Campania who he had commanded in the Social War. He convinced them to support him before Marius's own tribunes arrived, who were then killed when they tried to take control of the force. The importance of this cannot be underestimated, it being the first time the legions had chosen to side with a warlord against the Republic itself. Sulla now marched on Rome, joined by his fellow consul Quintus Pompeius Rufus. The pair fought their way into the city and a pitched battle ensued in the Esquiline Forum between the *optimates* and *populares*. There, after a promising start, Marius and Sulpicius suffered a resounding defeated. The latter was betrayed and executed, with Marius fleeing to Africa.

Sulla now took control of the city, posting troops throughout the capital to ensure order. He then addressed the popular assemblies to defend his own actions, before taking away their powers to legislate unless on a law already passed by the Senate. He then added 300 new members to the chamber to ensure its support. The power of the various public tribunes was also reduced. With peace restored in Rome, at least for now, he then sent his army back to Campania and resumed his post as consul.

However, all was not well. Another Roman army was at large in Italy under Gnaeus Pompeius Strabo, the father of Caesar's later rival Pompey. Sulla gave command of the force to his own ally Rufus, but when the latter arrived to take command, he was killed by Pompey Strabo's loyal legionnaires. This was only the first of several setbacks for Sulla, the most important being the failure of his candidates to replace himself and Rufus as consul for 87 BC. The winners were Lucius Cornelius Cinna and Gnaeus Octavius, the former a well-known opponent of his. To counter this Sulla forced Cinna to vow to support him. However, once in office Cinna immediately broke the oath. He tried to impeach Sulla, but the warlord ignored him. He took command of the army once more and marched east to fight Mithridates.

With Sulla gone Cinna tried to revive Sulpicius' voting plans for the Italians, with his fellow consul Octavius leading the opposition. On the day of the vote the tribunes vetoed the law and rioting ensued in the *Forum Romanum*, with Octavius's supporters chasing Cinna's men away. Cinna fled the pandemonium and headed for Capua in Campania where he won over the loyalty of a Roman force there (Sulla's troops there had already left), additionally recruiting Italians to swell his numbers. The old warrior Marius now returned from Africa to join him and together they besieged Octavius in Rome. The latter secured the backing of Pompey Strabo and his troops, but he died soon after helping repel a Marian assault on the city. Marius then cut off the food supply to the capital.

The armies of the two factions now confronted each other near the Alban Hills south-east of Rome, but before an engagement could occur the Senate turned on Octavian and entered negotiations with Marius and Cinna. The pair then took control of Rome without a fight, with Octavius beheaded. In a sign of things to come, his head was then displayed in the *Forum Romanum*. A massacre followed of Marius's and Cinna's opponents, with Sulla declared a public enemy. His house was burnt down and property confiscated, his laws repealed, and Marius (for the seventh time) and Cinna became the consuls for 86 BC.

The middle years of the first century BC were dominated by two further individuals of great significance to the story of Rome. The first was Pompey, the other arguably the greatest Roman of all, Julius Caesar. Though originally allies (Pompey married Caesar's daughter Julia in 59 BC), they later became the bitterest of enemies. Both had seen great military success, Pompey in Spain and the east, Caesar in Gaul where he famously defeated the Gallic leader Vercingetorix at the siege of Alesia in 52 BC, this the culmination of his conquest in Gaul. His campaigns there, within which sat his two incursions to Britain in 55 BC and 54 BC, are covered in detail in Chapter 6.

Both differed principally in their political powerbases, Pompey relying on the support of the *optimates* in the Senate while Caesar championed the *populares'* cause, following the path of radicals such as the Gracchi brothers and his great mentor Marius. Their rivalry was well recorded, particularly in the surviving letters of another contemporary politician, Marcus Tullius Cicero. Caesar himself also knew the power of a good press and made sure he recorded his victories for posterity, for example in his writing *The Conquest of Gaul*, a collection of his annual reports back to Rome while on campaign there.

Throughout most of the 50s BC Pompey and Caesar were kept in check by the First Triumvirate where Rome's richest man, Marcus Licinius Crassus, joined them to dominate public life. However, Julia died in 54 BC and then, when Crassus himself was killed campaigning against the Parthians at the battle of Carrhae in 53 BC, war between the two protagonists became inevitable. First blows were struck in January 49 BC when Caesar famously crossed the Rubicon river with his *legio XIII* Gemina against the express orders of the *optimates*-dominated Senate. This waterway, to the south of Ravenna in north-eastern Italy, marked the division between Italy proper and Cisalpine Gaul to the north. Caesar's move was a direct challenge to the Republic's authority, but instead of confronting him as he approached Rome Pompey fled to Greece where, after a lengthy campaign, Caesar finally defeated him at the crucial battle of Pharsalus in 48 BC (also detailed in Chapter 6). Pompey was beheaded soon afterwards as he arrived in Egypt, and within two years Caesar was the sole master of the Roman world after campaigning in Egypt, Asia Minor, North Africa and Spain. During his time in Egypt he became entangled in the politics of the Ptolemaic court in

Egypt. This included his infamous affair with the queen there, Cleopatra VII Philopator, with whom he had a son called Caesarion. When back in Rome he was declared dictator for life, receiving honours usually reserved for the Gods. He also embarked on a major programme of reform, including of the calendar, and settled thousands of landless veteran soldiers whose debts he cancelled. Such actions increasingly set him aloof from his noble peers of all factions. Friction with them soon grew to breaking point, despite Caesar filling the Senate with allies and courting the adulation of the masses. Matters finally came to a head with his assassination aged 55 on the Ides of March in 44 BC in the *curia* (senate house), then temporarily housed in the theatre of Pompey in the *Campus Martius* (Fields of Mars). The Liberators, as the protagonists dubbed themselves, were a posse of senators keen to turn the clock back to the 'great' days of the earlier Republic. However, their actions totally failed given the event martyred Caesar in the eyes of his contemporaries and started the final vicious round of civil wars that destroyed the Republic and created the Empire. In the decade after his death Caesar's supporters, led by his general Mark Antony, first fought and defeated his assassins, and then turned on themselves. A brief attempt to restore peace occurred through the Second Triumvirate, but again this failed. War broke out once more and by 31 BC there was again only one man left standing, Caesar's great nephew and adopted son Octavian, after he and his general Marcus Agrippa defeated Marc Antony and Cleopatra VII Philopator at the naval battle of Actium in northern Greece.

Octavian was keenly aware that the Roman political classes and wider population were exhausted after nearly a century of civil war, especially the recent brutal campaigns following the death of Caesar. A shrewd political operator, instead of announcing himself a 'dictator', he quietly started to gather the reins of power within Rome. Then, in 27 BC when it was obvious to all where the power in Rome now lay, the Senate declared him Augustus (from the Latin *augere* meaning 'illustrious one') and *princeps* (meaning 'master'). Thus, the Roman Empire was born, initially in the form of his Principate.

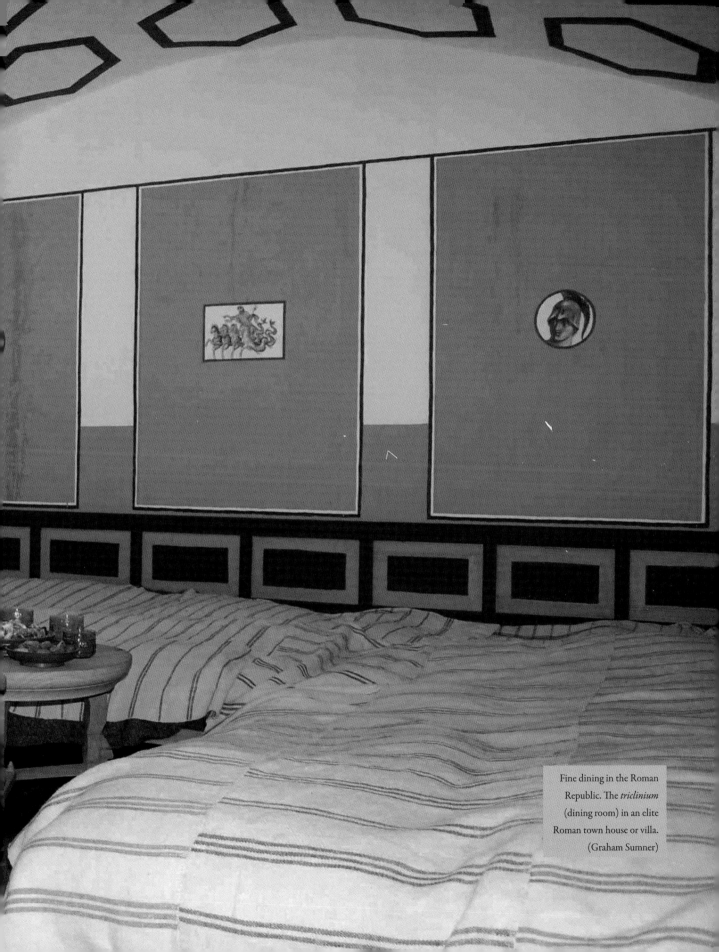

Fine dining in the Roman Republic. The *triclinium* (dining room) in an elite Roman town house or villa. (Graham Sumner)

CHAPTER 2 🗡
THE REPUBLICAN MILITARY

Greek warriors fight in Paestum, Magna Graecia. Note the *aspis* at right, plumed helmets and the greaves worn by the warrior at left.

Oscan warriors clash in Paestum, Magna Graecia. Note the warrior on the right, carrying a Greek *aspis*.

Greek or Oscan cavalryman at Paestum, Magna Graecia. Carrying an *aspis* and javelins. Note the lack of a formal saddle.

T he Roman military machine was pre-eminent in the ancient world. Even when it lost in campaign and battle, it learned from its mistakes and most often returned victorious. Yet the story of how the warriors of Rome became the elite soldiers of their time is far from straightforward. In this chapter I first trace the development of the iconic legionary from before the time of the Republic to the onset of the Principate Empire, this including an examination of their life experiences. I then consider the mercenaries and allies used by the armies of the Republic to bolster their military capability, before finally focusing on how the naval might of Rome evolved from the 4th century BC onwards.

Evolution of the Republican Legionary

The first insight we have into Roman military tradition comes from a time when the city was under Etruscan rule before the days of the Republic. This Etrusco-Roman army adopted the Greek-style hoplite phalanx as its main line of battle formation, it being introduced to the region when the Etruscans came into contact with the Greek colonies of southern Italy and eastern Sicily. The term phalanx references a deep formation of armoured spearmen whose front ranks fought with their long spears in an overarm thrusting position. Each front-rank warrior was protected by interlocking *aspis* (large round body shields) carried by the hoplite and his neighbours. Warriors in the rear ranks added their weight to the formation, and replaced those who fell in battle. This style of fighting is detailed in full in Chapter 8.

The Etrusco-Roman phalanx was supported on its flanks by Roman/Latin troops who still fought in a loose formation as did their Villanovan ancestors. Common weapons for these troops were short spears, axes and javelins. This way of fighting, with a solid phalanx of hoplites in the centre and lighter troops either side, was formalised by Servius Tullius, the first of the great reforming Roman military leaders. He instituted the Servian

Constitution in the mid-6th century BC that divided Roman society into seven different classes.

Tullian Military Classes

- The *equites*, the wealthiest citizens who could afford a mount and thus formed the cavalry.
- The First Class, the next wealthiest forming 80 centuries of hoplite-equipped spearmen fighting as a phalanx. Most troops here would have been of Etruscan origin.
- The Second Class, 20 centuries of spearmen with helmet, greaves and the *scutum* (rectangular shield).
- The Third Class, 20 centuries of spearmen with helmet and *scutum*.
- The Fourth Class, 20 centuries of spearmen with *scutum* only.
- The Fifth Class, 20 centuries of missile troops with slings and javelins.
- The *capite censi*, this translating as head count and referencing those in Etrusco-Roman society with little or no property. This class had no military commitment.

(*previous pages*)
The Second Temple of Hera at Paestum in the Bay of Salerno, Classical Greek culture in Magna Graecia dating to around 450 BC.

Each had a different military commitment to the Roman state based on wealth.

Armies formed in this way are often dubbed Tullian Roman (see on opposite page). Note *scutum* here refers to an Italian rectangular shield design rather than the much more substantial body shield of the mid to late Republic and Principate.

This military system began to evolve after Rome and its fellow Latin towns broke away from Etruscan control. As detailed in Chapter 1, they now faced the hill tribes of the Apennines, such as the Aequi, Umbri, Sabini and Volsci. These fought in a looser formation and often sought battle in rough terrain to negate the power of the First-Class phalanx, whose importance began to diminish. Then, after Rome became a Republic with the overthrow of Tarquin the Proud in 509 BC, three key events took place that had a big impact on the development of the Roman military system. The first was the initiation of the eight-year siege of Veii that ended in 396 BC. The second was the appointment of Marcus Furius Camillus as consular tribune in 401 BC, in the context of the increasingly unpopular siege. The third was the Roman defeat by the Senones Gauls at the battle of

Chariot of winged victory at Paestum, Magna Graecia.

Allia in 390 BC, and the subsequent sack of Rome.

These dramatic events led in turn to three developments within the Roman army, together called the Camillan reforms after Camillus. Firstly, in the context of the long siege of Veii, the army began to receive pay for the first time. This was in the form of the *stipendium* (cash allowance). Secondly, and crucially, the phalanx was formally abandoned. A key factor here was the height of the Gallic warriors the Romans faced at Allia, and their fighting technique. They were taller than their Latin counterparts and fought with long iron swords using a downward slashing technique. This rendered the *aspis*, designed to defend the user and his neighbours from frontal attack, less practical. The final, and connected, development was the abandonment of all previous line-of-battle shields – including the *aspis* – in favour of the *scutum*. Here it now references the famous specific type rather than the earlier generalised shield.

The outcome of all of these reforms was the appearance of the manipular legion to replace the Tullian Roman system, this early iteration called the Camillan system. Initially there were two such legions, each commanded by a consul with six

tribuni militum acting as subordinates. The early manipular legion numbered 3,000 infantry each, though this quickly increased with time, ultimately numbering over 6,000. Within this legion there were now three classes of line-of-battle troops, all termed for the first time legionaries. Based on experience and age rather than the equipment they could afford, these were:

- The *triarii*, veterans in helmet and body armour, carrying the *scutum*, *hasta* (thrusting spear) and sword. These replaced, in part, the old Tullian First Class.

- The *principes*, older warriors also in helmet and body armour, carrying the *scutum*, *pila* (heavy throwing javelin) and sword. These also replaced, in part, the old Tullian First Class.

- The *hastati*, 'the flower of young men', with helmet and lesser body armour, carrying the *scutum*, *pila* and sword. These replaced the old Tullian Second Class.

It is unclear how quickly the *pilum* replaced the spear among the new *principes* and *hastati*, though unusually, given they are clearly named after the *hasta*, it was the latter who converted first.

All three troops types formed up in a looser formation than the old Etrusco-Roman phalanx. This allowed free use of the sword and body shield. The *triarii* could be deployed in closer formation if a hedge of spears was required, for example against cavalry. The legion was completed with three lesser classes of warrior, the *rorarii*, *accensi* and *leves* who replaced, sequentially, the old Tullian Third, Fourth and Fifth classes. These troops became less important as the Republic progressed.

The manipular legion deployed in three lines. The first comprised 15 maniples of hastati, each of around 60 men and two officers. Each of these maniples had 20 *leves* attached to act as skirmishers. The second line then had 15 maniples of *principes*, again each of around 60 men and two officers. The third line comprised 15 *ordines*,

each *ordo* comprised of a *vexilla* of *triarii*, a *vexilla* of *rorarii* and a *vexilla* of *accensi*. Each *vexilla* numbered 60 troops and two officers, with the *triarii* additionally featuring a standard bearer. The term *vexilla* later evolved into the word *vexillation* used to describe detached regiments of Principate and Dominate legionaries and *auxilia*.

The *triarii*, as veterans, were the tactical reserve held back to exploit success, plug gaps in the first two lines or to cover a retreat. When not engaged, they deployed kneeling on their right knee. It is less clear how the *rorarii* and *accensi* were utilised, but a deployment on the flanks – as with the older Third and Fourth Tullian classes – or as camp guards seems most likely.

In terms of defensive equipment, the basic panoply of legionary protection for the Camillan *triarii*, *principes* and hastati was the *scutum*, helmet and armour of some kind for the upper torso and often also the lower legs.

The original Camillan legionary *scutum* was a large curved rectangular body shield, up to 120cm in length and 75cm in width. Made from planed wooden strips that were laminated together in three layers, the shield featured an *umbones* (iron boss) attached to the centre where the shield was slightly thicker. It was completed by fitting a calfskin/felt facing. This substantial shield was very heavy and could weigh up to 10kg, being held by a horizontal grip using a straightened arm. Crucially, rather than just being used for protection, it was also used as an offensive weapon in its own right, being smashed into opponents to push them over.

For body armour Camillan legionaries of all three classes wore a square bronze pectoral covering their heart and upper chest. This was held in place with leather straps. However, as the Republic progressed those who could afford it (usually *triarii* and *principes*) increasingly replaced these primitive pectorals with *lorica hamata* (chainmail shirts). Of Gallic origin and weighing up to 15kg, these offered greatly improved protection, covering the torso from shoulder to hip. They were made from interlinked iron rings 1mm thick and up to 9mm in external diameter, with up to 20,000 needed for each shirt. The name of the shirt was derived from the Latin *hamatus* meaning hooked, referencing the interlinked rings of iron or bronze.

This defensive panoply was completed with a helmet. These were made from bronze, fitting the cranium and providing good overall protection. Popular designs included those called Etrusco-Corinthian, Attic and Montefortino, the latter particularly popular in the Camillan legions. Additionally, if the legionary could afford it, his defensive equipment was completed with an iron or bronze greave on the leading left lower leg – both legs for the very well off. This was to prevent a debilitating blow to the shin that would open the legionary's guard to a mortal blow.

For his offensive weapon, as detailed, the *triarii* carried the *hasta*, up to 2.5m in length. Harking back to the hoplite origins of the old Tullian First-Class warrior, this featured a socketed iron spearhead up to 30cm in length and a bronze butt-spike, the latter acting as a counterweight to the spearhead. The weapon was usually wielded over the right shoulder to deliver a forceful overarm strike, although if used in the charge it could instead be deployed underarm.

Meanwhile, eventually all Camillan *principes* and hastati carried two *pila*, one heavy and one light. Each had a barbed head on a long, tapering iron shank whose weighted socket, attaching it to the wooden shaft, provided the punching force to hammer the weapon through enemy shields and armour. In terms of specific use, the lighter *pilum* was used as the *principes* and *hastati* approached the enemy. The heavier weapon was then used immediately prior to impact. The long iron shafts were specifically designed to bend after impact and so disable the use of the opponent's shield.

However, the principal weapon of the Camillan *principes* and *hastati* – and side arm of the spear-armed *triarii* – was the sword, with all legionaries trained to fight with a particular fencing technique. This involved taking the blow of an opponent on the large *scutum*, they then being dispatched with a swift upward or downward stabbing action to their exposed midriff or neck. Throughout much of the Camillan period such swords were comparatively simple leaf-shaped iron blades or the curved *kopis* favoured in Etruscan and Greek armies. The latter,

either of Etruscan or Macedonian origin, had a 65cm single-edged doglegged blade ideal for slashing.

After Rome's conflict with Pyrrhus in the early 3rd century BC the manipular legion further evolved into what historians call the Polybian system. This was named after the leading 2nd century BC Greek historian who narrated the story of Rome's conflicts in the 3rd and 2nd centuries BC. Legions of this period again deployed in three lines, featuring 1,200 *hastati* in 10 maniples of 120, 1,200 *principes* who were organised in the same way, and 600 *triarii* in 10 maniples of 60. Each maniple featured two centurions, two subordinates and two standard bearers. The major change was the disappearance of the *leves* who were replaced with 1,200 *velites*. These were elite specialist skirmishers, divided up among the other maniples for administrative purposes. Famous for their wolf-skin headdresses that set them apart on the battlefield, they carried bundles of javelins called *hastae velitares* that featured a 75cm shaft with 25cm iron tang and narrow armour penetrating blade. The formal transition from *leves* to *velites* was complete by 209 BC. The *rorarii* and *accensi* also disappear from this point.

The Polybian manipular legion also featured a formal cavalry component. This was 300 strong, divided into 10 *turmae* of 30 troopers. Like the high-status *equites* of the earlier Tullian army, this small force was actually the most prestigious within the legion. However, unlike the later auxiliary cavalry component of the Principate legions that served administrative and scouting functions, these young aristocrats were more likely to charge headlong into battle. Cato for example boasted his grandfather had had five horses killed under him in this manner.

The Polybian legion was highly efficient, and although it initially struggled against Hannibal in Italy in the later 3rd century BC, was ultimately his nemesis at the battle of Zama in 202 BC where its flexibility was the key to a crushing victory. It was also a military system the Hellenistic kingdoms in the eastern Mediterranean never came to terms with, they being repeatedly defeated by it in set-piece battle as detailed in Chapter 1. There were four reasons why this later manipular legion was so successful:

Polybian legionaries and
an officer at the time of the
Punic Wars.
(Graham Sumner)

- The manipular legion was very flexible, deploying in its three lines when opportunity allowed. This ensured the troops in the second and third lines were fresh until needed as the battle progressed, unlike the opposing troops who might all be engaged from first contact (particularly Hellenistic armies). Further, given the wider spacing of the legionary compared to say the Carthaginian spearman or Macedonian phalangite, more complex manoeuvres could be carried out and rough terrain exploited. The former was key at the battle of Cynoscephalae against Philip V in 197 BC, the latter at the battle of Pydna against Perseus in 168 BC.

- Roman military psyche. In short, reflecting Roman culture more broadly, the manipular legions possessed true grit and were renowned for never giving up. Thus defeat, even if writ large on the battlefield, was never accepted and the Romans kept coming back. This is no more evident than in the context of the Second Punic War (see Chapter 1).

- As set out earlier, the Roman military was adept at seamlessly assimilating enemy military tactics and technology. Thus, Roman naval power had its origins in the First and Second Punic Wars, where the maritime prowess of the Carthaginians provided the template for ultimate Roman naval supremacy. This is detailed in full later in this chapter.

- Loot and plunder. Roman society was heavily structured and based on wealth qualifications, particularly among the aristocracy. Thus, although Rome was initially hesitant to engage in the western and eastern Mediterranean, the enormous wealth of Carthage and particularly the Hellenistic kingdoms ultimately proved an enormous draw. The more successful aristocratic military leaders, effectively independent warlords with private armies from the later 2nd century BC as detailed in Chapter 1, thus made huge fortunes

in their campaigns of conquest, with the soldiery equally well motivated through the promise of fabulous plunder.

The *triarii*, *principes* and *hastati* of the Polybian legions were broadly equipped in the same way as their Camillan predecessors. However, they featured three new innovations in terms of equipment. Firstly, as the Republic progressed and the legionaries came into more contact with the Gauls and later Galatians, two new helmet types appeared. These were the Coolus design with a round cap of bronze and small neck guard, and the iron Port type with a deep neck guard. A particularly fine example of a Gallic Coolus helmet was excavated in 2008 at North Bersted, West Sussex by Thames Valley Archaeological Services. This featured an enormous crest that would have set the wearer out as a man of great importance, showing how versatile this helmet design was. However, it was ultimately the Port type that came to dominate Roman helmet design given it evolved into the classic 'imperial' Gallic helmet often associated with the later Principate Roman legionaries of the 1st and 2nd centuries AD. Etrusco-Corinthian, Attic and Montefortino designs continued to be used by the Polybian legionary, but most had disappeared by the beginning of the 1st century BC.

Secondly, a further new addition to the Polybian legionary's panoply was the *gladius Hispaniensis*. This proved so successful that it had replaced all earlier types by the mid-3rd century BC and was to remain the standard legionary weapon through to the later Principate period. As the name suggests the *gladius* was of Spanish origin, and rather than being the short stabbing sword of popular legend, in the Polybian period it was instead a cut and thrust design up to 69cm long and 5cm in width. The *gladius* featured a tapering sharp stabbing point and was worn on the right-hand side unless by an officer, who wore it on the left as a mark of differentiation. Many have questioned how a legionary could draw the weapon smoothly into an en-guard position from the right-hand side, especially as the large pommel sat just below the armpit. However, experimental archaeology with well-equipped re-enactors has shown that it can easily be drawn by inverting the right hand, thumb downwards, then grasping the handgrip and pulling straight upwards. It is then a natural progression to continue this movement forwards to bring the sword down to the side, point forward, in the characteristic legionary fencing stance. Those *gladii* used in the Polybian legions inflicted gaping injuries that shocked their opponents in the Second Macedonian War when its widespread use is first noted. This was because it lacked any blood runnels to let air into a wound. Therefore, the sword had to be viciously twisted to release it. The final new addition at this time was the equipping of the Polybian legionaries with a *pugio*, a 30cm long dagger.

The final reform of the legions prior to the onset of the Principate were those carried out by the seven-time consul Marius, he completely reorganising the Roman military establishment in 107 BC at the height of the Cimbrian Wars which had tested the manipular legions to destruction. His aim was to turn each individual legion into a self-contained fighting force. To do this he standardised the legionary on the *gladius*- and *pilum*-armed *principes* and *hastati* (these terms now being dropped), with the spear-armed *triarii* and javelin-armed *velites* disappearing entirely. From this point, all of the fighting men in the legion were simply called legionaries, numbering 4,800 out of a total 6,000 men in each legion. The remaining 1,200 troopers were support personnel who carried out a wide variety of roles that enabled the legion to function autonomously (see Chapter 6 for full detail).

Marius also replaced the old Camillan and Polybian manipular system with centuries, each comprising 80 legionaries and 20 support staff, sub-divided into units of 10 (8 legionaries and two non-combatants). Each century was commanded by a centurion, having specific titles which reflected their seniority based on the old Camillan and Polybian manipular legions. The names, with seniority in ascending order, were:

- *hastatus posterior*
- *hastatus prior*
- *princeps posterior*
- *princeps prior*
- *pilus posterior*
- *pilus prior*

The Marian legionaries lived, fought and ate together, with each legion developing their own identity around the new *aquila* (eagle standards) introduced by Marius. Training was also regularised, with Marius insisting on regular fitness drills to ensure the legionaries were always physically fit. This was to ensure they could carry their own equipment on campaign, with the troops earning the nickname *muli mariani* (Marius's mules). One should perhaps envision the Marian legionary as having the same body shape as a modern Olympic weightlifter, square and all muscle. His training particularly focused on martial skills, based on the methods used to instruct gladiators. As an example, for sword drill a large stake the size of an opponent was set up in the training ground. The trooper then practiced his *gladius*- and *scutum*-based fencing technique as detailed above using a wooden replica sword and

A late republican/early Principate senior centurion. (Graham Sumner)

(*opposite*)
A late republican/early Principate *cornicen* (horn blower), tasked with pacing the legionaries on the march and issuing orders in battle. (Graham Sumner)

wicker shield, with the stake being 'the enemy'.

One of the main advantages of the new Marian legions, as set out in Chapter 1, was that they didn't have to rely on long lines of supply given they were self-contained units with integral specialists. This allowed late republican warlords like Marius, Sulla, Pompey and Caesar to amalgamate a large number into huge armies owing their loyalty to a specific leader, especially when campaigning on the frontiers of the growing Republic well away from Rome. In such circumstances it became common for the various warlords to actually raise their own legions without the approval of the Senate, often using their own or supporter's money to finance them.

In terms of equipment, these Marian legionaries were all equipped in the same way, with *scutum*, *lorica hamata*, Coolus and Port-type helmets, two *pila*, the *gladius* and the *pugio*. By doing away with differentially armed troop types within the legions, Marius therefore made them much easier to maintain in the field.

The standard deployment in battle for the Marian legions, including those of Caesar and Pompey, remained the three lines of the earlier manipular system. The first two were deployed to sequentially engage the enemy (second-line units replacing the front-line units as the latter tired), while the third acted as a reserve, just as the *triarii* had in the manipular legions. Caesar himself provides direct insight into this tactical approach, describing how when fighting the supporters of Pompey in Spain in 49 BC, he deployed four cohorts of legionaries in his front line and three in the second and third.

The Life of the Republican Legionary

Until the reforms of Marius, the Camillan and Polybian manipular legions were formed by a compulsory levy of Roman citizens who met a minimum wealth/property qualification. These formations were raised whenever necessary rather than being forces in being. Recruitment into their ranks was usually authorised by the Senate, with the legion later being disbanded once the need for its existence had passed.

A key aspect of Marius's reforms in 107 BC was to realise that, given Rome's by then widespread military responsibilities, this early republican system was no longer sustainable. He determined standing units were required that could remain in existence for years or even decades, and the Marian legions were born. To man these he principally relied on volunteer recruits usually aged between 17 and 23, though some were as young as 13 and or as old as 36. Additionally, in times of crisis, the number of legionaries was bolstered by conscription under a levy called the *dilectus*.

Each Marian legionary, whether recruit or conscript, signed up for a minimum term of six years. This length of service lasted until at least the battle of Actium in 31 BC. Land was then offered to them upon retirement as a stipend, these veterans often being settled in colonies. Caesar provides a good example: his retirees after the campaign in Greece against Pompey were settled in the Hellenistic city of Butrint (*Buthrōtum*) in modern Albania.

As detailed, Marius also abolished the wealth/property requirement for the legionary, and from that point most recruits came from the landless lower classes. This was a shrewd move that increased the sense of identity within each individual legion, with the legionaries now increasingly 'other' when compared to the rest of society. At a stroke the warlords of the later Empire were therefore able to wield armies that owed more loyalty to them than to the Senate and people of Rome. Julius Caesar then set a trend which underpinned the success of his own legions, regularising pay levels for his troops at 225 *denarii* a year. It is unclear if his opponents immediately copied the move, but this amount became standard legionary pay through to the time of Emperor Domitian in the late 1st century AD. Caesar was also adept at spreading the plunder from his campaigns among his troops, always going out of his way to ensure he didn't appear to be amassing wealth for his own ends.

Like all armies, the republican legions marched on their stomachs. Later the 4th-century AD writer Vegetius said in his military manual that troops should never be without corn, salt, wine and vinegar and that would certainly have been

the case for Caesar's legions, with beans, bread, porridge, vegetables and eggs forming the core diet. Meat would be added on feast days, with the wider diet supplemented by local produce and hunting. On campaign, the daily staples were whole-wheat biscuits and hard tack, together with bread baked in the marching camp at the end of the day's march.

Such marching camps were also a key feature in the life of the republican and later Principate and Dominate legionary when on campaign, from the time of Rome's conflict with Pyrrhus of Epirus. These large-scale temporary fortifications were built by the legionaries at the end of each day's march in enemy territory. They were constructed in a few hours and came in a variety of sizes dependent on the scale of the force that needed protection, with at the larger end those of almost 70 ha found in the Scottish Borders used there during the Severan campaigns in the early 3rd century AD. Almost always playing card in shape, Roman marching camps generally featured a deep ditch between one and two metres wide, with the spoil then being used to create an internal rampart. Atop this ran a palisade created by the stakes the troops carried as part of their specialist engineering equipment (see Chapter 7), either a continuous wooden barrier or one created by the stakes being lashed together to form large caltrops. Within this barrier the camp would then be set out for the night, effectively recreating the interior layout of a permanent Roman fortification. The next day (or longer if the camp was occupied for more than a night), the camp was struck in swift order. This was in a very specific way, with the first trumpet call from the *cornicern* signalling the legionaries to strike their tents, the second telling them to ready the pack animals and destroy the camp, and the third to fall into marching ranks.

Meanwhile, religion was a key feature in the daily lives of the republican legionary, playing a major role in their appreciation of belonging and belief, especially later in the Marian legions when they served for lengthy periods of time. Roman society, within the military and without, was very conservative and in that regard each legionary was obliged to honour the gods of the Roman

pantheon, in particular the Capitoline triad of Jupiter, Juno and Minerva given their association with Rome. We can add to these Mars, given he was the god of war.

For non-military kit all republican legionaries carried their equipment on a T-shaped pole resting on their shoulders when on the march, with the shield held in place across the back. Helmets were usually strung from the neck across the chest. The marching kit also included a *paenula* (hooded woolen bad weather cloak) made from thick wool that fastened with a button or toggles on the centre of the chest. The officers wore a shorter rectangular cloak called a *sagum* that fastened on the right shoulder with a brooch. A very important piece of kit for the legionary was his hobnailed *caligae* (sandals). Typically these featured a leather upper made from a single leather piece which was sewn at the heel. This was then stitched to a multiple layer hide sole shod with many iron studs, each sandal weighing up to 1kg. From the time of the Marian reforms each legionary was also a skilled engineer in his own right, with building and engineering playing an enormous part of his working life. To enable the warriors to fulfill such a roll they also carried a stake (as used in the marching camp defences), saw, pickaxe, chain, sickle, basket and leather strap. Finally, these late republican legionaries also carried a sturdy cross-braced satchel for their personal effects, a water skin in a net bag, a *patera* (bronze mess tin), a cooking pot, canvas bags for grain rations, spare clothing, and bespoke engineering equipment.

Other Troops in the Republican Roman Military

Republican Roman armies after the Camillan reforms were predominantly based on legionary heavy infantry. Roman commanders therefore recruited mercenary and allied troops to supply other capabilities on campaign and in battle, for example most of their cavalry and much of their specialist skirmishing light infantry. Many of the types detailed below are considered in far more

The city of Butrint in modern Albania, where Julius Caesar settled many of his veterans after defeating Pompey at the battle of Pharsalus.

detail in Chapter 8 in my full review of the allies and enemies of the Roman Republic and Empire.

Early on in the Republic, such troops were recruited from Italy. Examples included Latin neighbours, or the hill tribesmen of the Hernici, Aequi, Umbri, Sabini and Volsci. These were soon joined by warriors from Samnium and Magna Graecia. However, from this point as Rome began its irresistible advance across first the western and then eastern Mediterranean, the mercenaries and allies began to be recruited from much further afield. This was to have a dramatic effect not only on the make-up of the mid and later republican armies, but also on the equipment of the legionaries themselves as the Romans began to adopt the tactics and technology of their mercenaries, allies and enemies.

In its wars against Carthage the Romans first came up against troops from Germany, Gaul, Spain and North Africa. Impressed, they recruited them in large numbers. The Gauls were renowned for their fierce charge, their elite warriors wearing coats of mail and iron helmets that soon found their way into the legionary panoply. Meanwhile the Spaniards, equally fierce, provided the inspiration for the *scutum*, *pilum* and *gladius*. Both also supplied the bulk of the cavalry used by the mid and later republican armies in the western Mediterranean, with Gallic cavalry particularly feared as trophy headhunters. Meanwhile, from North Africa Rome recruited Numidian light horses, famous for skirmishing with javelins with which they showered their foes. They were particularly known for their practice of hamstringing opposing foot troops when pursuing a broken enemy. It was also from North Africa that republican Roman armies sourced their elephants. The Romans first encountered these terrifying beasts of war when fighting Pyrrhus of Epirus, and later Carthage and Numidia, they making a huge impression on contemporary audiences. Two different elephant types were used in a military context in the classical world. The first was the Indian variety first encountered by Alexander the Great in the early 320s BC when fighting in India. He was so impressed that he created his own elephant corps, this becoming a key feature of many later Hellenistic armies including that of Pyrrhus. Meanwhile, the second type was the smaller African forest elephant used by Ptolemaic Egypt, Carthage and Numidia. These were initially sourced from the Horn of Africa after

By the late republican period the legions of Rome were based in legionary fortresses set out along the borders of its various conquered territories. Here we see a typical barrack block for legionaries in such a fortress.
(Graham Sumner)

the Ptolemies were cut off from supplies of Indian elephants by the Syrian Wars with the Seleucid Empire. They proved easy to breed in captivity and their use quickly spread westwards through North Africa. The largest variety of elephant, the African bush type, was untrainable for war.

Elephant use by the Roman military was mostly restricted to the mid-republican period, with 20, for example, being fielded by Titus Quinctius Flaminius against the Macedonian King Philip V at Cynoscephalae in 197 BC during the Second Macedonian War. There is some doubt as to whether they were still in use by the mid-1st century BC. The 2nd century AD Macedonian author Polyaenus (*Stratagems*, 8.23.5) records that 'Caesar' had one large elephant when campaigning in Britain, which he used to force a crossing over a large river, often identified as the River Thames. Caesar himself doesn't mention this in his own writing, which I believe he would have given his obsession with prestige, and most historians don't give the reference any credit. Polyaenus was most likely confusing his source material with Claudius's successful AD 43 invasion when elephants are

certainly recorded arriving with the emperor prior to the submission of the regional British tribes at the Catuvellauni capital of Camulodunum (modern Colchester, see Chapter 6 for detail). It should be noted it is not clear if these were trained war elephants, they most likely being obtained from the emperor's personal menagerie to 'shock and awe' the native Britons. Alternatively, Polyaenus may have simply used the term 'Caesar' to directly refer to Claudius as the emperor. Caesar did actually obtain elephants from Italy to use during his Thapsus campaign in North Africa in 46 BC, using them to train his troops in how to engage the beasts. However, these are again not thought to have been trained war elephants and may have been animals originally destined for the arena. Caesar subsequently captured Pompey's elephants after defeating him at Pharsalus in 48 BC, the elephants originally supplied by Pompey's Numidian ally Juba. These are last mentioned at the battle of Mutina in 43 BC after Caesar's death. It is of course possible Caesar intended to take these elephants to Parthia with him where he next intended to campaign before he was assassinated.

Interior of a temple in Herculaneum with portrait showing the Capitoline Triad – Jupiter, Juno and Minerva.

A pair of reproduced *caligae*, heavy-soled hobnailed military boots, a vital piece of legionary kit. (Trimontium Trust)

However, war elephants were always a double-edged sword in the ancient world, difficult to control and expensive to maintain. Often a bigger threat to their own troops than the enemy, it seems likely that the pragmatic Caesar distrusted them and preferred to rely on his legionaries and supporting mercenaries and allies.

To these troops, exotic and otherwise, the Romans added other specialist troop types in the western Mediterranean, particularly light infantry. These included javelinmen from Germany, Spain and Numidia, bowmen from across the region and slingers from Syracuse and the Balearic Isles, the latter particularly skilled with their weapon and much in demand as mercenaries.

Once Rome turned its attention to the Hellenistic kingdoms of the eastern Mediterranean even more troops types began to bolster the ranks of the legionary spearheads as they knocked out the successor kingdoms of Alexander and their neighbours one by one. The most ubiquitous were the Hellenistic *thureophoroi* who strengthened the legionary line-of-battle from the mid-3rd century BC. These were named after their *thureos* (oval shield), a development of the Celtic infantry shield. This was smaller and less substantial than the hoplite's *aspis* but was more flexible. Armed with long spear and javelin, though unarmoured except for a helmet, the *thureophoroi* were initially light troops equipped

for close combat in a secondary role but whose flexibility saw them used more and more in front line combat.

Interestingly given the Roman propensity for osmosing the tactics, techniques and equipment of their opponents, in the republican period they never tried to adopt the pike that was the weapon most associated with Hellenistic armies. Phalanxes of pikemen 16 deep, wielding weapons up to 6m in length and with the pikes of the front five ranks set at the charge, were the hallmark of the armies of Macedonia, and later Greece, Epirus, the Seleucid Empire and Ptolemaic Egypt. Polybius, in his *Histories* (18.28–32), describes the imperviousness of this dense, bristling formation:

> ... so long as the phalanx retains its characteristic form and strength nothing can withstand its charge or resist it face to face ... we can easily picture the nature and the tremendous power of a charge by the whole phalanx, when it advances 16 deep with levelled pikes.

Yet when the legionaries faced the pike phalanx in the crucial battles of conquest in the region, for example at Cynoscephalae as detailed above, Magnesia and Pydna, they won every time. This was largely due to the inherent flexibility of the Camillan and Polybian manipular system that enabled the legions to make better use of tactical advantages. Given the scale of these and other victories over the pike phalanx, the republican Romans were clearly deterred from trying to equip even a few legionaries with the pike. In fact, the only attempt to arm legionaries with pikes would come much later when the emperors Caracalla and Severus Alexander tried in the early 3rd century AD, using Alexander the Great as their role model. Both failed.

Back to the mid and late republican periods in the eastern Mediterranean, Thracian peltasts were also popular as mercenaries, armed with the wicked-looking *rhomphia* (two-handed cutting weapon), javelins, and protected by the *pelta* (wicker shield). These were bolstered by other specialist troop types, for example highly sort after bowmen from Crete and slingers from Rhodes.

In terms of cavalry in the region, republican armies sourced mercenaries and allies from across the eastern Mediterranean, the principal suppliers being Macedonia and Greece. These mounted troops were armed in a very different fashion to the warriors that had fought with Alexander and his immediate successors. The latter had been shock troops equipped with the 4m *xyston* (lance), charging the enemy battle line in wedge formation and often delivering the battle-winning blow. However, by the time Macedon faced the growing might of Rome from the later 3rd-century BC Hellenistic line-of-battle cavalry had diminished to a skirmishing force using light spears and javelins. These only engaged enemy cavalry in hand-to-hand combat when necessary. Such a change in role is often associated with the introduction of the large cavalry shield in the 3rd century BC. This followed Pyrrhus's campaigns in Italy where he was suitably impressed by their use when fighting the Romans. The Galatian invasion of Greece in 279 BC was another catalyst. The advent of these shields made using the long *xyston* problematic for cavalry given the saddle technology of the day, and certainly by the time they were employed by the legions of Rome mercenary cavalry from the region they had a very secondary role, scouting and protecting flanks.

A last point of reflection here concerns formal allies. It was in the eastern Mediterranean where these fought most visibly with the legions. Prominent examples included Rhodes, the Aitolian League from mountainous central Greece, the Galatians (eastern Gauls) and Bithynians from Asia Minor, Armenians from the southern Caucasus Mountains and Judeans from the Levant. However, the best-known example is the Pergamene force of Eumenes II that formed the left wing of the Roman army at Magnesia in 190 BC. This played a crucial role in the overwhelming Roman victory over the Seleucids, including facing down a terrifying scythed chariot charge.

The Republican Roman Navy

Rome came late to naval warfare. The earliest record we have of a Roman warship dates to 394 BC, this referencing the transport of three senators to the Oracle at Delphi to present a votive offering. The trip ended badly when the vessel was captured on its journey. By 349 BC the nascent Roman navy was still too small to engage a single squadron of Greek pirate vessels cruising up the Italian peninsula, they instead being encouraged to depart by a legionary force. A growing capability does emerge by 338 BC when a first Roman naval victory is recorded in the context of conflict with its Latin neighbours shortly after the First Samnite War. This event was significant enough to prompt Taranto, the major regional naval power, to invite Rome to sign a treaty limiting the latter's naval activity off its coast in return for the provision of naval support when requested. This was a good deal for the Romans at the time given their fleet was still small, numbering only 20 vessels by the time of the Second Samnite War. However, the navy did grow sharply in size as the Republic matured, particularly when Rome expanded its influence south along the Italian peninsula into Magna Graecia where the Greek Italiote colonies were increasingly obligated to provide additional naval resources for their newly powerful northern neighbour. Rome then continued to flex its growing naval power as the century drew came to a close, with a Roman fleet seizing the Pontine Islands to protect the coast between the Bay of Naples and Ostia in 312 BC.

The growing importance of this fledgling part of the Roman military establishment was officially recognised in 311 BC when a 'navy board' comprising two officers called the *duoviri navales* was established. Their role was to ensure that the newfound Roman naval capability was fit for purpose when called on for action. By the end of the 4th century BC the Roman fleet had grown to over 40 vessels of various sizes, this being used to varying degrees of success, but it was the next century that was to see Roman naval power mature in the context of the Punic Wars.

By 272 BC, with the end of the Pyrrhic Wars detailed in Chapter 1 and the capture of Taranto, Rome was now the dominant power in the Italian peninsula south of the River Po. This led to a vast increase both in the coastline it controlled and associated maritime trade, causing an inevitable

Early Roman warriors fighting in the Tullian system. The soldier at right is a First-class Etrusco-Roman hoplite fighting in a classical Greek phalanx, while those at centre and left are Second-class warriors supporting the elite spearmen on the flanks. (Graham Sumner)

(*opposite*)
The business end of a Roman war galley, its ram, designed to smash through the hull of an opposing galley or rake the oars down its side.

clash with Carthage, the existing regional superpower in the western Mediterranean. By this time the Carthaginian Empire, which reflecting its Phoenician origins relied heavily on its maritime prowess, included its core territory along the Tunisian North African coast, part of Corsica, most of Sardinia and a large swathe of southern and eastern Spain. As such it presented a solid barrier to any Roman expansion westwards into the Mediterranean and soon the two were at war, with the First Punic War breaking out in 264 BC. The pretext for this was control over the key Sicilian city of Messina, with Rome making the first move. Spotting an opportunity when the Carthaginian squadron there left on patrol, the Romans transported a consular army by sea which quickly occupied the city and ejected the Carthaginian garrison. The latter responded by deploying their regional fleet to raid up and down the Italian coast, this highlighting the disparity in the number of ships in their respective navies. Rome responded in turn with typical robustness, the Senate approving the construction of the first 'official' Roman fleet. This comprised 100 quinqueremes to fight as line-of-battle ships and 20 *trireme*s to act as fast scouts (see below for ship details), their design based on captured Carthaginian vessels. Here we see that remarkable Roman propensity for copying the successful tactics and technology of their opponents yet again. However, here they went further, with Roman innovation now coming to the fore. Recognizing that they lacked the nautical skills at the time to tackle the Carthaginians in a full naval battle, the Romans played to their main strength. This was in land warfare where they considered themselves superior to the Carthaginians. To that end they fitted their new ships with the *corvus*, a 11m boarding ramp fitted to the bow, this featuring a large iron spike designed to penetrate the deck of the vessel being engaged when the ramp was dropped. Roman marines would then board the enemy vessel, engaging opposing crew in hand-to-hand fighting. Equipped in the same manner as the legionaries of the period, the Roman troops would usually overwhelm the defending Carthaginians given the superiority of their fighting technique in such close quarters.

Things didn't always go the Roman way, and in an early encounter a small Carthaginian fleet managed to capture 17 Roman vessels, though the Carthaginians came off the worse in a subsequent minor engagement. However, the first major naval action of the war took place in 260 BC when 143 Roman ships engaged 130 Carthaginian vessels at the battle of Mylae off the Sicilian coast. Here the Romans used the *corvus* for the first time en masse, securing the capture of 50 Carthaginian vessels. At a stroke Punic control of the oceanic western Mediterranean had been overturned. Further engagements over the next few years saw Rome taking Corsica and most of Sardinia, then defeating the Carthaginian fleet twice at Sulci in 258 BC. In 257 BC Malta was captured, with the Roman fleet again victorious. By 256 BC the respective fleets had reached 300 ships each in number, and the Romans decided to take the war to the Carthaginian homeland in North Africa. This crossing was made carrying a huge force of 50,000 troops, the Romans successfully avoiding the Punic fleet sent to intercept it, with the subsequent landing carried out unopposed on the North African coast. However, against expectations the legions were then beaten by the Carthaginian army and had to fall back on the town of Nabeul on the Tunisian coast which they fortified. The following spring a Roman fleet of 200 vessels plus transports set off to carry out an evacuation, heavily defeating a Carthaginian naval force sent to intercept it. In this engagement, which featured an additional 40 Roman vessels that had sallied from Nabeul, 114 Carthaginian ships were driven ashore and destroyed or captured. A successful evacuation followed, though this relative success turned into a monumental disaster when the returning fleet of up to 400 vessels (including those captured from the Carthaginians) ran into a great storm which destroyed all but 80 vessels. The loss of life of around 100,000 (including many of the most experienced sailors and veteran soldiers) was the largest in a single seafaring event in history and may be an indication that, while Roman military prowess at sea had clearly grown, they still had much to learn about long-range nautical skills. Despite this catastrophe the Romans again showed true grit

and managed to gather a new fleet of 170 warships within a year that, despite having untrained crews, helped capture the major Sicilian city of Palermo before successfully raiding the North African coast. However, on the return journey fate intervened again, with 27 Roman vessels lost on the rocky coastline off Cape Palinuro.

The war dragged on, with the new Roman fleet defeated in 249 BC in its first naval engagement. The surviving vessels yet again succumbed to a storm that reduced the overall Roman fleet to only 20 vessels. The growing Republic soon replaced the losses though, and this time with an improved line-of-battle design which featured better handling characteristics and a new, lighter version of the *corvus*. Major naval success followed in 241 BC when a Roman fleet intercepted a Punic resupply fleet destined for Sicily where the Carthaginian garrison was in desperate need of resupply. When this failed to get through, with the loss of 120 Punic vessels, the Carthaginians sued for peace.

The war ended in 240 BC with the withdrawal of Carthaginian troops from Sicily.

The First Punic War was a dramatic coming of age for Roman naval power. From a standing start, with no fleet capable of operating in the oceanic zone in the western Mediterranean, the Romans had established complete blue water sea control in the open ocean around Sicily, as well as control of the littoral zone around the coast of the island and most of the Italian peninsula. In terms of naval losses in the war, the Carthaginians lost more vessels to naval combat, though Rome lost more overall given their extensive storm casualties. However, Rome finished the conflict with the larger navy, and within a few years had added the remainder of Sardinia to its capture of Sicily (excepting Syracuse).

After its first war with Carthage Rome continued to expand its influence, with naval power playing a major role. One fleet campaigned in Liguria in the north-west of the Italian peninsula in the 220s

Roman war galley, merchant ship and pharos lighthouse, Ostia Antica.

A Roman *trireme* wall painting from Pompeii, view from the rear with steering oars in view, depicting a classical scene from the time of the Republic.

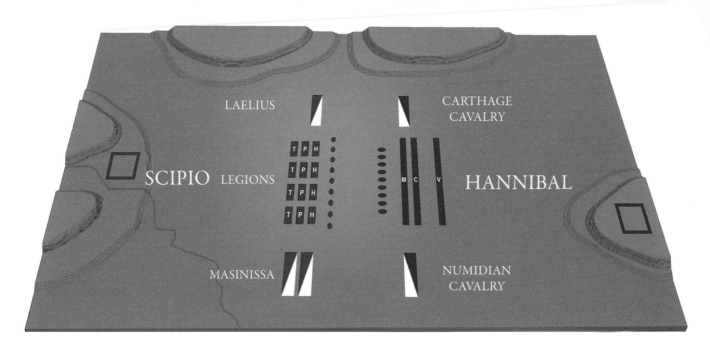

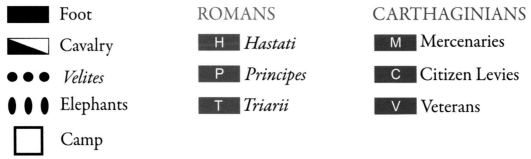

	Foot	ROMANS		CARTHAGINIANS	
■	Foot		Hastati	M	Mercenaries
◥	Cavalry	H			
●●●	*Velites*	P	*Principes*	C	Citizen Levies
❚❚❚	Elephants	T	*Triarii*	V	Veterans
□	Camp				

The battle of Zama in 202 BC where Publius Cornelius Scipio defeated Hannibal, setting up the Roman Republic for ultimate victory in the Second Punic War. (Nigel Emsen)

BC, while another tackled Illyrian piracy in the Adriatic. The latter saw Rome establish a physical presence in the Balkans for the first time in what is now modern Albania. With the Republic continuing to flex its power to satisfy its ever-growing regional ambitions, renewed conflict with Carthage was inevitable and the Second Punic War broke out in 218 BC.

Rome began the war with two fleets. One, of 60 ships, campaigned off the coast of Spain, while another was held in reserve to threaten the Carthaginian North African homeland. In this way Carthage was cut off from its colonies, forcing its leader Hannibal into his great gamble in invading Italy across the Alps in 218 BC. Despite tactical victories of huge proportions over the next two years, detailed in Chapter 1, he failed to bring Rome to heel and soon the legions were on the march again. As the tide in the conflict slowly

turned the way of Rome, its fleet now came to the fore, winning the first major naval engagement of the war at Lilybaeum off the Sicilian coast. Building on its success, Rome then established a naval base at Tarragona (*Taraco*) in Spain that cut Hannibal off from the Punic colonies there. A naval battle followed at the mouth of the River Ebro in 217 BC where the Romans were again triumphant, breaking the last vestiges of Carthaginian naval power in the western Mediterranean and capturing 25 Punic ships in the process.

Naval conflict continued to play a major role as the war progressed, with Hannibal now stranded outside Taranto in southern Italy, which he failed to capture given his lack of siege equipment. The city held out against him through supply by sea while the Roman navy denied him access to the city's extensive harbouring facilities. Rome later captured the key Sicilian city of Syracuse in 212

BC after seeing off a last desperate Carthaginian naval resupply attempt. Naval exchanges continued for the next decade, with the Roman fleet usually dominant as at the battle of Carteia in 206 BC, before the final defeat of Hannibal at the battle of Zama in 202 BC.

To show that Rome was once and for all the dominant naval power in the western Mediterranean, the remaining Punic vessels in Carthage were then towed out to sea and burned. This was very fitting, for in final analysis of this important conflict, while Hannibal was able to achieve the spectacular victories on his march down the Italian peninsula which have since resonated throughout history, it was actually Rome's aggressive dominance at sea which meant that the Carthaginians never had a chance of ultimate strategic victory.

As detailed in Chapter 1, an additional outcome of the Second Punic War was that Rome next turned its attention to the Hellenistic kingdoms of the eastern Mediterranean after Philip V's abortive attempt to form an alliance with Hannibal.

From this point onwards, the next fifty years of Roman expansion eastwards saw the Republic in conflict with the various successor kingdoms to Alexander the Great's empire. Naval campaigning again played a major role as, over time, the various opponents were beaten one by one, such that by 146 BC the Macedonian and Seleucid kingdoms and various combinations of Greek city-states had been vanquished.

The Roman fleets of this period in the early-to-mid-1st century BC were considerably smaller than at their height during the Second Punic War, with many ships decommissioned as Rome's opponents were successively defeated. A by-product of this was an increase in piracy, particularly along the Anatolian coast as the former sailors and marines in the defeated Hellenistic navies now looked to brigandage as a new way to make a living. They found ready employment manning the pirate vessels that began to plague the regional sea routes, challenging Roman sea control in the eastern Mediterranean and threatening its grain supply from Egypt. The Republic ultimately turned to Pompey to deal with the problem once

and for all, the Senate granting him unheard of powers, including command of a huge fleet and an *imperium* (area of control) stretching out 80km out from the Anatolian shoreline. He launched his campaign in 67 BC and within a year was victorious, using a highly organised campaigning strategy that saw him dividing the Mediterranean into 13 zones, seven in the east to target the pirates directly and six in the west to prevent them fleeing there. This sophisticated approach proved highly successful, with Pompey's campaign credited with killing 10,000 pirates, capturing another 20,000 and taking or destroying 600 vessels.

The next character to enter the stage of Roman naval history was Julius Caesar, in the form of his conquest of Gaul in the 50s BC, including his two incursions to Britain. In the first instance, as his Gallic campaign progressed into north-western Gaul, Caesar came into contact with the tribes of the Atlantic seaboard who had a totally different shipbuilding tradition to that of the Mediterranean. Preeminent were the Veneti of southern Brittany who controlled much of the cross-Channel marine traffic between Gaul and Britain. This trade had long thrived, as evidenced by LIA emporia sites at locations such as Hengistbury Head and Poole Harbour in Dorset, where large quantities of pre-conquest wine amphora and elite pottery have been found. Although the Veneti submitted to Roman authority in 57 BC after Caesar's second year campaigning in Gaul, they rebelled in 56 BC and became the main target of Roman campaigning that year. This culminated in Roman victory at the naval battle of Morbihan Gulf where Caesar had to innovate to defeat his Gallic opponents given their vessels were more suited to northern waters than the Mediterranean-built galleys used by Caesar. This innovation took the form of sickle-shaped hooks on the end of long poles which the Romans used to cut the rigging of the Veneti vessels, making them more vulnerable to boarding where once again the Roman marines were far better equipped than their opponents. Caesar's subsequent invasions of Britain are fully detailed in Chapter 6.

Caesar concluded his conquest of Gaul in 52 BC, though his success inevitably led to conflict

The island of Farmakonisi (*Pharmacussa*) off the coast of south-western Anatolia. Near here Julius Caesar was seized by Cilician pirates in 75 BC.

with his rivals back in Rome, most notably Pompey as detailed in Chapter 1. The latter's attempts to exercise control of the Tyrrhenian Sea after fleeing to Greece ultimately failed, with Caesar able to pursue him by transporting his army to the Balkans in a very risky mid-winter crossing. After a number of setbacks, Caesar was then ultimately victorious at the battle of Pharsalus in 48 BC (this fully detailed in Chapter 6).

Naval power again played a major role in the final next phases of republican civil war following Caesar's assassination in 44 BC, first between Mark Anthony and Octavian against the Liberators, and finally when Octavian fought the alliance of Mark Anthony and Cleopatra. The future first emperor was the ultimate victor at the crucial naval battle of Actium in 31 BC when his military commander Marcus Agrippa first achieved sea control around the coast of Greece to choke off his opponent's supply routes, and then forced the decisive engagement at Actium on his own terms. This left Octavian as the last man standing, with the Senate finally acknowledging him as Augustus in 27 BC, initiating the onset of the Principate Empire.

The vessels used by the navies of the Roman Republic had their origins at the beginning of the 1st millennia BC, in the form of pentaconter galleys featuring a single bank of oars either side. By the time of the Greek and Persian Wars in the 5th century BC these lines of battle ships had grown in size and were now styled *biremes* and *triremes*, so called because they featured two and three banks of oars respectively. As the millennia progressed, larger and larger polyremes appeared, including quadiremes (the '4', and so on), quinqueremes (allegedly invented by Syracusian dictator Dionysius 1 in 399 BC), hexaremes, septiremes, octeres, enneres and deceres. The evident pattern here was for vessels to get larger and larger, clearly a symptom of an arms race in the fairly symmetrical conflicts between the Hellenistic kingdoms, and later during Rome's expansion across the Mediterranean and its civil wars. In the case of the wars in the eastern Mediterranean in the 3rd and 2nd centuries BC even bigger ships were built, most notably by Demetrius the Besieger, his son Antigonus Gonatas, and Ptolemy IV, the latter

apparently constructing a '40'. However, these larger vessels would have been much fewer in number, serving principally as flagships, with the main line of battle war galleys at the time of the Punic Wars still being the quinquereme, and the main scout ship the *trireme*.

In terms of the naming of the vessel types based on the oaring system, the larger polyremes derived their names not from the number of banks of oars but from the number of men rowing on a given bank. In this context a quinquereme would feature a *trireme* arrangement but with two oarsmen rowing the top two tiers of oars. Whatever their size, the vessels would come in aphract (oarsmen unprotected), semi-cataphract (oarsmen partially protected) and cataphract (oarsmen fully protected) versions.

As detailed above, the Romans also came into contact with a totally different ship building tradition through Caesar's conquest of Gaul in the 50s BC. Such vessels were typified by those used against the Romans by the Veneti. Caesar himself provides a detailed description of these, saying (3:1):

The Gaul's own ships were built and rigged in a different manner from ours. They were made with much flatter bottoms, to help them ride shallow waters caused by shoals or ebb tides. Exceptionally high bows and sterns fitted them for use in heavy seas and violent gales, and the hulls were made entirely of oak, to enable them to stand any amount of shocks and rough usage. The cross-timbers, which consisted of beams a foot wide, were fastened with iron bolts as thick as a man's thumb. The anchors were secured with iron chains instead of ropes. They used sails made of raw hides or thin leather, either because they had no flax and were ignorant of its use, or more probably because they thought ordinary sails would not stand the violent storms and squalls of the Atlantic and were not suitable for such heavy vessels.

Caesar learned from their use and built 600 vessels to this design for his second incursion to Britain in 54 BC. Then, as Roman *imperium* unfolded throughout north-western Europe, the new provinces there made their own use of this ship-building technology, largely for merchant vessels. Ships built in this way are dubbed

Romano-Celtic in design. This tradition has been identified through the examination of over 30 wrecks found in the Severn Estuary, the Thames, the Channel Islands, the Schelde/Meuse/Rhine Delta, the Rhine at Xanten, and at Mainz. Roman ships constructed in this way broadly have the following features, setting them apart from galleys and merchant vessels built in the more common Mediterranean tradition:

- A framing of closely spaced, large timbers with half-frames spanning the sides and bottom, and with a floor covering the bilges and bottom (the individual timbers often not being fastened together).

- Planking which is flush-laid and fastened to the frame with large iron nails.

- Caulking within the plank seam using macerated twigs, moss or twisted fibre.

- Where a mast is used, the mast step being well forward.

It is a combination of such Mediterranean and Romano-Celtic designed vessels that came to dominate the regional fleets in the northern waters of the Empire, these detailed in full in the next chapter.

Julius Caesar, whose campaigns in Gaul introduced the Romans to a new, northwestern European boat-building tradition. (Livius.org/Jona Lendering)

CHAPTER 3 ✝
THE ROMAN EMPIRE

The Roman Empire was one of the longest surviving political institutions of world history. It came into being in the form of the Principate Empire following the Senate's acclamation of Augustus as the first emperor in 27 BC. This phase then lasted through to the end of the hugely damaging 'Crisis of the 3rd Century' in AD 284 when Diocletian became emperor. The latter realised that the Empire had been so damaged by the crisis that drastic action was required to restore order to its political institutions and economy. He therefore set about a programme of reform dubbed the Diocletianic Reformation. This transformed the Empire into something very different, it now entering what today is called its Dominate phase. In the west this lasted until the overthrow of Romulus Augustulus, the last emperor there, in AD 476. In the east the Empire was to continue in one form or another through the various iterations of the Byzantine Empire until AD 1453, when the Ottoman Turks finally sacked Constantinople.

In this chapter I detail the Roman Empire in both its principate and dominate phases sequentially. For both I additionally provide a detailed breakdown of its geographical organization at the time to provide context for the later detailed discussions regarding the Roman military. Under the Principate entry I also take the opportunity to provide a thorough description of Rome as it reached its Principate zenith towards end of the 2nd century AD.

The Roman Principate

As detailed above, the first phase of the Roman Empire is styled the Principate.

The name is derived from Augustus's title *princeps*, used by Augustus to reference himself as the 'first among equals', or, more accurately, first citizen of the Empire. It was then assumed by each subsequent emperor on their accession, though in reality was a conceit, allowing the Empire to be explained away as a simple continuance of the Republic when in reality it was a true dictatorship.

Thanks to Augustus and his stealthy gathering of the levers of imperial supremacy, future emperors had few checks and balances on their authority. Their powers now included:

- Regulating the Senate, including convening its sessions and setting the agenda for all of its meetings. From this time the emperor also had total control over who was appointed a senator.
- Controlling the Roman calendar.
- The authority to consecrate temples and oversee religious ceremonies as the *Pontifex Maximus* (leader of the college of priests).
- Being the supreme commander of the Roman military.
- Assuming the powers of *tribunicia postetas* (the power of coercion) and *sacrosanctity* (legal inviolability through sacred law).
- Exercising regional authority through the appointment of governors in imperial provinces, approving the appointment of proconsuls in senatorial provinces, and appointing the *procurator* in all

provinces. Governors exercised military and legal authority in their province, while *procuratores* were charged with making the province pay and ensuring it was *pretium victoria* – worth the conquest.

Using these powers, each emperor exercised imperial authority through three main bodies, which remained in place throughout the Principate. The first was the *Consilium Principis* (main council), created to be the central imperial advisory body. This was effectively always in session, providing the emperor with advice on military, legal and diplomatic matters. Next came the *fiscus* (imperial treasury), controlled by an a *rationibus* (financial officer) (later replaced by one styled an *a rationalis*). This was the magnet for the wealth generated by each province and was used to fund all of the emperor's activities, including the use of the Roman military. The word *fiscus* is very specific and refers to the personal treasury of the emperor, literally translating as 'basket' or 'purse'. Finally came the Praetorian Guard, founded by Augustus and institutionalised later by Tiberius. This is fully detailed in Chapter 2.

Power was devolved from the emperor into the provinces through their governors/proconsuls and *procuratores* in these two separate chains of command, this system designed to prevent one or the other accruing too much power and challenging imperial authority. Appointment as a governor/proconsul was the most senior post on the *cursus honorum* (aristocratic career path) for a senator, usually following a term as consul in Rome.

To exercise their authority in the province, each governor/proconsul headed an executive body called the *officium consularis*. In most provinces this included an *iuridicus* (legal expert), *legates* from any legions based there, senatorial-level military tribunes from any auxiliary units, and equestrian-rank officers. Meanwhile the *procurator*, always an equestrian, had a personal staff of equestrian and freedmen administrators called *procutatores*, known collectively as his *Caesariani*. These personnel were registrars, finance officers and superintendents. The *procurator*'s specific responsibilities included the collection of all taxes within the province, for example the *tributum soli* (land tax), the *portorium* (duty on the carriage of goods on public highways) and the *tributum capatis* (poll tax). They were also responsible for the collection of rents from any imperial estates in the province owned by the emperor, the management of all major *metalla* (mines) and quarries (to run these the *procurator* appointed one of his staff as a *procurator metallorum*) and distributing pay to public officials and the military.

The Severan Buildings on the Palatine Hill in Rome. Septimius Severus and his wife Julia Domna rebuilt much of the imperial palace after he became emperor in AD 193, founding the Severan Dynasty.

Dynasties of the Principate

- The Julio-Claudian Dynasty, lasting from the accession of Augustus in 27 BC to the death of Nero in AD 68. This period included the beginnings of the Empire, the loss of Varus's three legions in the Teutoburg Forest in AD 9, and the initial campaigns of conquest in Britain from the Claudian invasion of AD 43 onwards.

- The 'Year of the Four Emperors' in AD 69, with Vespasian the ultimate victor.

- The Flavian Dynasty, from Vespasian's accession to the death of his younger son Domitian in AD 96. This included the defeat of the Batavian Revolt under Gaius Julius Civilis in AD 70, the later campaigns of conquest in Britain including the governor Agricola's campaigns in the far north, and the First 'Great' Jewish Revolt which lasted AD 66–73.

- The Nervo-Trajanic Dynasty, from the accession of Nerva in AD 96 to the death of Hadrian in AD 138. This included the campaigns of Trajan, comprising his conquest of Dacia in two campaigns AD 101–102 and AD 105–106, his Parthian campaign AD 114–117, and the associated Second Jewish Revolt (the Kitos War) AD 115–117. The Dynasty also featured the Third 'bar Kokhbar' Jewish Revolt AD 132–135.

- The Antonine Dynasty, from the accession of Antoninus Pius in AD 138 through to the assassination of Commodus in AD 192. The lengthy 23-year reign of Antoninus Pius was one of relative peace, with the Empire at its most stable (though much campaigning still took place in Britain). However, the accession of the diarchy of Marcus Aurelius and Lucius Verus in AD 161 marked the beginning of a lengthy period of trouble across Rome's far-flung frontiers. Most notable were the Roman–Parthian War from AD 161–166, and the lengthy Marcomannic Wars along the Danube that began in AD 166 and lasted well into the reign of Commodus. Campaigning also occurred throughout this dynastic period in Britain.

- The 'Year of the Five Emperors' in AD 193, and the subsequent civil wars. The latter ranged from the accession of Pertinax through to the death of British governor and usurper Clodius Albinus in AD 197 at the battle of Lugdunum (modern Lyon), this detailed in full in Chapter 6.

- The Severan Dynasty, from the accession of Septimius Severus in AD 193 through to the assassination of Severus Alexander in AD 235. This included Severus's two campaigns in Parthia between AD 195 and AD 197, his campaigning in North Africa against the Garamantes Berber tribe, and his two attempts to conquer Scotland in AD 209 and AD 210 (these also detailed in Chapter 6). Later Severus's elder son Caracalla also campaigned in Parthia, while Severus Alexander fought unsuccessfully against the newly emerged Sassanid Persian Empire (which had replaced the Parthian Empire from AD 224) and the Alamanni Germans and their Sarmatian allies.

- The 'Crisis of the 3rd Century', from the death of Severus Alexander to the accession of Diocletian in AD 284. This was a time when the Empire was under great stress, racked with external conflict and civil war, pestilence in the form of the Plague of Cyprian, and economic depression. All ultimately led to change within and outside its borders and the onset of the Dominate phase of Empire. Much campaigning took place in this period, particularly against the newly emergent Goths, and once more the Sassanid Persians. The low point was the capture and humiliation of the Emperor Valerian by the Sassanid Persian King Shapur I at Edessa in AD 260.

Exquisite living in the Roman Principate. Interior of a large villa at Oplontis in the Roman Bay of Naples.

One might note here how small the executive teams of the governor/proconsul and *procurator* were, in total no more than 60 staff in a normal province. To give context, in Roman Britain this amounted to only 0.0017% of the estimated population of 3.5 million, compared to around 25% in public employ today. Clearly this was an insufficient number of officials to run the province, and therefore both teams were bolstered by the appointment of military personnel assigned from the provincial military presence to assist with official duties. Those appointed to the *officium consularis* were known as *beneficiarii consularis*, and those to the *procurator's* staff *beneficiarii procuratores*. A good example of an actual individual fulfilling one of these roles can be found in today's Museum of London, where the funerary monument of centurion Vivius Marcianus from *legio II Augusta* is displayed. Seconded from his legion's fortress at Caerleon in south-eastern Wales, this man served as a *beneficiarii* based at the Cripplegate vexilation fort in London in the early 3rd century AD. The role of legionaries as administrators is discussed in full in Chapter 7 when I consider the Roman military in their non-conflict roles.

Provincial Structure of the Principate Empire

Talk of proconsuls, governors and *procuratores* elegantly leads to a detailed description of the provincial structure of the Principate Roman Empire at its height, during the later 2nd century AD. By this time the Empire had grown to cover a vast geographic area. Encompassing the entire Mediterranean basin, English Channel and much of the North Sea, it stretched all the way from Hadrian's Wall in the north of far-flung Britain to the *limes* of distant Arabia. This was a distance of some 4,200km as the crow flies. The Empire's population at this time was around 65 million people, some 21% of the entire world's population.

At this time the Empire was divided into 44 provinces, both senatorial and imperial. These broadly broke down into seven regions, namely Britannia, Gaul and Germany, Spain, the Danube and Italy, Greece and Asia Minor, the east, and North Africa.

Britannia encompassed the main island of Britain up to the line of Hadrian's Wall, built around the time of this emperor's visit in AD 122. It ran west to east along the Solway Firth–Tyne line. For much of its 117km length it tracked the earlier Flavian Stanegate Road. From around AD 142 the northern border actually moved further north to the line of the Clyde–Firth of Forth, the fortification built there known as the Antonine Wall. However, this was abandoned after only eight years of occupation in the early AD 160s, with the border once more moving back south to Hadrian's Wall again.

Britannia was the wild west of the Roman Empire. A marginal province at best, it was always a place of difference, the never-conquered far north requiring an exponentially large military presence. This was some 12% of the Empire's entire military complement in what was only 4% of its geographic area. This radically altered the geography of the province, with the south and east a fully functioning part of the Empire but the north and west a heavily militarised zone. Given Britannia was also far from Rome, this combination made the province a hotbed for usurpers and troublemakers later in the Empire.

Britain was difficult to invade in the first place, with Caesar himself failing (if his intention was to stay) in 55 BC and 54 BC, and the great Augustus and mad Caligula (AD 37 to AD 41) both planning but abandoning conquest. Even the Aulus Plautius-led invasion of Claudius was problematic, the troops weary of crossing terrifying *Oceanus* until shamed into boarding the invasion fleet by one of the emperor's senior freedmen, Tiberius Claudius Narcissus. In this story, when the legionaries refused to clamber onto the invasion vessels in north-western Gaul, the former slave himself boarded a ship. Shouting '*Io Saturnalia*', referencing the end-of-year role-reversing winter festival, the chastened soldiery followed, and the invasion proceeded. The story of Caesar's two incursions, set within his conquest of Gaul, and the later successful Claudian invasion are told in full in Chapter 6.

The story of Roman Britain through to the late 2nd century AD is also one of many famous individuals well recorded in the primary sources. Think Caratacus who opposed Aulus Plautius, Vespasian who conquered the south-west in the late AD 40s, Boudicca who nearly destroyed the province in AD 60/61, her nemesis Suetonius Paulinus, the Brigantian Queen Cartimandua, and Lollius Urbicus who drove the border north to the Antonine Wall in the mid-2nd century AD.

By the later 2nd century AD Roman Britain was at the height of its provincial success, such as it was. The province was threaded with a well-built system of military trunk roads, a legacy of the lengthy campaigns of conquest there. A prime example was Watling Street that started at the imperial Gateway of Richborough (*Rutupiae*) on the east Kent coast, resplendent with its Flavian Carrera marble-clad monumental arch. From there it headed west to the provincial capital of London (*Londinium*), then on to the *municipium* of St Albans (*Verulamium*), and thence to the far off *civitas* capital of Wroxeter (*Viriconium*) in the Welsh Marches. Here it branched north and south, to the legionary fortresses at Chester (*Deva Victrix*) on the River Dee and Caerleon (*Isca Augusta*) on the River Usk. Meanwhile, Ermine Street linked London with the *colonia* at Lincoln (*Lindum Colonia*, originally a legionary fortress) and the legionary fortress and *canabae* (civilian settlement) at York (Eboracom, later to become a *colonia*). Its extension Dere Street then headed even further north, through the fort and small town at Corbridge (*Coria*), then through Hadrian's Wall before traversing the Scottish Borders, reaching the Firth of Forth at Inveresk (Roman name unknown). Another key route was the Fosse Way, linking Lincoln with the south-western *civitas* capital of Exeter (*Isca Dumnoniorum*, also originally a legionary fortress), passing through Cirencester (*Corinium*) on the way. The Fosse Way crossed Watling Street at modern High Cross in Leicestershire, one of the major transport intersections of Roman Britain. As one can see, this was a very militarised province, with its conquest and later military establishment literally etched across its landscape in the form of roads, fortifications of all kind, and in most cases their civilian settlement successors.

At this time there were three long-established legions in the province. These were *legio II Augusta* at Caerleon, *legio XX Valeria Victrix* at Chester and *legio VI Victrix* at York, the latter replacing the earlier incumbent *legio IX Hispana* in the early 2nd century AD. *Vexillationes* (companies) of each rotated through postings to the north, either along Hadrian's Wall and the Stanegate forts immediately to its rear (for example Vindolanda), or mounting incursions into the unconquered far north. They were joined on the border, and on campaign, by numerous auxiliary cavalry and infantry units (see Chapter 2 for detail). All were supported by the *Classis Britannica* (provincial regional navy). Headquartered in north-western Gaul at Boulogne-sur-Mer (*Gesoriacum*), this fleet operated principally from bases around

Provinces of the Principate Empire in the Early 2nd Century AD

Sarmatia

Iberia

Dacia
Sarmizegetusa
• *Tomis*

Artaxarta •

Moesia Inferior

Armenia

Bithynia et Pontus

Cappadocia

Naissus

Thracia
• *Philippopolis*

Ancrya

• *Caesarea*

• *Nisibus*

Macedonia

essalonica

Galatia

Achala
Athens

Asia
Miletus

Lycia et Pamphylia

Tarsus

Cilicia

Antiochia

Syria

Mesopotamia

Patara

Salamis

Cyprus

Caesarea

• *Bostra*

Judea

Cyrene

Alexandria

Creta et Cyrene

Aegyptus

Arabia

Arabia Felix

the south and west coast of Britain including Dover (*Dubris*), Richborough, Caerleon and Chester. Then, when supporting Roman military operations in the north, it forward deployed to naval bases at Maryport (*Alauna*) on the west coast, and in the east South Shields (*Arbeia*) and Wallsend (*Segedumum*) on the River Tyne, Cramond (Roman name unknown) on the Firth of Forth and Carpow (Roman name unknown) on the River Tay.

The economy of Roman Britain was dominated by agriculture, as with the rest of the Empire. Much new land was reclaimed during the occupation that helped to greatly increase agricultural output, for example in the Fenlands around the Wash on the east coast. Agricultural yield was also increased by the introduction of new farming technology and techniques. The produce from this farming boom helped the population to grow to some 3.5 million by the late 2nd century AD, up from around 2 million in the Late Iron Age (LIA) immediately prior to the arrival of the Romans.

Industry also featured in the province, including the iron industry in the Weald and the ragstone quarrying industry of the upper Medway Valley. These two vast *metalla* were among the largest industrial enterprises anywhere in the Empire. The former provided all of the iron utilised by the military in the north, while the latter supplied all of the stone used to build and maintain the new urban environment in the south-east, including London. Other industries that flourished under the Roman occupation of Britain included indigenous pottery manufacturing, glass making, mosaic manufacture, brewing, mill and quern stone manufacture and textile production. It was the latter that provided the Roman world with its best-known British exports, namely the *birrus* (rain-proofed hooded cloak) and the *tapetia* (fine quality woollen rug).

The Romans named the fort *Trimontium* after the three Eildon Hills there. Here in the foreground Eildon Hill North. (Trimontium Trust)

Compared to the rest of the Empire Britain made little contribution to its political life, except through the numerous usurpation attempts. We know of no native British senator, and indeed the most famous Romano-Britons were religious figures, namely St Alban, St Patrick and the controversial theologian Palagius, accused by St Augustine of Hippo of denying that good deeds required divine intervention.

Moving on to Gaul and Germany, the rich provinces here illustrated how quickly indigenous territories could be culturally assimilated into the Roman way of life. Real Roman interest in the region began in the mid-2nd century BC through mercantile engagement with the Greek colony of Marseille (*Massilia*), with a treaty being signed to protect the town from Iberians to the west, Gauls to the north and Carthaginians across the Mediterranean. Further Roman interest there led to the creation of a new province in 122 BC along the Mediterranean coast called Transalpine Gaul (also called *Provincia Nostra*, translating as 'our province'), this later being renamed Gallia Narbonensis after its regional capital of Narbonne was founded in 118 BC.

The province then became the springboard for

Roman amphitheatre at the Caerleon legionary fortress, south-eastern Wales. This was the home of *legio II Augusta* who built the structure.

Interior view of the Roman amphitheatre at the Caerleon legionary fortress, south-eastern Wales.

Barrack blocks and ovens at the legionary fortress at Caerleon.

Detail of barrack blocks at the legionary fortress at Caerleon. All built by *legio II Augusta* legionaries.

Julius Caesar's conquest of Gaul when he became its governor in 58 BC, along with Cisalpine Gaul. In pursuit of glory and wealth, Caesar lost no time in campaigning north and by the end of the decade had reduced the Gallic kingdoms there to Roman vassalage, this fully detailed in Chapter 6. From that time, they became new Roman provinces, these revised by Augustus in 22 BC, with more territory added to the north and east later. By the late 2nd century AD there were nine provinces in the region, these being:

- Germania Inferior in the Rhine Delta and lower Rhine valley.
- Germania Superior in the upper Rhine valley.
- Gallia Belgica, broadly the area of modern Belgium.
- Gallia Lugdunensis, a broad strip through modern central France ranging from Brittany in the west to the provincial capital of Lyon (Lugdunum) in the east.
- Gallia Aquitania along the Bay of Biscay.

- Gallia Narbonensis in modern Provence, a senatorial province.
- Three small provinces bordering Gallia Narbonensis and Italy, from north to south Alpes Graiae et Poeninae, Alpes Cottiae and Alpes Maritimae.

This large region featured distinct cultural and economic differences across its wide geography. The far north and east were more militarised given the provinces there featured the *limes Germanicus* separating the world of Rome from *barbaricum* (as viewed by contemporaries) to the north. Further south, the northern Gallic provinces were nicknamed Gallia Comata, meaning 'long haired Gaul.' This territory featured fine quality agricultural land heavily exploited for arable and fruit crops, including the fine quality wines associated with the region to this day. It was also the home to a dense network of *fabricae* (state-run manufactories) around Autun (*Augustodunum*) in the modern Bourgogne-Franche-Comté region of modern France. These produced much of the

Bartlow Hills in Cambridgeshire, a series of elite monumental barrow burials dating to the early Roman occupation of Britain. The Principate Empire ruled with a light touch and was relaxed about native populations worshipping their own gods and burying their dead as they wished, provided they worshipped the imperial cult and paid their taxes.

equipment for the military in the region. This region of non-Mediterranean Gaul also developed a reputation as the Principate progressed for social conservatism in its arts and culture, and was home to a substantial commercial class whose goods were traded across the Empire. Pre-eminent among these were the Samian-ware ceramic works at La Graufensque near Millau, Lezoux and Clermont-Ferrand. These made high-quality tablewares using a glossy red surface slip which was popular across the Empire. By way of contrast the far south of Gaul was far more urbanised, reflecting the longevity of large-scale stone-built settlement there dating back to the early period of Greek expansion in the western Mediterranean.

In addition to Lyon, key cities in Gaul and Germany included Cologne (*Colonia Agrippina*) that became the provincial capital of Germania Inferior, Mainz (*Mogantium*) with its legionary fortress which was the provincial capital of Germania Superior, Reims (*Durocotorum*) which was the provincial capital of Gallia Belgica, Trier (*Treverorum*) also in Gallia Belgica, Narbonne (*Narbo*) which was the provincial capital of Narbonensis, and the key Mediterranean port city of Marseille.

The Rhine frontier featured a dense chain of fortifications to maintain the northern *limes* that ran for over 570km from the Rhine Delta to the Danube. The key bases were the legionary fortresses, with sites at Nijmegen (*Noviomagus*), Xanten (*Vetera*) and Neuss (*Novaesium*) joining those already detailed at Mainz and Cologne. A further 55 forts of various sizes and over 1,000 watchtowers completed the defensive frontier here. The *limes Germanicus* was divided into three sections, these being:

- The Lower Germanic *limes* extending from the North Sea coast to the Rheinbrohl municipality in the Rhineland Palatinate of modern Germany.
- The Upper Germanic *limes* from Rheinbrohl to Lorch am Rhein near Darmstadt in Hesse.
- The Rhaetian *limes*, with only the section on the Rhine detailed here, the Danubian length covered in the next section.

By the late 2nd century AD, the *limes* of the first two sections were home to some of the crack legions of the Roman Empire. These included *legio VIII Augusta* and *legio XXII Primigenia pia fidelis* in Germania Inferior, and *legio I Flavia Minervia pia fidelis* and *legio XXX Ulpia Victrix* in Germania Superior. The military establishment here also featured the usual complement of auxiliaries, and the *Classis Germanica* regional fleet. This large navy was responsible for patrolling the Rhine from deep within the continental interior at its confluence with the Vinxtbach stream in the modern Rhineland Palatinate through to the Zuiderzee and the North Sea coastlines in the Rhine Delta area. It also had responsibility for the Rhine's many tributaries and was later tasked with patrolling the rivers Meuse and Scheldt. Together the legions, auxiliaries and fleet faced off against multiple threats to the north, including the Germanic Saxons, Thuringii and Alamanni (see Chapter 8).

Heading to the far south, the Iberian Peninsula featured three provinces that were formed in 14 BC when Augustus reorganised the territory of his new Empire. These were Hispania Tarraconensis in the north-west and east, Hispania Baetica in the south and Hispania Lusitania in the south-west. The peninsula as a whole was well known in the Roman period as an exporter of fine wine, olive oil, *garum* (fish sauce) (all made in industrial quantities), and precious metals and copper. The latter extractive industries featured some of the largest *metalla* operations in the entire Empire, including the Rio Tinto mines in the region of modern Andalusia and the Vispaca mines in Portugal. Hispania Tarraconensis was a province of contrasts. The eastern Mediterranean seaboard was largely Punic in origin, with key towns like Cartagena (*Carthago Nova*) dating back to the time of Hannibal, though the provincial capital of Tarragona (*Tarraco*) was an earlier Spanish founding. Meanwhile the mountainous north retained much of its pre-Roman Basque character. Unusually for a province away from the frontiers of Empire, Hispania Tarraconensis also featured a legion. In the late 2nd century AD this was *legio VII Gemina*, based at León (*Castra Legionis*) to

maintain order among the troublesome native northern Lusitanians.

Next, in the far south of the Iberian Peninsula, the senatorial province of Hispania Baetica was one of the richest Roman provinces, featuring the key Atlantic port of Cádiz (*Gades*, originally a Phoenician founding). With its provincial capital at Cordoba (*Corduba*), Hispania Baetica was most notable in the Roman world for being the birthplace of Emperor Trajan.

Meanwhile Hispania Lusitania, sitting on the Atlantic seaboard, encompassed much of the territory of modern Portugal. Its provincial capital was located at Mérida (*Emerita Augusta*). The region had proved particularly difficult to conquer during the republican wars, but by the late 2nd century AD it was a sleepy backwater, not requiring the close military attention needed in northern Tarraconensis.

Moving on to the Danube frontier and Italy, the former was another key military border zone while the latter was the centre of the Empire, featuring the imperial capital of Rome.

This region of the Empire was particularly complex in terms of wealth and culture, given the Danubian provinces spanned the whole range of Roman civilization from the settled Celtic tribes in the west to the urbanised seaboard of Dalmatia, and on to the ancient Greek colonial cities along the Black Sea coast. There, the Thracian regions east of the pass of Succi were Greek-speaking and their cities had Greek names. Meanwhile, the Latinisation of Dacia after an occupation of 150 years is reflected in modern Romanian.

The key cities in the region included Augsberg (*Augusta Vindelicorum*) which was the provincial capital of Raetia, Wels (*Ovilava*) which was the provincial capital of Noricum, Vienna (*Vindobona*), Roman *Carnuntum* which was the provincial capital of the vital province of Pannonia Superior where Septimius Severus (AD 193–211) was later proclaimed emperor, Split (*Aspalathos*) on the Adriatic coast where Diocletian later built has palace when he retired, Budapest (*Aquincum*) which was the provincial capital of Pannonia Inferior, Kostolac (*Viminacium*) which was the provincial capital of Moesia Superior, Roman *Ulpia Traiana Sarmizegetusa* which was the provincial capital of the redoubt province of Dacia following Trajan's two wars of conquest there, Konstantsa (*Tomis*) which was the provincial capital of Moesia Inferior, and Roman *Perinthus* which was the provincial capital of Thracia.

As with the Rhine, the Danubian provinces were defined by the northern *limes* here which ran for much of the river's 2,860km length. These fortifications were divided into four sections:

- The Rhaetian *limes*, here only the section on the Danube.
- The Noric *limes* in Noricum.
- The Pannonian *limes* in Pannonia Superior and Inferior.
- The Moesian *limes* in Moesia Superior and Inferior, running down to the Black Sea. From AD 106 during the reign of Trajan (AD 98 to AD 117) to AD 275 in the reign of Aurelian (AD 270 to AD 275) this section actually ran far to the north, encompassing the salient province of Dacia which stood proud to the north of the Danube.

The Danubian *limes* by the late 2nd century AD were also home to some of the most experienced legions of the Empire, battle-hardened during the

Nine provinces of the Danube region (from west to east)

- Raetia, the province linking the Rhine and Danube
- Noricum
- Pannonia Superior
- Pannonia Inferior
- Dalmatia
- Moesia Superior
- Dacia
- Moesia Inferior
- Thracia

Marcomannic Wars. These were based in a string of legionary fortresses along the *limes*, ranging from Vienna in the west to *Troesmis* in the east. At this time the legions here included *legio III Italica concors* in Raetia, *legio II Italica* in Noricum, *legio X Gemina, legio XIV Gemina Martia* and *legio I Adiutrix pia fidelis* in Pannonia Superior, *legio II Adiutrix pia fidelis* in Pannonia Inferior, *legio IV Flavia felix* and *legio VII Claudia pia fidelis* in Moesia Superior, *legio XIII Gemina pia fidelis* in Dacia and *legio I Italica, legio V Macedonia* and *legio XI Claudia pia fidelis* in Moesia Inferior. As with the Rhine frontier, they were joined by an equivalent number of auxiliaries, while the two regional fleets here were the *Classis Flavia Pannonica* on the upper Danube and the *Classis Flavia Moesica* on the Lower Danube. They faced off against yet more aggressive northern neighbours. These included the Germanic Marcomanni, Juthungi and Quadi, various Sarmatian tribes including the Iazyges and Rhoxalani, remnant Dacians and Bastarnae, and later various Gothic confederations.

Moving south, the provinces of Italy were Italia itself, the twin island province of Corsica et Sardinia, and Sicily. Italia had been one political entity encompassing the whole Italian Peninsula since the incorporation of Cisalpine Gaul in 42 BC. Rather than being an imperial or senatorial province run by a governor or proconsul, it was actually administered directly by the Senate. To claim to be a Roman citizen before Caracalla's AD 212 *constitutio Antoniniana* one had to be a freeman born in the peninsula, or a former slave manumitted there. Across Italy nearly all roads literally did lead to Rome, including the *via Appia* to *Capua* and then Brindisi (*Brindisium*), the *via Aurelia* to Pisa (*Pisae*), and the *via Cassia* to Genoa (*Genua*). By the late 2nd century AD Rome had grown to an immense size, with a population of nearly one million, being styled by its inhabitants the *caput mundi* (head of the world). Its twin ports of Ostia and Portus were fully occupied importing vast quantities of grain from Egypt, North Africa and Sicily to feed its bourgeoning population.

In terms of a military presence, aside from the Praetorian Guard there was no significant land-based military unit in Italy until Septimius Severus established the newly raised *legio II Parthica* in Albanum 34km from Rome in the late AD 190s to keep an eye on the elite classes there. The province did feature the two most prominent regional fleets of the Principate Empire, however. These were the *Classis Ravennas* based at Ravenna in the north-east with responsibility for the Adriatic Sea, and the *Classis Misenensis* based at Miseno (*Misenum*) on the north-western tip of the Bay of Naples with responsibility for Tyrrhenian Sea.

Moving further south, Sicily was one of the wealthiest provinces in the Empire and was for most of the Principate peaceful and so little mentioned by primary sources. As detailed above, it was one of the key sources of grain for Rome, featuring an intensive agricultural economy that included many huge imperial estates own by the emperor. Meanwhile, the senatorial province of Corsica et Sardinia is similarly little mentioned by contemporary sources, being equally peaceful and agrarian in nature. Corsica was famed at the time for its wax exports, while Sardinia was a major supplier of lead and silver to the western Empire.

Further east in Greece and Anatolia were located some of the most important provinces of the Empire. The former was divided into four provinces, with Macedonia to the north including the broad plains of Thessaly, Achaia including the Peloponnese, Euboea and Boetia, Epirus to the west on the Adriatic coast, and Thracia to the east stretching to the Black Sea.

Macedonia was one of the larger Roman provinces, and senatorial in nature. It was also one of the earliest created, in 146 BC after the final destruction of the preceding Hellenistic kingdom. Except for its eastern seaboard, it was rather remote and agrarian, with a social structure based on its many villages. The provincial capital Thessalonica was a striking exception, the city prospering as it sat astride the *via Egnatia*, a major trunk road which linked the Adriatic coast of the Balkans with the Bosporus. In the Dominate period of empire it rose to even greater prominence as an imperial capital in the east when Diocletian (AD 286 to AD 305) created his tetrarchy.

Achaia was also a senatorial province but far different in character, featuring some of the greatest

Roman amphitheatre at Pompeii. Entertainment for the masses in the Principate Empire.

The forum in Pompeii with Vesuvius still looming in the background. The destruction of the Roman Bay of Naples by the AD 79 eruption was the greatest natural disaster in the 1st AD Principate.

cities of the classical world, particularly Athens which styled itself a leading centre of culture and arts. Many of the great intellectual figures of the Empire studied, taught or sought an audience there. It was also a key place for Roman emperors to visit, for example the philhellene Hadrian (AD 117 to AD 138) who built the fine Arch of Hadrian, still a key feature of the city to this day, linking the centre of Athens with its religious precinct. Here Hadrian also completed the Temple of Olympian Zeus,

600 years after its construction had begun. Other examples of his imperial patronage in Athens included a gymnasium, the Panhellenion shrine (of all of the Greeks), and a huge library. Such benefactions were just the latest in a long history of Roman largesse in the city, which had included the construction of the Roman agora (market place) and the Odeon of Agrippa. Meanwhile the provincial capital of Corinth also prospered under Roman rule, it being re-founded in 44 BC after its

destruction by republican Rome in 146 BC (see Chapter 1).

Meanwhile Epirus, also a senatorial province, extended from the Acroceraunian Mountains and Gulf of Aulon on the Adriatic coast to the Acheloos River in the south. This was a fairly unremarkable province in the Principate, with its provincial capital located at Nicopolis from where the Ionian islands were also administered.

To the east, Thracia had originally been the kingdom of Thrace, famous for its *rhomphaia*-wielding peltasts who had served as mercenaries across the eastern Mediterranean in the mid and later republican period. This became a Roman client kingdom in 20 BC and was fully annexed into the Empire by Claudius (AD 41 to AD 54) after the death of its last King Rhoemetalces III in AD 46. Given it sat well within the Empire far away from its borders, Thracia remained prosperous and peaceful until the 'Crisis of the 3rd Century', after which it frequently found itself a border zone during the frequent Gothic incursions into the Balkans. In the late 2nd century AD it featured no

permanent military units, though occasionally the *Classis Pontica* (Black Sea regional fleet), normally based at Trapzon (*Trebizond*) on the north coast of Anatolia, forward deployed to Byzantium when needed to guard the entrance to the Bosporus.

Moving across this waterway into Asia, Anatolia was a thriving economic and cultural powerhouse in the Roman Empire. The imperial presence here had its origins in the kingdom of Pergamum, left as a legacy to Rome by its last king Attalus III upon his death in 133 BC. Rome used this as a springboard for the various campaigns of conquest eastwards by later republican warlords including Marius, Sulla, Pompey and Caesar. Sequentially they targeted the various kingdoms of Anatolia including Bithynia in the north-west, Pontus in the north (fighting no fewer than three wars against Mithridates VI) and the Galatians in the centre.

By the late 2nd century AD, the most westerly province in Anatolia was that of Asia. Senatorial in nature, its geography centered on the lands of the old kingdom of Pergamum. This featured some of the Empire's leading cities, including the provincial

The Temple of Apollo at modern Didim (ancient *Didyma*) in southwestern Turkey, one of the most important temples in the province of Asia.

capital of Ephesus (its Temple of Artemis one of the seven wonders of the ancient world), Pergamum itself, Priene, Miletus and Halicarnassus.

To its north was the smaller senatorial province of Bithynia et Pontus, sitting on the Asian side of the Bosporus. Its provincial capital Izmit (*Nicodemia*) was one of a number of major cities there. The province of Galatia to the south was far more agrarian, with its provincial capital at Ankara (*Ankrya*), while the south coast featured two other small provinces. These were Lycia et Pamphylia to the west, and Cilicia in the east. The former was governed from Demre (*Myra*), the latter *Tarsus*.

Roman Anatolia was far more militarised on its most easterly flank, where sat the province of Cappadocia. Aside from a short period from AD 114 to AD 118 when Armenia, Assyria and Mesopotamia were incorporated into the Empire following Trajan's eastern campaigns, the province was the border territory facing some-time friend, some-time enemy Armenia, and further east the Arsacid Parthian Empire.

The latter were the nearest to a symmetrical enemy faced by the Principate military. Originating in north-eastern Iran, from the 3rd century BC they had expanded westwards at the expense of the various Hellenistic kingdoms in the region and soon encountered the eastward expansion of the Romans. The Parthian army featured a very effective combination of armoured noble lancers and a multitude of lightly armoured horse archers, the latter famous for their 'Parthian Shot' tactic of approaching enemy formations at speed and then losing arrows over the croup of their mount as they wheeled away. This mixture of shock cavalry and missile troops proved highly effective against the Romans time and again, for example almost wiping out the republican army of the triumvir Crassus in 53 BC at the battle of Carrhae, where he and his son lost their lives.

Cappadocia featured the key crossing points in the upper Tigris and Euphrates valleys and was often the launch point for Roman campaigns eastward against Parthia and later Sassanid Persia. Its key industry was olive oil production. While the provincial capital was at Kayseri (*Caesarea*),

The Library of Celsus at Ephesus. One of the lintels carries a dedication to Julius Caesar as *Pontifex Maximus*.

the most important settlements were the two legionary fortresses and their *canabae*s at Sadak (*Satala*) in the north-east and Malatya (*Melitene*) in the south-east. The former was home to *legio XV Apollinaris*, the latter to *legio XII Fulminata*. These were the key anchor points of the Cappadocian *limes*, with the Black Sea port of Trabzon the regular home to the *Classis Pontica*. The province's military component was completed by a large number of auxiliaries, including many locally recruited mounted bowmen.

Moving south to the eastern frontier proper, this featured the key barrier provinces of Syria and Arabia Petraea, Syria Palaestina on the Mediterranean coast and the island of Cyprus in the western Mediterranean. Syria was the major bulwark against the Parthians in the east for much of the Principate. It was also highly fertile, sitting as it did on the western arc of the Fertile Crescent. The province was governed from the huge metropolis of Antakya (Antioch on the Orontes), which by the later 2nd century AD had a population of 250,000.

In addition to the northern section of the *limes Arabicus*, the border territory also featured a system of defence-in-depth based on client and allied kingdoms that often formed a buffer between the Empire and the Parthians. These included Palmyra, Osrhoene, Adiabene and Hatra. The principal legionary fortresses in Syria were at Zeugma (originally the Hellenistic Seleucia-on-the-Euphrates) in the north, Raphanaea near the Mediterranean coast and Danaba to the south. These were home to some of the most battle-hardened legions in the Empire, sequentially *legio IV Scythica, legio III Gallica* and *legio XVI Flavia Firma*. In addition to the usual auxiliary complement, the military presence in the province was completed by the *Classis Syriaca* that operated out of the port of *Seleucia Pierra*.

The province of Arabia Petraea was the opposite of abundant Syria, being largely a desert inhabited by nomadic and transhumant Arab peoples. For commerce it relied on desert caravans operating through trading centres such as Petra. This town was annexed by Trajan during his eastern campaigns, initiating the creation of the province.

One legion was based here, *legio III Cyrenaica* at Bosra (*Bostra*), which was also the provincial capital. From here the legionaries and their supporting *auxilia* (including camel-riding *equites Dromedarii*) had the unforgiving task of manning the southern *limes Arabicus*. Defence-in-depth is also evident here, with the Romans frequently making use of their Ghassanid Arab allies to repel the Lakhmid Arabs who were supporters of the Parthians and later the Sassanid Persians.

Heading west to Syria Palaestina, this was formerly the province of Judaea. It proved to be one of the most troublesome provinces of the Roman Empire, and like Britain had a disproportionately large military presence. The province incorporated the territories of the former Hasmonean and Herodian kingdoms of Judaea, including Judaea itself, Samaria and Idumaea. The major issue for the Romans here were the native Jewish inhabitants who proved the most recalcitrant adherents to the ways of Rome following the formation of the province in the early AD 40s. Three desperate Jewish Revolts were put down by the Romans in the most brutal fashion, the first featuring the siege of Masada and destruction of the Second Temple in Jerusalem and the last effectively triggering the Jewish diaspora given the exceptionally harsh Roman reprisals afterwards. It was after Hadrian crushed the last revolt that the provincial name was changed, with Jerusalem renamed *Aelia Capitolina* (the provincial capital was actually at *Caesarea Maritima* on the coast). Despite the defeat of the last revolt, the province still featured two legions in the late 2nd century AD, these being *legio VI Ferrata fidelis constans* based at *Caparcotna* near Megiddo and *legio X Fretensis* based in *Aelia Capitolina*. Given their proximity to Syria proper and Arabia, these were frequently used as a strategic reserve when the eastern frontier was threatened, and to campaign in the east during Roman incursions into Parthia and later Sassanid Persia.

Finally in the region, the province of Cyprus was as far within the Empire as it was possible to get. It was originally incorporated into the republican province of Cilicia, becoming an independent senatorial province in 22 BC under Augustus.

There was little Roman military presence there, with the provincial capital located at Paphos (*Nea Pafos*) famous for its 'Tombs of the Kings' Hellenistic and Roman necropolis.

Heading south once more, Aegyptus was one of the powerhouse provinces of the Empire, established in 30 BC after Octavian and his general Marcus Agrippa defeated Mark Antony and Cleopatra. Given its economic might, the province was always a place of difference within the Empire, this based on the abundantly fertile Nile Valley that provided much of the grain supply to Rome and elsewhere across the Mediterranean. Aegyptus was also unique among Roman provinces in being considered the emperor's own imperial domain where he was styled the successor to the preceding system of Pharaonic rule. Here the governor was a titled *praefectus augustalis*.

We have great insight into the life experiences of all levels of society in Roman Egypt thanks to the thousands of surviving papyrus documents that detail every aspect of life there, many found at the key Roman site of *Oxyrhynchus* near modern El-Bahnassa, 160km south-east of Cairo.

The capital of the province was Alexandria, located on the Mediterranean coast of the Nile Delta. This vast city had been founded in 332 BC by Alexander the Great. Given it was also the location of his *Soma* (mausoleum), the city was a particular draw for Roman emperors when touring the east, with many stopping off here to view his body in its glass covered golden sarcophagus. By the late 2nd century AD, the city's population had reached around 600,000, making it the largest urban centre in the Roman world outside of Rome itself. Roman Alexandria was best known for its 130m-tall Hellenistic *pharos* (lighthouse), (another of the seven wonders of the ancient world), and its great library, the largest in the ancient world. Further south, the Great Pyramid of Khufu at the Giza Pharaonic necropolis was another of the seven wonders of the ancient world.

Aegyptus had enjoyed a century of prosperity by the late 2nd century AD. This included Hadrian founding the city of Antinopolis to commemorate his lover who drowned in the Nile in AD 130. However, it was also a source of continuing trouble, with a full revolt breaking out when Antoninus Pius (AD 138 to AD 161) raised taxes in the Middle Nile Valley in AD 139. This conflict, known as the Bucolic War, lasted several years during which Alexandria was besieged. The rebellion was eventually put down by the Syrian *legate* Gaius Avidius Cassius, who later usurped in AD 175 when mistakenly told Marcus Aurelius (AD 161 to AD 180) had died. Initially successful, he was recognised by the regional legions, but was then killed by a centurion when word reached the province that Marcus Aurelius was approaching with a huge army.

The province featured one legion, *legio II Traiana Fortis*, originally founded by Trajan in AD 105 for his Dacian campaigns. This performed with distinction during the Bucolic War, deploying from its legionary base at Nicopolis to defend Alexandria during the siege. The region also featured significant auxiliary forces. The provincial capital was also home to the *Classis Alexandrina Augusta* that patrolled the south-eastern Mediterranean and River Nile. This was one of the first regional fleets created by Augustus, in this instance in the later 20s BC. It received its imperial title after supporting Vespasian in AD 69, the 'Year of the Four Emperors'.

In addition to countering the frequent native insurgencies in the province, the military forces here also fought the nomadic Blemmye and Nobatae who lived in the desert between the Nile and Red Sea. Though not a sophisticated opponent in terms of tactics and technology, they often raided Roman Egypt in such numbers that they presented a real danger. The Romans countered this threat with a series of fortifications and watchtowers to protect the rich agricultural land in the Nile Valley. Most Blemmye and Nobatae warriors were unarmoured bowmen, often mounted on mules and donkeys, though they occasionally used elephants trained for war.

To the west of Aegyptus was the twin senatorial province of Cyrenaica et Creta. The former was named after the Pentapolis of five cities that sat along the Mediterranean coast in a well-watered fertile region known as the Gebel el Akbar. These cities, all originally Greek colonies, were Cyrene itself (the provincial capital), Ptolemais, Barca, Berenice and Belagrae. Elsewhere Cyrenaica was unremarkable, the south mainly unpopulated desert. It featured no significant military establishment. The latter was also true of Roman Crete, though this island economically thrived during the Roman period given its imperious location for trade in the central eastern Mediterranean.

Continuing west one next comes to the vast and wealthy senatorial province of Africa Proconsularis. This featured a number of densely settled coastal regions where many of the cities had Punic foundations, with a desertified interior. Its geography roughly comprised the coast of modern western Libya, north-eastern Algeria and Tunisia. The climate at the time was kinder to intensive agriculture there than today, and along with Egypt and Sicily the province was a key supplier of grain to Rome. It was also home to a thriving olive oil industry, and a key source of gold and slaves from sub-Saharan Africa.

The provincial capital of Africa Proconsularis was located at Carthage (*Carthago*), re-founded in 49 BC by Julius Caesar after its obliteration in 146 BC at the end of the Third Punic War when the original province here was created. By the late 2nd century AD, the city had a population of 100,000, and was likely home to the *Classis nova Libyca*. Some believe this was actually based in Cyrenaica, but I feel this unlikely given the proximity of the *Classis Alexandrina Augusta* in Aegyptus, and the need to patrol the central and western North African littoral along the coast. Nearby cities included Thapsus, Cirta and Hippo Regius, the latter later home to St Augustine.

The Numidian west of the province was effectively a separate entity after being placed under the control of an imperial *legatus* in AD 40 by the Emperor Caligula, though nominally remained within Africa Proconsularis until the reign of Septimius Severus in the late 2nd century AD when it was officially detached as the new province of Numidia. Meanwhile, further east, the region known as Tripolitania included the city of Lepcis Magna, Septimus Severus's birthplace.

Africa Proconsularis was one of the most articulate of provinces, renowned for its literature and as a source of leading lawyers in the Empire. It was also home to some of its wealthiest senatorial and equestrian families who ran huge agricultural estates there, many often owned by the emperor.

The province was protected in the south by the *limes Tripolitanus* series of fortifications built to defend the region from frequent raiding by the Garamantes and Musulamii Berber tribes. The *limes* were manned by North Africa's only legion, *legio III Augusta pia fidelis*, and supporting auxiliary units. The legion was originally based in the Numidian west at Haidra (*Ammaedara*) in the Aures Mountains but was later moved further south to nearby Tebessa (*Thevestis*) where it remained in Numidia after the region was officially separated away from Africa Proconsularis.

Moving further west, the final two Roman provinces in the late 2nd century AD were Mauretania Caesariensis and Mauretania Tingitana. Both were created by Claudius when he divided the original single province there into two. The former occupied the territory of the modern Mahgreb in Algeria, with its provincial capital at Cherchell (*Caesarea*). The latter then extended west to the Atlantic coast of modern Morocco, with its capital at Tangiers (*Tingi*). The main threat to both provinces came from the Mauri Berber tribe in the southern desert, with the *limes Tripolitanus* extending west from Africa Proconsularis to protect the rich agricultural strip along the Mediterranean coast there.

Rome in the Late 2nd Century AD

As with the wider Principate Empire, Rome was at the height of its power in the later 2nd century AD, with between 750,000 and 1 million inhabitants sprawling across seven hills on the eastern bank of the Tiber. By this time each summit had long been a distinct district in its own right with a well-recognised unique character. It is therefore important to set each hill in context. (More information can be found in the box on the next page)

By the late 2nd century AD Rome had evolved dramatically from the time of the late Republic.

Draining of the marshland around the extensive *Campus Martius*, which sat between Servian Walls and the Tiber, had begun at the beginning of the 1st century BC. Prior to this the area had featured few buildings except the four modest temples today found in the modern Lago de Torre Argentina, given the unhealthy location. The *Campus Martius* now became the focus for an architectural arms race as late republican warlord after late republican warlord raced to outdo each other by building monuments and temples of increasing grandeur. Pompey set the standard with his monumental theatre built at the foot of the Capitoline Hill in the early 50s BC, later renovated by his nemesis Julius Caesar who then built the Theatre of Balbus and the Theatre of Marcellus nearby. The latter two were part of a complex masterminded by his general Marcus Agrippa that also included the enormous cylindrical Pantheon temple (later completed by Emperor Hadrian) and an enormous public bathing complex stretching south-east towards the *Forum Romanum*. One innovation of Augustus's grand building programme was the use of new sources of marble. This included a local white marble from Carrara (*Luna*) in northern Italy, and brightly coloured marbles from Egypt and Anatolia. Before this time much of the marble used in Rome had come from Greece.

However, it was the *Forum Romanum* that was the centre of political and religious life in Rome. Given its opulent splendour the *Forum Romanum* proved an irresistible draw for late republican leaders and Principate emperors who wanted to monumentalise their own achievements. First

The Pantheon in Rome, started by Marcus Agrippa, finished by Hadrian. A superb example of Roman monumentalism.

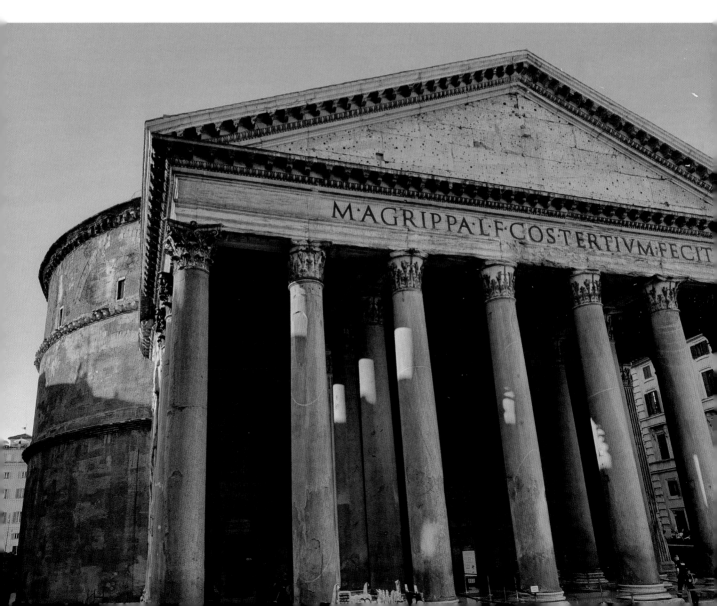

The Hills of Rome

Rome was famously built across seven hills on the eastern bank of the Tiber. These, each with their own distinct character, were;

- The Aventine Hill at the south-eastern extremity that lay outside of the original sacred boundary of the city. This hill had a long-standing association with Rome's Latin allies, and with eastern deities and the lower classes. It was also the hill favoured by Remus in the Roman founding myth.

- The Palatine Hill to its north, the centremost of the seven. This was by far the most salubrious of the seven hills, and from the time of Augustus home to the imperial palace atop its 40m peak. Such was its fame across the empire at the time and subsequently that the hill has given us the name palace, derived from the original *palatinus*. The Circus Maximus ran down its western side and the *Forum Romanum* its east. It was the Palatine Hill that was favoured by Romulus in the Roman founding myth.

- The Caelian Hill to the east, originally settled in the 7th century BC by the population of the Alba Longa when forced there after the city's defeat by Tullus Hostilius, third king of Rome. In both the republican and imperial periods, the Caelian hill was very fashionable and home to many of Rome's wealthiest citizens, it only a short walk to the Palatine Hill and *Forum Romanum*.

- The Capitoline Hill, to the north-west of the Palatine Hill. This steep knoll featured a vertical cliff overlooking the *Forum Romanum* called the Tarpeian Rock after a treacherous Vestal Virgin executed there. It was the site of many key temples in Rome to deities of the Classical Roman pantheon, and originally called *Mons Saturnius* after an early temple there. The hill was later renamed *Mons Capitolium* after a temple to Jupiter Optimus Maximus, the senior deity in the Capitoline Triad, was built there in the later 6th century BC. Contemporary tradition had it that the name originated from the finding of a human skull (hence caput, meaning head or summit) when the foundations of the latter were being built. Other key temples included the 8th century BC vulcanal shrine of Vulcan on the hill's lower eastern slopes overlooking the head of the *Forum Romanum*, a key temple to all of the Capitoline Triad (one of the largest in the city), the Temple of Virtus, a later Temple of Saturn and the Temple of Juno Moneta. With the *Campus Martius* running along its south-eastern foot, adjacent to the Palatine Hill, the Capitoline Hill was seen as a symbol of strength and eternity in the city. Indeed, it was here that many Romans came to seek shelter during the sack of the city in 390 BC by Brennus's Senones Gauls given its steep, easily defendable slopes.

- The Esquiline Hill, to the north-east of the Palatine Hill. This was a very fashionable district to live in, overlooking the valley where the Colosseum was later built. The hill consisted of three spurs, these being the *Cispian* northern spur, the *Fagutal* western spur and the *Oppian* southern spur. It was on the latter that Nero built his 1.6km-long *Domus Aureus* (Golden House), and where Trajan built his public bathing complex. However, this chic place had another, much darker side, for on the far side of the Esquiline Gate along the *via Labicana* and its various branches were the ditches where the bodies of the dead slaves from the city were unceremoniously dumped. By the late 2nd century BC, though some of the land here had been reclaimed from this grim land use as the fine living atop the hill spread beyond the city walls, the area was still notorious as the *Sessorium*, the place where troublesome slaves were executed by crucifixion, a punishment usually reserved for this lowest level of society.

- The Quirinal Hill, to the far north of the Palatine Hill, originally a Sabine settlement from the 8th century BC. The hill was named after Quirrinus, thought to be the Sabine god of war, himself named after the Sabine word for spear. Livy (1.44) says the Quirrinal became part of the expanding city of Rome during the reign of Servius Tullius in the 6th century BC (along with the Viminal hill, see below) and was later associated with a Temple of Mars built by Augustus, and Constantine I's bathing complex.

- The Viminal Hill, to the immediate south-east of the Quirinal Hill and with the Esquiline Hill to its south. This was the smallest of Rome's seven hills, later featuring the 110,000m² Baths of Diocletian on its north-eastern slopes. The unfashionable Subura district with its many brothels where Julius Caesar first set up home in the city, a deliberate gesture to show his *populares* sympathies, was located in the valley between the Viminal Hill and Esquiline Hill.

A slice through the Roman Imperial palace atop the Palatine hill, with corridors and reception rooms visible in cross section.

The *Forum Romanum*

The key buildings of the forum in the later 2nd century AD included:

- The *Tabularium* (official records office)

- The Arch of Titus

- The Temple of Concord

- The Temple of Saturn

- The *Basilica Julia*

- The *rostra* (public speaking platform)

- The Temple of Castor and Pollux

- The Arch of Augustus (now lost except its travertine foundations)

- The Temple of Deified Julius Caesar

- The Temple of Vesta

- The *regia* (office of the *Pontifex Maximus*)

- The *Basilica Aemilia*

- The *Curia Julia*, begun by Julius Caesar and finished by Augustus

At the very end of the 2nd century AD the great warrior Emperor Septimius Severus would add to these his own monumental arch, built to commemorate his two eastern campaigns against the Parthians and their allies. This fine monument, still standing proud today, was constructed next to the entrance to the Senate House to remind the political elites of the imperial capital who the boss was.

The Temple of Vesta in the *Forum Romanum*, Rome. As rebuilt by Julia Domna, wife of Septimius Severus, after it had burnt down in the reign of Commodus.

The *Forum Romanum* as seen from the Palatine Hill.

up, Julius Caesar built an enormous forum that stretched the entire length of the *Forum Romanum* on its north-east side, much of it completed after his death. At its centre was the Temple of Venus Genetrix, referencing his family's association with the goddess. Next, Augustus went further by building his own forum adjacent to that of Caesar, featuring the vast Temple of Mars Ultor. Not to be outdone, Trajan later built his own forum to the immediate north of those of Caesar and Augustus. This featured Trajan's Column, the towering memorial commemorating his Dacian conquests.

Meanwhile, standing proud above the *Forum Romanum* atop the Palatine Hill stood the imperial palace. The original 'palace' here was built by Augustus, a deliberately modest structure to bolster the conceit that he was simply the *princeps*. This building was formed by combining several 1st-century BC houses into one structure. It featured the House of Augustus, with several fine staterooms, and the House of Livia. The latter was a peristyle-type town house with a range of family rooms running off the central courtyard. This palace was enlarged by Tiberius (AD 14 to AD 37), and then extended west across the summit of the Palatine Hill by Nero (AD 54 to AD 68). However, his palace burned down in AD 65, after which he moved the imperial residence to the vast *Domus Aureus*, which he built on the *Oppian* spur of the Esquiline Hill. After his suicide this was then abandoned, and by the late 2nd century

AD the only surviving element was the 36m-high bronze-clad Colossus of Nero, an immense statue of the mad emperor sited between the *Forum Romanum* and the Colosseum that had later been modified into a monument to the sun-god Sol. Vespasian, victor in the 'Year of Four Emperors' in AD 69, moved the palace back to the Palatine Hill and there it was to remain, his utilitarian structure later vastly expanded by his younger son Domitian (AD 81 to AD 96) into a monumental range of buildings with an extensive suite of lavish reception rooms.

Vespasian's major contribution to central Rome was initiating construction of the Colosseum, built at the foot of the *Forum Romanum* between the Palatine and Caelian Hills. This vast amphitheatre, constructed on the site of the lake Nero had built in his *Domus Aureus*, was the largest in the Roman world and could hold up to 80,000 spectators. It was only bettered in terms of size as a place of entertainment in Rome by the 621m-long Circus Maximus chariot-racing stadium built on the western side of the Palatine Hill beneath the imperial palace. This could hold 150,000 spectators. Both the Colosseum and Circus Maximus were used primarily to stage *Ludi* (public games) associated with the Roman religious calendar.

Meanwhile, nearby to the west in the *Campus Martius* was the *Ara Pacis* (altar to peace), a large rectangular structure covered in reliefs celebrating

The Circus Maximus in Rome, as seen from the imperial viewing platform.

Augustus's *Pax Romana* and constructed next to his circular tomb. Nearby was the *Horologium* (or *Solarium*) *Augusti* that used an ancient Egyptian obelisk as a sundial marker to show the time of day on an inscribed marble plaza. On the western bank of the Tiber was the imposing Mausoleum of Hadrian, while a final key feature of late 2nd-century Rome was the legionary fort-sized *Castra Praetoria* (Praetorian camp), built on the eastern slopes of the Quirinal Hill outside of the Servian Walls there.

Aside from its grand imperial precincts Rome lacked the precise grid-pattern layout of classical towns and cities of Greek and Etruscan origin. Much of Rome was a heaving, overcrowded web of lanes and thoroughfares, with only the major trunk roads to and from the city cutting through the vast urban sprawl. While the better off could afford fine town houses in the finer districts, housing a million inhabitants proved a huge problem. The Roman solution, as with today, was to build upwards. To that end they constructed thousands of *insulae* (literally meaning island in Latin) tower blocks up to seven-storeys high. With the wealthiest living at the bottom and the poorest the top, many were badly designed and built, leading to frequent collapses and fires. Meanwhile, at street level all kinds of dwelling and commercial activity competed for the limited space, with most citizens eating out rather than cooking in their own dwellings given the fire hazard.

With this level of urban density, disease was rife, with frequent epidemics culling the population. As with the rest of the Empire, Rome suffered from the various plagues that came and went, but the real killers there were more common diseases. These included tuberculosis, typhoid fever, gastroenteritis and malaria. The latter was rife in Rome, especially its most dangerous Plasmodium Falciparium form, given the huge stretches of marsh on the banks of the Tiber.

Public health in Rome was helped by its fresh water supply, this facilitated by 10 aqueducts by the late 2nd century AD. These were, in order of date completed, the *Aqua Appia, Aqua Anio Vetus, Aqua Marcia, Aqua Tepula, Aqua Julia, Aqua Virgo, Aqua Alsietina, Aqua Claudia, Aqua Anio*

Novus and *Aqua Traiana*. Together they supplied at least 1,127,000m^3 of water per day to meet the demands of the city, with a senatorial-level *curator aquarum* charged with their maintenance. Rome also had one of the best-designed wastewater systems in the Empire, with a complex system of stone-slab covered sewers draining waste into large trunk sewers which carried the effluent into the Tiber and its tributaries. The largest was the *Cloaca Maxima*, originally built by the Etruscans to drain the *Forum Romanum*, which later became a principal sewer. However, given its immense growth by the late 2nd century AD, large areas of the city lacked any wastewater provision at all. In these areas effluent was simply thrown from upper story windows, with water-borne diseases rife given the high levels of pollution.

Criminality was also endemic in Rome given its enormous population, with security provided by the Praetorian Guard on special occasions, and the *cohortes urbanae* (urban cohorts) created by Augustus to counterbalance the power of the former. The latter were the equivalent of modern *gendarme* (armed police) and originally numbered three cohorts of 500 men with six centurions and commanded by a tribune. An additional cohort was added in the Flavian period. Fire was also an ever-present danger in Rome given the dense living conditions for most citizens, with the *vigiles urbani* (watchmen of the city) providing the main firefighting service and also being an additional law and order resource. The latter were commanded by a *praefectus vigilum*.

A final feature of Rome in the late 2nd century AD was its twin ports Ostia and Portus, the vital routes through which the grain supply from Egypt, North Africa and Sicily arrived in the imperial capital via the Tiber. Ostia, founded in the 4th century BC, was originally a fort at the mouth of the Tiber which quickly developed into a major port. However, by the beginning of the 1st century AD it could no longer cope with the immense demand for the wheat shipped there for use in Rome. Claudius therefore built a new harbour 3km to the north called Portus, which was then greatly expanded by Trajan, including the installation of a new pentagonal harbour basin.

Ostia Antica today, the original port of Rome.

Roman merchant ship carrying grain for the *cura annonae* in Rome at Osta Antica.

The Dominate Empire

The 'Crisis of the 3rd Century' changed the very nature of the Roman Empire. Such were the multiple shocks experienced by all levels of Roman society that Diocletian was forced to take drastic action in order to drag the Empire out of the maelstrom it found itself in. In attempting to remedy the Empire's downward spiral, he was preceded by a number of noteworthy emperors who, despite their best efforts, ultimately failed. Aurelian (AD 270 to AD 275) provides a good example, as he tried to reform the shattered Roman economy by improving the quality of the coinage with new, improved issues. He also recognised the now real threat to the Italian peninsula from predating Germans and Goths and so built the 19km Aurelian Walls in Rome to replace its now outdated Servian predecessor. It was also he who finally defeated the breakaway Gallic Empire in the west, and defeated the Palmyrans in the east. The latter, under its queen Zenobia, had carved out an Empire of its own incorporating much Roman territory after the capture of Valerian in AD 260, adding a further threat in the region to Roman interests.

However, it ultimately fell to Diocletian to rectify the situation. Once emperor he quickly

Late republican and principate Rome on view. The *Porta San Paolo* in the Aurelian Wall circuit adjacent to the Pyramid of Caius Cestius.

Rear of the Aurelian Walls
in Rome, with bastion in
view.

realised that the political structures of the Principate were no longer fit for purpose, and from the point we refer to the Empire as the Dominate. This referenced a much more authoritarian style of imperial control, with the name itself based on the word dominus, meaning master or lord in Latin. Gone was the conceit of the Principate with the emperor the principal citizen of the Empire but still 'one of us'. Now, with control of the military and political classes vital to the survival of the Empire, he became more akin to an eastern potentate.

Diocletian specifically reformed the Empire in three ways, in what later became known as the Diocletianic Reformation:

- Firstly, by instituting the tetrarchic system of political control that divided power across his vast Empire between first two and then four (two senior and styled Augustus, and two junior and styled Caesar) brother-emperors. Note he retained overall control.
- Secondly, by completely reordering the provincial structure of the Principate in order to secure much firmer control of the tax base of the Empire. He now created a

The Portrait of the Four Monarchs at St Mark's Basilica, Venice. Most likely statues of Diocletian, Maximian, Galerius and Constantius Chlorus, the original tetrarchy. This is from the Philadelphion in Constantinople, looted during the Fourth Crusade sack of the city and taken to Italy. (Guy Esnouf)

A late Roman shieldwall, note the mix of ridge helmets and Spangenhelms (see Chapter 5 for detail). (Graham Sumner)

new system of diocese, these much larger units of economic control, to replace the older provinces. Each diocese was then broken down into a number of new, much smaller provinces.

- Thirdly, by adding extra layers of public administration to support the above, increasing the coercive power of the Roman state. This allowed a fully systemised taxation regime to be introduced on all economic production, called the *annona militaris*.

Throughout the Dominate period the Empire was constantly under military pressure along its far-flung frontiers, particularly by Germans and Goths over the Rhine and Danube, and by the Sassanid Persians in the east. By this time Roman military supremacy wasn't all but guaranteed as previously, at least in the long run in a conflict, and so the Roman military machine had to change as radically as the Empire itself had. Soon Germans and Goths in particular were settling within its borders, and from that point onwards their influence became increasingly visible in Roman military units stationed in both the west and east. In the first instance they were recruited as *foederate* mercenaries and allies (see Chapter 5 for full description). Then later, as manpower pressures began to grow, they began to increasingly fill the ranks of regular units (see Chapter 5 for detail). Additionally, the civil wars that Diocletian had done so much to stop soon returned with a vengeance as political and military leaders took advantage of periodic instability to usurp. This put a huge strain on the Roman military establishment, with thousands of regular troops often killed in these conflicts.

There were a number of the principal dynasties, time periods and large-scale military campaigns in the Dominate phase of Empire, these are fully detailed on p. 122.

The Diocene Structure of the Dominate Empire

As detailed earlier, Diocletian completely reorganised the political and economic structure of the empire into new diocese. These were much larger regional units than the earlier Principate provinces. Each of the bigger units was controlled by a *vicarius* (sometimes called an *exarch* in the Greek-speaking east), a senior official appointed by the emperor who combined the power of the earlier provincial governors and *procuratores*. The *vicarii* were usually based in the most significant city or town in the diocese, for example in Britain, *Londinium*. Meanwhile those appointed to run the new, smaller provinces within each diocese retained the title governor, though now had far less authority within the rigid new administrative structure of the Empire.

One more reform of the geographic organization of the Dominate Empire occurred under Constantine I. This saw the large diocese themselves set within even larger units of control with the creation of four prefectures which effectively quartered the Empire, roughly tracing the tetrachic system of imperial rule set up by Diocletian. These were, in the north and west the *Praefectura praetorio Galliarum*, in the imperial centre (including North Africa) the *Praefectura praetorio Italiae*, along the Danube frontier and in the Balkans the *Praefectura praetorio Illyrici*, and in the east (including Egypt) the *Praefectura praetorio Orientis*. The first two were under the ultimate control of the western emperor, the latter two the eastern emperor. Diocletian originally created 12 diocese, these are all detailed on pp. 124ff.

Statue of Constantine the Great, founder of the Constantinian Dynasty, in York. Here he usurped as emperor after the death of his father Constantius Chlorus.

CONSTANTINE·THE·GREAT
A.D. 274~337

PROCLAIMED ROMAN EMPEROR
IN YORK A.D. 306

The Dominate Empire

- Diocletian's tetrarchy, from his accession in AD 284 until Constantine I secured control of the entire Empire in AD 324. Military activity at this time included the western Caesar Constantius Chlorus's successful campaign in AD 296 to return Britain to the imperial fold after the usurpation of Caurausius and later Allectus, and successful Roman campaigning against Sassanid Persia.

- The Constantinian Dynasty from AD 324 through to the death of Jovian in AD 364. This dynastic period initially featured much civil war, with Constantine I seeking over time to control the entire Empire following *legio VI Victrix* proclaiming him emperor in York in AD 306. There was also continual trouble with the Germans and Goths along the Rhine and Danube, with Julian the Apostate's campaigns against the Alamanni in Gaul, featured in detail in Chapter 5, and with Sassanid Persia in the east.

- The Valentinian Dynasty from the accession of Valentinian I in AD 364 through to the death of the usurper Eugenius in AD 394. This period included the disastrous Gothic Wars of eastern Emperor Valens that culminated in the shattering defeat of the eastern field army at the battle of Adrianople in AD 378 at the hands of a combined Visigoth and Ostrogoth army. Here the emperor himself lost his life, and such were the Roman losses that the Empire – both west and east – struggled to recover militarily afterwards.

- The Theodosian Dynasty, from the accession of Theodosius I the Great in AD 392 to the death of Valentinian III in AD 455. Theodosius I was the last emperor to rule both halves of the Roman Empire at the same time. This dynastic period was dominated in the west by the widespread migration of Germans and Goths into the western Empire, under pressure from the Hunnic expansion from the Asian steppe. It was bookended by two dramatic sackings of Rome, the first by Alaric I's Visigoths in AD 410 and the second by the Vandals under Genseric in AD 455. However, it was Hunnic predations in both the western and eastern Empire that were to prove most problematic to the survival of the Empire in the first half of the 5th century AD, with a military highpoint being the defeat of Attila the Hun by the *magister militum* Flavius Aetius at the battle of the Catalaunian Plains in AD 451.

- The Fall of the West, from the accession of Petronius Maximus in AD 455 to the abdication of Romulus Augustulus as the last western emperor in AD 476 on the orders of Odoacor, a senior officer in the Roman army. The latter, leading a revolt of *foederates* and regular units, had shortly beforehand been proclaimed rex *Italiae* (king of Italy). One of his first acts once in power was to send the regalia of western imperial authority to eastern Emperor Zeno, this officially marking the ending of the western Empire. However, in the east the Empire was to continue in one form or another until AD 1453 when the Ottoman Turks under the Sultan Mehmed II finally sacked Constantinople, destroying the last vestiges of the Byzantine Empire.

A Dominate-period late Roman legionary. Note he wears a simple ridge helmet with cheek guards and *lorica hamata* and carries a large round body shield and a long spear. (Graham Sumner)

Diocese and Provinces of the Dominate Roman Empire

Diocese	Province
Britanniae	Maximia Caesariensis
	Britannia Prima
	Flavia Caesariensis
	Britannia Secunda
	A fifth province in the diocese called Valentia (thought to translate as 'land of Valens') is detailed on the late 4th/early 5th century AD *Notitia Dignitatum*, though its existence is problematic
Galliae (the Rhine frontier and northern Gaul)	Germania Prima
	Germania Secunda
	Lugdunensis Prima
	Lugdunensis Secunda
	Belgica Prima
	Belgica Secunda
Viennensis (southern Gaul)	Aquitanica Prima
	Aquitanica Secunda
	Novem Populi
	Narbonensis Prima
	Narbonensis Secunda
	Viennensis (which gave the diocese its name)
Hispaniae	Gallaecia
	Tarraconensis
	Carthaginiensis
	Lusitania
	Baetica
	Mauretania Tingitana (across the modern Straits of Gibraltar in North Africa)
Italia	Liguria
	Transpadana
	Rhaetia
	Venetia et Histria
	Aemilia

	Tuscia et Umbria
	Flaminia
	Latium
	Samnium
	Apulia et Calabria
	Lucania et Bruttium
	Sicilia
	Corsica et Sardinia
Pannoniae	Noricum Ripense
	Noricum Mediterraneum
	Pannonia Prima
	Pannonia Secunda
	Valeria
	Salvia
	Dalmatia
Moesiae	Moesia Prima
	Dacia
	Praevalitana
	Dardania
	Epirus Nova
	Epirus Vetus
	Macedonia
	Thessalia
	Achaea
Thraciae	Moesia Secunda
	Scythia
	Thracia
	Haemimontius
	Rhodope
	Europa
Asia	Asia (which gave the diocese its name)
	Hellespontus

	Lydia
	Caria
	Phrygia Prima
	Phrygia Secunda
	Pisidia
	Lycia and Pamphylia
Pontica	Bithynia et Pontus
	Paphlagonia
	Galatia
	Cappadocia
	Diospontus
	Armenia Minor
	Pontus Polemoniacus
Oriens	Isauria
	Cilicia
	Augusta Euphratensis
	Syria Coele
	Osrohoene
	Mesopatamia
	Pheonicia
	Augusta Libanensis
	Palaestina
	Arabia Prima
	Arabia Secunda
	Thebais
	Aegyptus Iovia
	Aegyptus Herculia
	Libya Superior
	Libya Inferior
Africa	Africa Proconsularis
	Byzacena
	Mauretania Sitifensis

Mauretania Caesariensis

Numidia Cirtensis

Numidia Militian

Tripolitania

Roman legionary shield
cover from Leiden, modern
Netherlands.
(Livius.org/Jona Lendering)

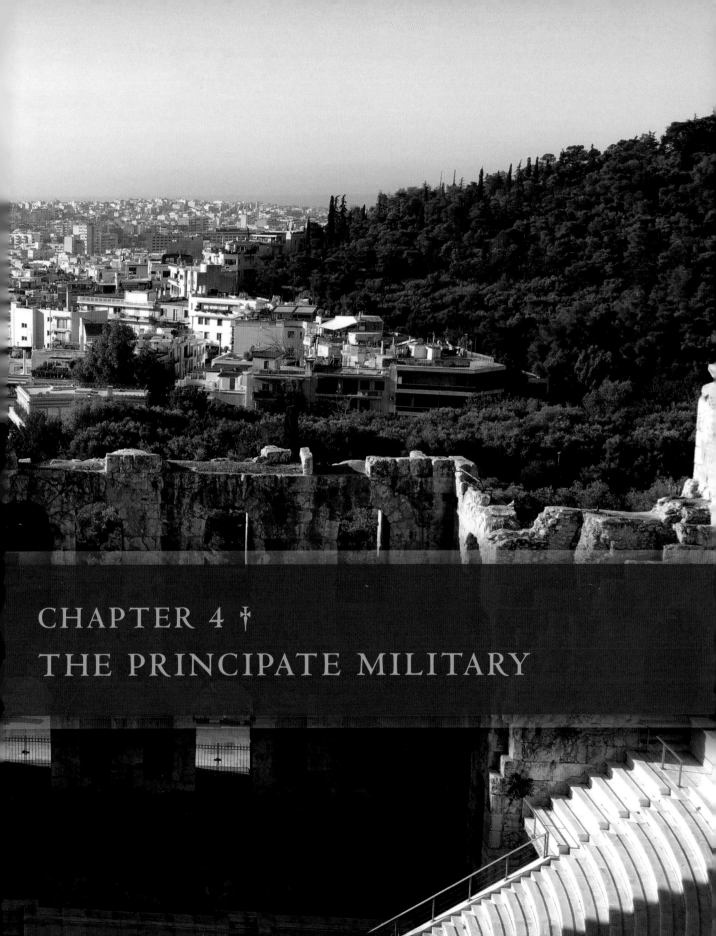

CHAPTER 4 ⸸
THE PRINCIPATE MILITARY

A senior legionary
centurion of the Principate.
(Graham Sumner)

T he Roman military in the Principate phase of Empire was pre-eminent in a world where at that time it lacked a true symmetrical threat (one whose military tactics and technology matched its own, unless through weight of numbers) until the advent of the Sassanid Persians in the early 3rd century AD. Most often on campaign and in battle it won. When it did lose to Germans, Sarmatians or Parthians, it always learned from its mistakes and came back the better for it, showing true Roman grit. This is the Roman military most recognisable to the general public. Think of legionaries resplendent in torso-covering *scutum*, fine *lorica segmentata* and bright-crested imperial Gallic helmets, their *gladii* at the ready.

In this chapter I set out the Principate Roman military in detail. First, I consider the legionary from the time of Augustus through to the accession of Diocletian in AD 284. I then focus on a brand-new institution in the Roman military, the *auxilia*. Next, I detail Roman naval power in the Principate phase of Empire, before closing the chapter with a review of one of the Empire's most enigmatic institutions, the Praetorian Guard.

The Principate Legionary

Augustus carried out the next major reformation of the Roman military. Given the enormous military establishment he inherited at the end of the last round of republican civil wars, this was very extensive and designed to reduce this hugely expensive complement to manageable numbers. The reforms included the legions, their supporting troops (most, from this time onwards, becoming the full-time *auxilia*) and regional fleets. The latter two are considered in more detail later in Chapter 2.

His first move with the legions was to tackle the huge number he now had scattered around his new Empire, these numbering an improbable 60. Over a five-year period he reduced this total to 28, it then falling to 25 after Varus's losses in Germany in AD 9. Subsequent emperors increased the number again, with the total hovering around 30 for the next 250 years, for example 29 were in existence at the time of the accession of Marcus Aurelius and Lucius Verus in AD 161. The total only rose above

30 during the Severan dynasty after Septimius Severus created *legio I Parthica*, *legio II Parthica* and *legio III Parthica* for his eastern campaigns, bringing the total then to 33.

The Principate legions after the Augustan reforms numbered 5,500 men, organised into ten cohorts. Of these, the first had five centuries of 160 men (*legio II Parthica*'s first cohort had six such centuries), with the other cohorts having six centuries of 80 men. Each century was then broken down into ten eight-man sections called *contubernia*, whose men shared a tent when on campaign and two barrack block rooms when in their legionary fortress. Additionally, the legions also featured 120 auxiliary cavalry, these acting as dispatch riders and scouts. We know specifically of one such individual who actually served in this latter role in *legio IX Hispana*. This is Quintus Cornelius whose now-lost tombstone was found around 1800 on the south side of the churchyard of St Peter-at-Gowts church in Lincoln. His inscription (RIB 254) reads:

Legionary artillery, in this case an *onager* (stone thrower). Each later Principate legion had 10. (Graham Sumner)

Quintus Cornelius, son of Quintus, of the Claudian voting-tribe, trooper of legio IX from the century of Cassius Martialis: aged 40 years, of 19 years' service, lies buried here.

The numbering and naming of the legions seems confusing to us today, reflecting their being raised by different republican leaders (especially in the civil wars of the 1st century BC) and emperors, and at different times. Therefore, many shared the same legion number (always permanent) but had different names, for example there were five third legions. Others shared the same name but had different numbering, for example Septimius Severus's three Parthian legions. The longevity of this numbering, and the clear differential in the naming, suggests that the strong sense of identity of the republican Marian legions was certainly carried over into their Principate counterparts.

In that regard, the standards carried by the legions were very important and had expanded in number by the time of the Principate into a formal complement comprising four different types. First and most important was the *aquila* (eagle standard) first introduced into the late republican legions by Marius and carried by the *aquilifer*. The eagle by this time was made entirely of gold, and only left camp when the entire legion was on the move. Another standard, the *imago*, featured an image of the emperor and was carried by the *imaginifer*, while signa standards were allocated to each individual century and featured the legion's battle honours. These were carried by the *signifer*. Flag-based standards were also used, called *vexilla*, one of which showed the name of the legion, while others of the same type were allocated to legionary detachments, hence their naming as *vexillationes*. The *vexilla* were carried by *vexillarii*. These various standards were joined in their signalling role in the legions by the *cornicen* (musician) who played the *cornu*. The latter always marched at the head of the centuries, with the *signifer* or another appropriate standard bearer.

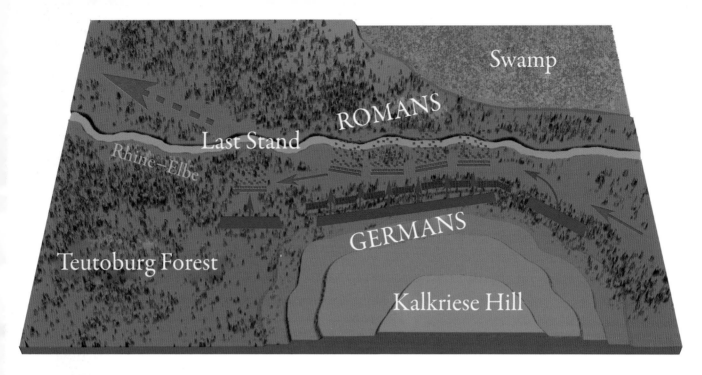

Swamp

ROMANS

Last Stand

Rhine–Elbe

Teutoburg Forest

GERMANS

Kalkriese Hill

Open

Forest

Contour

Swamp

River

Germans

Romans

Principate legionaries could be volunteers or conscripted (the latter again under the *dilectus*), depending on the circumstances, although by the time of the diarchy of Marcus Aurelius and Lucius Verus they were increasingly enrolled as conscripts given the losses suffered first in the Roman–Parthian War and later the Marcomannic Wars. Such conscripted recruitment was usually on a regional basis, as with their foundings *legio II Italica* and *legio III Italica*, who were recruited in Italy. Those recruited by either means were exclusively Roman citizens for most of the Principate, originally being all Italian at the end of the Republic, although increasingly they came from Gaul and Spain as citizenship spread, and later came from North Africa and the

The battle of Teutoberg Forest in AD 9 when the three Roman legions plus auxiliaries of Varus were annihilated by Arminius' Germans in a large scale ambush. (Nigel Emsen)

Roman medics at work on the battlefield as the legionaries advance. (Andy Singleton)

Legatus legionis with *aquilifer, legio II Augusta.* (Andy Singleton)

eastern Mediterranean. The recruiting base for legionaries then increased even further with the Edict of Caracalla in AD 212, as this made every freeman living in the Empire a citizen. Meanwhile, throughout the Principate phase of Empire there was a height requirement for the legionary, this being 1.8m.

Augustus greatly increased the term of service for the legionaries in his reforms from the six years of the late Republic to 20 years, designed to maintain a stable base of highly experienced troops in the legions. The last four years were served as a veteran, excused from fatigues and guard duty, such troops called *vexillum veteranorum*. This length of service was then later extended by Augustus to 25 years, with five as a veteran, a term which lasted well into the Dominate phase of Empire. The increase was due to a shortage of recruits (Augustus being too successful when slimming the number of legions down), and because of the strain placed on the imperial *fiscus* to pay the *praemia* retirement gratuity for retiring legionaries given the very large

number of troops Augustus inherited.

Such gratuities could now be money (3,000 *denarii* in the late 1st century BC, this rising to 5,000 *denarii* by the time of Septimius Severus), or land as in the later Republic. In the latter case this was now in the form of centuriated land parcels designed to set the retiree up as a farmer, or in *coloniae* (veteran settlements) as in the later Republic. Such retired legionaries often settled near to their former legionary bases, these settlements then developing into *coloniae* towns as happened with Gloucester (*Glevum*), Lincoln and York in Britain.

In terms of pay the Augustan legionary received the same 225 *denarii* as introduced by Caesar, from which deductions were now formally made for arms, clothing and food. This was increased to 300 *denarii* by Domitian, a level it remained at until the reign of Septimius Severus who increased it to 450 *denarii*. His son Caracalla increased legionary pay even more, by a further 50%, following his father's advice to keep the soldiery

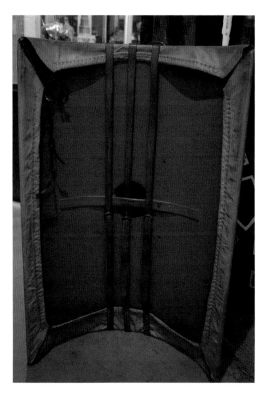

Rear view of a reproduction of a classic Principate legionary *scutum*, this in travel mode. Note the left-handed hand-grip. (Trimontium Trust)

Reproduction of a classic Principate legionary *scutum* with travel cover. (Trimontium Trust)

Front view of a
reproduction of a classic
Principate *scutum*.
(Trimontium Trust)

Lorica segmentata

Lorica segmentata was a type of armour constructed of articulated iron plates and hoops. The origins of *lorica segmentata* are unclear though it may have originally been a form of gladiator armour. The first types emerge in the archaeological record at the end of the 1st century BC when it began to replace *lorica hamata* as the main type worn by the legionary, and from that point the armour evolved through three specific versions, these being (all named after the location where examples were found):

- The Dangestetten–Kalkriese–Vindonissa type, those found dating to between 9 BC to AD 43.

- The Corbridge–Carnumtum type, those found dating to between AD 69 to AD 100.

- The Newstead type, those found dating to between AD 164 to AD 180.

Each successive version was less complicated than that which preceded it, for example that found in the principia of the *vexillation* fort at Newstead (*Trimontium*) in the Scottish Borders in 1905 featuring rivets to replace earlier bronze hinges, a single large girdle plate to replace the two previous ones, and hooks to replace earlier and more complicated belt-buckle fastenings.

A recreation of the Newstead late *lorica segmentata* found at the Flavian and Antonine fort there. (Trimontium Trust)

happy above all else. This basic pay was also often increased through donatives such as the 75 *denarii* left by Augustus to all of his legionaries in his will. Even at its most basic level this was a good salary for a Roman citizen, and in an age before popular banking the legionaries often handed their savings to their unit standard bearers, a duty which placed a huge amount of trust upon them. We have a direct example of one such standard bearer performing this role. This is Rufinus, a *signifer* with *legio IX hispana*, whose tombstone was found in York. His image on the monument shows him holding a *codex ansantus* (case of writing tablets) in his left hand, there to record his fellow legionaries' accounts.

Meanwhile, to provide some context here as to the impact legionary and other military expenditure had on the imperial *fiscus*, in the 2nd century AD the overall annual cost of the Roman military was 150 million *denarii* (this comprising the salaries and retirement gratuities for legionaries, *auxilia* and the milites of the regional fleets).

The diet of the Principate legionary was very similar to that of his later republican predecessor, though by this time more care was taken when on campaign to ensure the security of their grain supply. This is well evidenced by the Scottish campaigns of Septimius Severus in Scotland where he expanded the size of the granaries at the key naval supply base at South Shields by a factor of 10 (see Chapter 6 for detail).

Meanwhile, religion continued to play a major role in the daily lives of the Principate legionary, with the obligation to worship the gods of the Roman pantheon now joined by the even more important requirement to worship the imperial cult of the sitting emperor. Additionally, the worship of certain gods that had a specific association with the Roman military now also appeared. These were often eastern in origin and included Mithras, Bacchus and Isis. The worship of all of these gods, and also the dates of the traditional festivals of Rome (together with the accession days and birthdays of emperors), structured the religious year for the Principate legionary.

Elsewhere in the Principate legionary's daily life, he was officially unable to marry until he retired,

(*left*)
Side view of a reproduction of a classic 'imperial' Gallic helmet. Note the cheek guards and extensive neck guard. (Trimontium Trust)

(*above*)
A variety of types of reproduced 'imperial' Gallic helmets. (Trimontium Trust)

though legionaries often contracted technically illegal marriages. Septimius Severus changed this, granting the soldiers their right to marry and at the same time giving the formerly illegal spouses and offspring legal rights for the first time.

In terms of command structure, the legions from the early Principate were led by a senatorial-level *legatus legionis*. His second-in-command was also of senatorial-level, called the *tribunus laticlavius*, a younger man gaining the experience needed to command their own legion in the future. Third in command was the *praefectus castrorum* (camp prefect), a seasoned former centurion responsible for administration and logistics. Below this level there were five younger equestrian-level tribunes, called the *tribuni angusticlavii*, these allocated tasks and responsibilities as necessary. The actual control of each cohort in the legion remained the responsibility of the centurions, as with the late republican legions.

Equipment of the Principate Legionary

As with the late republican legionary, those of the Principate were for the most part specialist heavy infantry whose arms and armour were always geared towards defeating their opponents through the shock of impact and discipline (although see below regarding the new legionary *lanciarii*).

In terms of his defensive panoply, for a shield the Principate legionary was still equipped with the curved, rectangular *scutum* (though squarer in design than those of their republican counterparts). As before it was used as an offensive weapon in its own right, and in defence allowed the legionaries to adopt a number of defensive formations including the *testudo*. This featured interlocking shields providing full cover on all sides, including from above. Other formations that made great use of the shield included the *orbis* to provide all round defence and the *cuneus* (swine head) wedge formation used to puncture an opponent's battle line.

In terms of armour the legionaries of the Principate wore a variety of types of full body armour. The most commonly depicted in contemporary culture and found in the archaeological record is the famous *lorica segmentata*. Other types of armour continued to be worn, including *lorica hamata* that stayed in use throughout the Principate, and came back into full favour in the 3rd century AD. A further variant was *lorica squamata* (scalemail) (cheaper than chainmail but inferior in flexibility and protection) made from small bronze or iron interlocking scales, while in the provinces even

Roman legionaries on the Arch of Septimius Severus. Note the 'imperial' Gallic helmets they are wearing.

more exotic types were to be found, for example a suit of crocodile skin armour found in a 3rd-century AD context in Manfalut, Egypt, and now housed in the British Museum. It is not clear in such cases if the function of the armour was more religious than military, in this instance perhaps referencing a military crocodile cult associated with the goddess Isis. Additionally, when fighting certain types of opponent, such as the Bastarnae using the two-handed *falx* (slashing weapon), extra armour was fitted including articulated iron *manicae* (arm guards), thigh guards and greaves. Specific troop types within the Principate legions were also often differentially equipped with armour when compared to the rank and file legionaries to mark them apart, with officers frequently shown wearing iron and bronze muscled cuirasses and centurions and signifers wearing chainmail (even when the majority of legionaries were wearing *lorica segmentata*).

Finally, in terms of defensive military equipment, the helmet of the legionary also evolved throughout the Principate. At the time Augustus became the emperor the Coolus and

Port types were still the most common to be found in the legions. However, the latter soon developed into the much more substantial classic 'imperial' Gallic helmet. In particular this featured a much larger neck guard. A final 'imperial' type originated in Italy, hence it being called 'imperial' Italic. This was a bronze compromise between the new designs of Celtic origin and the more traditional Roman types of the Republic. All of these helmets featured prominent cheek guards (again of Celtic provenance), neck guards and often a reinforcing strip on the front of the cap to deflect downward sword slashes. Ear guards were added from the AD 50s.

The Principate legionary also still carried his two *pila*, again one light for use in the approach and one heavy for use immediately prior to impact. However, the principal weapon was still the *gladius*, worn as before on the right-hand side for rank and file troopers. When Augustus took office, the main type was still the *gladius Hispaniensis*. This developed during his reign into the Mainz-type *gladius* that was broader and shorter, featuring a longer stabbing point. A further development,

A dense mass of Severan legionaries with round shields and spears fighting Parthian cataphracts. Tactical and technological change shown in real time on the Arch of Septimius Severus in Rome.

An early Principate legionary, still in his *lorica hamata*. Soon this was replaced with *lorica segmentata*, and from the reign of Septimius Severus in the later 2nd century AD many began to replace their *pila* with spears. (Livius.org/Jona Lendering)

adopted towards the close of the 1st century AD, was the Pompeii-type *gladius*, this being slightly shorter than Mainz type with a squatter, triangular stabbing point. All of these swords were still used in the same cut-and-thrust combat routine, this continuing to dominate Roman fencing techniques even when the length of the swords began to

Late Principate Roman legionary on the Arch of Septimius Severus, Rome. Military technology can be seen in transition here, with him wearing classic *lorica segmentata* armour but carrying the new round shield which increasingly replaced the traditional *scutum*.

increase again in the later 2nd century AD. The weapons complement was completed by the *pugio*. Both this and the *gladius* were suspended from two individual belts that crossed over front and back.

This traditional Principate legionary panoply was beginning to change by the late 2nd/early 3rd centuries AD. This was largely a response to a change in the nature of their opponents. Previously, the legions had most often faced a similar infantry-heavy force (excepting the Parthians in the east), but were now tackling a multitude of threats, many of a differing nature that required a more flexible response. In particular, the heavily armoured charging lancers of the Sarmatian tribes faced by the Romans in the Marcomannic Wars made a strong impression.

This change is shown in real time on four of the monuments set up in Rome by four great warrior emperors – Trajan's Column, the Column of Marcus Aurelius and the Arches of Septimius Severus and Constantine. The latter is particularly important given it is in effect a time machine, built in AD 315 in the Dominate phase of Empire to celebrate Constantine's victory over Maxentius at the battle of Milvian Bridge in AD 312. At the time the imperial *fiscus* was running low, as it had been used by Maxentius to fund his failed defence of Rome. Therefore, the architects of the new arch sourced panels from existing monuments to complement its new and contemporary depictions of his martial success. These included four panels called the Great Trajanic Frieze which comprised slabs from a monument to celebrate victory in Trajan's two Dacian campaigns, and similar panels from a lost Arch of Marcus Aurelius to celebrate his successes in the Marcomannic Wars.

The change in the equipment of the later Principate legionary was initially evident in their weaponry. First, from the reign of Septimius Severus the longer cavalry-style *spatha* sword began to replace the shorter *gladius* for all Roman foot soldiers. This weapon was up to 80cm in length, although some of 1m length have been identified. The new sword was suspended from a baldric on a Sarmatian-type scabbard slide and came to dominate Roman military equipment in the west until the Empire's end there, continuing in use in the east afterwards. It seems likely the adoption of this weapon had its origins in the need for more reach to tackle armoured mounted opponents.

A similar change is also evident in the use of the *pila*, being gradually replaced by a thrusting spear of between 2m and 2.7m in length in the same time period. This change is visible actually taking place on the four monuments detailed above. Thus Trajan's Column, the Column of Marcus Aurelius and the reused panels on the Arch of Constantine show legionaries in classic *lorica segmentata* armour mostly armed with *pila*, while on the Arch of Septimius Severus and on the contemporary

panels of the Arch of Constantine they have been replaced by spears. This was again a response to the experiences fighting mounted opponents more frequently, as with the longer sword. A legionary spear wall made much more sense engaging such opponents than the use of *pilum* impact weapons, with one such legionary phalanx actually depicted on a panel on the Arch of Septimius Severus, there countering Parthian cataphracts.

Moving to the defensive panoply, this change is also evident with the shield. In the later 2nd century AD, the traditional *scutum* began to be replaced by a large flat (and sometimes slightly

Roman legionaries of *legio II Parthica* from the later Principate Empire, fighting on the eastern front against the Parthians. Note the *lanciarius* with his quiver of javelins. (Graham Sumner)

dished) oval body shield, confusingly still called a *scutum*. This new design was of simple plank construction, with stitched-on rawhide, and was strengthened with iron bars. The two types appear to have been used side by side for some time, with examples of both found at the fortified frontier-trading town of Dura-Europos in Syria dating to AD 256. This transition is also very evident on the four monuments detailed above, with many of the large round shields featuring on the Severan arch, and even more on the contemporary panels of the Arch of Constantine. Once again, this change seems to have been associated with the type of opponent more commonly faced by the Romans, the round shield perhaps more suited to dealing with a mounted threat. It certainly gave greater freedom of movement for the new swords and spears coming into use with their greater reach and would also have been cheaper to produce.

Not surprisingly, a change is also evident in the body armour of the legionary as the Principate approached its end. Thus, on Trajan's Column and the Column of Marcus Aurelius most are wearing *lorica segmentata*, as they are on the reused panels on the Arch of Constantine. However, on the Arch of Septimius Severus there is a much higher proportion wearing *lorica hamata* and *lorica squamata*, this proportion increasing yet again on the contemporary panels of the Arch of Constantine.

Roman Principate legionaries in *lorica segmentata* on the Arch of Constantine in Rome. These are reused from a lost Arch of Marcus Aurelius.

The Principate Legions of Rome

Legion	When founded	Destroyed/disbanded
legio I Germanica	Later republic	Disbanded AD 70 after Civilis Revolt
legio I Adiutrix pia fidelis	Provisionally recruited by Nero, then made a regular legion by Galba	
legio I Italica	Under Nero	
legio I Macriana	Under Nero	Civil war legion, disbanded AD 69/70
legio I Flavia Minervia pia fidelis	Under Domitian	
legio I Parthica	Under Septimius Severus	
legio II Augusta	Later Republic/under Augustus	
legio II Adiutrix pia fidelis	Under Nero	
legio II Italica	Under Marcus Aurelius	
legio II Parthica	Under Septimius Severus	
legio II Traiana fortis	Under Trajan	
legio III Augusta pia fidelis	Later Republic/under Augustus	
legio III Cyrenaica	Later Republic	
legio III Gallica	Under Caesar	
legio III Parthica	Under Septimius Severus	
legio IIII Flavia felix	Under Vespasian	
legio IIII Macedonica	Under Caesar	Disbanded AD 70
legio IIII Scythica	Under Mark Antony	
legio V Alaudae	Under Caesar	Destroyed under Domitian
legio V Macedonica	Later Republic	
legio VI Ferrata fidelis constans	Under Caesar	
legio VI Victrix	Later Republic	
legio VII Claudia pia fidelis	Under Caesar	

legio VII Gemina	Under Galba	
legio VIII Augusta	Later Republic	
legio IX Hispana	Later Republic	Disappears in the early 2nd century AD
legio X Fretensis	Later Republic	
legio X Gemina	Under Caesar	
legio XI Claudia pia fidelis	Later Republic	
legio XII Fulminata	Under Caesar	
legio XIII Gemina pia fidelis	Later Republic	
legio XIV Gemina Martia Victrix	Later Republic	
legio XV Apollinaris	Under Augustus	
legio XV Primigenia	Under Caligula	Disbanded AD 70
legio XVI Flavia Firma	Under Vespasian	
legio XVI Gallica	Under Augustus	Disbanded AD 70
legio XVII	Under Augustus	Destroyed in AD 9 in Germany
legio XVIII	Under Augustus	Destroyed in AD 9 in Germany
legio XIX	Under Augustus	Destroyed in AD 9 in Germany
legio XX Valeria Victrix	Under Augustus	
legio XXI Rapax	Under Augustus	Possibly destroyed under Domitian
legio XXII Deiotariana	Under Augustus	Possibly destroyed under Hadrian
legio XXII Primigenia pia fidelis	Under Caligula	Possibly destroyed under Hadrian
legio XXX Ulpia Victrix	Under Trajan	

After Goldsworthy, A. 2003. *The Complete Roman Army*. London: Thames and Hudson.

Meanwhile, as the Principate progressed, legionary helmets also became increasingly substantial, with the Italic 'imperial' type disappearing entirely by the early 3rd century AD. The Gallic 'imperial' style did continue in use, but was increasingly supplemented by heavier, single bowl designs reinforced by cross-pieces and fitted with deep napes, leaving only a minimal T-shaped face opening. These helmets provided exceptional levels of protection.

A final change in this time period was the appearance of a new type of legionary. This was the *lanciarii* (light trooper) armed with a quiver of javelins and lighter armour than their front-rank line-of-battle equivalents. Such troops, who operated like the *velites* of the Polybian legions, skirmished forward to deter mounted bowmen and other lightly armed missile troops. They are first attested in gravestone epigraphy serving in the ranks of *legio II Parthica* in the context of Caracalla and Macrinus's AD 215–218 Parthian War.

Not surprisingly, a change is also evident in the body armour of the legionary as the Principate approached its end. Thus, on Trajan's Column and the Column of Marcus Aurelius most are wearing *lorica segmentata*, as they are on the reused panels on the Arch of Constantine. However, on the Arch of Septimius Severus there is a much higher proportion wearing *lorica hamata* and *lorica squamata*, this proportion increasing yet again on the contemporary panels of the Arch of Constantine.

Meanwhile, as the Principate progressed, legionary helmets also became increasingly

A reproduction of a Roman auxiliary cavalry 'sports' helmet, used in displays of mounted martial prowess. Based on the Newstead Helmet, found at the Flavian and Antonine fort there. (Trimontium Trust)

with deep napes, leaving only a minimal T-shaped face opening. These helmets provided exceptional levels of protection.

A final change in this time period was the appearance of a new type of legionary. This was the *lanciarii* (light trooper) armed with a quiver of javelins and lighter armour than their front-rank line-of-battle equivalents. Such troops, who operated like the *velites* of the Polybian legions, skirmished forward to deter mounted bowmen and other lightly armed missile troops. They are first attested in gravestone epigraphy serving in the ranks of *legio II Parthica* in the context of Caracalla and Macrinus's AD 215–218 Parthian War.

Roman legionaries also provided the battlefield and siege artillery component of Roman armies when on campaign. Such weapons included light *scorpiones* (dart-throwers) and the larger *ballistae*, the latter firing large bolts and shaped stones. When at full strength, each cohort fielded one of the latter and each century one of the former. This gave an impressive total of ten *ballistae* and 59 *scorpiones*. A final development with regard to

substantial, with the Italic 'imperial' type disappearing entirely by the early 3rd century AD. The Gallic 'imperial' style did continue in use, but was increasingly supplemented by heavier, single bowl designs reinforced by cross-pieces and fitted

Principate legionary artillery was a move to replace the *ballista* with the *onager* (catapult), the latter larger and better suited to siege warfare, from around AD 250.

Meanwhile, one area where the equipment of the republican legionary remained broadly the same through to the later Principate was with regard to his non-military and engineering kit. Over 300 years later, they still remained *muli mariani*.

The *Auxilia*

Legionaries were not the only soldiers in the Roman military during the Principate phase of Empire. As detailed in Chapter 2, republican Roman armies had always used mercenary and allied auxiliary troops to support the legions. These were recruited to fulfil a wide variety of supporting roles on the battlefield, fighting under their own officers and in their own native formations.

However, this all changed as part of the Augustan reforms of the military. In addition to his rationalisation of the legions, the first emperor

The tombstone of a Roman auxiliary cavalry officer called Insus, son of Vodullus, who was born in Trier. The funerary relief shows him carrying a severed head. Found in four pieces in Lancaster city centre.

also formalised the supporting troops in the Roman military establishment, and from this time they were called auxiliaries (or *auxilia* in shortened

Principate auxiliary foot troops making initial contact with the enemy before the legionaries to their rear. (Graham Sumner)

form, as used in this book). These were now regular troops and featured both cavalry and infantry, recruited from *peregrini* (non-Italian) freemen, often from recently conquered new provinces as the new Empire expanded. The number of *auxilia* quickly grew, with Tacitus (*Annals*, 4.5) saying that by AD 25 there were as many in the Roman army as legionaries, the latter number at that time around 175,000.

Though *auxilia* were full line of battle troops, they were the junior partners to their legionary counterparts. Foot troops were paid 100 *denarii* per annum from the later 1st century AD, with cavalry paid 200 *denarii* (those based on the wing of a battle formation being paid 333 *denarii*). Terms of service were similar to those of the legionaries, with auxiliaries normally serving 25 years. Upon retirement the trooper was given a citizenship diploma that granted Roman citizenship to himself and his heirs, the right of legal marriage to a non-citizen woman, and citizenship for existing children.

The *auxilia* provided most of the cavalry and much of the foot complement of Roman armies. Auxiliary cavalry were organised into *quingenary alae* of 512 men or *milliary alae* of 768. Each was commanded by a *praefectus alae*. The basic cavalrymen were called *equites*, their defensive panoply featuring flat oval or hexagonal shields,

short *lorica hamata* and a variety of types of bronze and iron helmets, often with cheek and neck guards. For offensive weaponry they were equipped with a *hasta* that could be thrown or used as a short lance, and a *spatha*. Many *equites* armed in this way were among the most feared units in the Principate military, specifically recruited from regions famous at the time for their formidable mounted warriors. A good example is the auxiliary cavalry of Gallic origin, descendants of Caesar's mercenary warriors referenced in Chapter 2, who were known for their predilection for trophy headhunting.

In the early Principate the *equites* were supported by a variety of different types of light cavalry fighting in the style of their native region. Examples included Moorish *symmachiarii* javelin-armed skirmishers, and eastern horse archers. By the later 2nd century AD such specialist light cavalry had been fully integrated into the Roman military establishment. Examples included javelin-armed *equites illyriciani* and bow-armed *equites sagittarii*. Specialist shock cavalry had also begun to appear by this time, initially in the form of *numeri* temporary units of indigenous troops recruited in the east, often called *contarii* referencing their long *contos* (lances). A fine example is found in Britain where in AD 175 Marcus Aurelius sent 5,500 of the 8,000 Iazyges lancers supplied to the Roman military as part of a peace treaty with the

Roman Principate *auxilia* infantry on the Arch of Septimius Severus in Rome. Note the short *lorica hamata*.

Sarmatians during the Marcomannic Wars. These were based at Ribchester (*Bremetennacum*) in modern Lancashire from where they helped defend the northern provincial frontier in the province.

As the later Principate progressed such shock cavalry were quickly formalised into full auxiliary *ala*, for example the lancers as *equites contariorum* and heavily armoured cataphracts as *equites cataphractarii*. The latter were based on the Parthian cataphracts Rome often encountered in the east and were again armed with the *contos*, wearing a suit of scale armour called *lorica plumata* which covered the entire body, with a substantial helmet with gilded face plate. Their horses were often similarly fully armoured.

In terms of *auxilia* foot troops, although these were the junior partners to their legionary counterparts, they were still among the best soldiers of the ancient world. There were many occasions when the fighting was done by the *auxilia* alone, for example at the battle of Mons Graupius in AD 83 when Agricola finally managed to bring the Caledonians to battle south of the Moray Firth in the Grampians (Tacitus, *The Agricola*, 36.1–2).

Auxilia infantry formations in the Principate were based on a single *quingenary* cohort of 480 troops, or a double-sized *milliary* cohort of 800 troops. These cohorts (both the small and large) were divided into centuries of between 80 and 100 men, these under the command of a centurion,

they clearly replicating the similar structure in a legionary formation. However, the centurions, unlike the auxiliary troopers, were sometimes Roman citizens appointed from the legions. Others were drawn direct from the rank and file of the auxiliary unit. Above this level the cohort was commanded by an equestrian, a praefectus for a *quingenary* unit and a tribune for a *milliary* unit.

Auxilia foot troops fought in both close and loose formation, the latter making them especially useful in difficult terrain. As with the cavalry they often retained the skills associated with their place of origin, for example the Batavian *auxilia* used by Aulus Plautius in the famous river crossing battle described by Dio (*Roman History*, 60.19–60.23) in Kent during the AD 43 Claudian invasion of Britain. This was most likely the River Medway. The Batavians originated in the Rhine Delta and were renowned for being able to swim in full armour. Dio says Plautius deployed them in a flanking manoeuvre after the first day's inconclusive fighting, downriver of the native Britons defending the western bank. The Batavians swam across the river, probably using inflated animal skins, and attacked the Britons from the rear. Plautius then forced the crossing with his legionaries, winning the battle.

When in close order auxiliary foot troops were line of battle troops who fought in a similar manner to the legionaries. The auxiliary shield throughout

Detail of Principate *auxilia* on the Arch of Septimius Severus in Rome, note the shield grips.

An *equites cataphractarii*,
the fully armoured shock
cavalry that came into being
in the later Principate and
then thrived in the later
Dominate phase of Empire.
(Graham Sumner)

Auxiliary Cohorts and *Alae* of the mid-Principate Empire

Unit	Location	Date
Brittones Aurelianensis	Upper Germany	AD 200
Cohors Sagittariorum	Hispania Baetica	Later 2nd century AD
Cohors I Aelia Brittonum milliaria	Noricum	Later 2nd century AD
Cohors I Dacorum Brittonum millaria	Britannia and Noricum	Later 2nd century AD
Cohors I Dardanorum Aurelia	Dalmatia	Later 2nd century AD
Cohors I Sacorum Aurelia Nova	Dalmatia	Later 2nd century AD
Cohors I Septima Belgarum	Upper Germany	AD 200
Cohors I Tungrorum mil.	Britannia	2nd century AD
Cohors I Ulpia Tiaiana Cugernorum CR	Britannia	2nd century AD
Cohors I Ulpia Traiana Campestris Voluntariorum	Dalmatia	2nd century AD
Cohors II Aforum Flavia	Mauretania	Late 2nd century AD
Cohors II Astorum Equitata	Britannia	2nd century AD
Cohors II Dacorum Aurelia	Pannonia Inferior	Late 2nd century AD
Cohors II Gallorum Equitata	Britannia	2nd century AD
Cohors II Tungrorum mil.	Britannia	2nd century AD
Cohors III Aquitanorum equitata CR	Upper Germany	Late 2nd century AD
Cohors III Gallorum	Hispania Baetica	Late 2nd century AD
Cohors III Nerviorum CR	Britannia, Hispania Baetica	Late 2nd century AD
Cohors III Breucorum	Britannia	2nd century AD
Cohors III Tungrorum mil.	Mauretania	Late 2nd century AD
Cohors IV Gallorum	Gallia Lugdunensis	Late 2nd century AD
Cohors IV Tungorum mil.	Lower Germany	2nd century AD

Cohors V Baetica	Hispania Baetica	Late 2nd century AD
Cohors VI Raetorum	Britannia	Late 2nd century AD
Cohors VII Delmatorum eq.	Mauretania	Late 2nd century AD
Ara Colonia Ulpia Traiana	Lower Germany	Late 2nd century AD
Ala Asturum	Gallia Lugdunensis	2nd century AD
Ala (Gallorum) Placentia	Britannia	Late 2nd century AD
Ala (Hispanorum) Vettonum CR	Britannia	2nd century AD
Ala Noricorum	Lower Germany	Late 2nd century AD
Ala (Gallorum) Sebosiana	Britannia	2nd century AD
Ala I (Hispanorum) Aravacorum	Pannonia	Late 2nd century AD
Ala I Asturum	Britannia	2nd century AD
Ala I Britannica	Mauretania	Late 2nd century AD
Ala I Caninafatium	Pannonia	Late 2nd century AD
Ala I Contaforium	Pannonia	Late 2nd century AD
Ala I Ituraeorum	Pannonia	Late 2nd century AD
Ala I (Pannoniourum) Sebosiana	Britannia	2nd century AD
Ala I (Pannoniorum) Tampiana	Britannia	Later 2nd century AD
Ala II Asturum	Britannia	2nd century AD
Ala II Pannoniorum	Pannonia	2nd century AD

After D'Amato, R. 2016. *Roman Army Units in the Western Provinces* (1). Oxford: Osprey Publishing.

the Principate was usually an elongated oval plank design covering the torso and featuring a central iron or bronze boss, the shield smaller in size than the legionary *scutum*. In terms of armour *auxilia* are most frequently shown wearing *lorica hamata* or *lorica squamata*, these shorter and less sophisticated than those worn by their legionary counterparts. *Auxilia* helmets were also less sophisticated, often-cheaper bronze versions of those worn by the legionaries. They were armed with short, throwable spears called *lancea* rather than *pila*, and a sword similar to the legionary *gladius*, this later replaced by the longer cavalry-style *spatha* as with the legionaries. The *auxilia* also provided the majority of the specialist warriors in Roman military formations, for example archers, slingers, staff slingers and javelinmen.

The former, called *auxilia sagittarri* and organised into *cohortes sagittariorum*, were a particularly important component of Roman armies and wore distinctive uniforms that distinguished whether they had been recruited in the west or east. Those from the east, where they had to contend with Parthian and other eastern horse archers, often had better protection than their line-of-battle *auxilia* counterparts, wearing long *lorica squamata*

Regional Fleets of the Roman Principate

Fleet	Annual Stipend
Classis Ravenna	300,000 *sesterces*
Classis Misenensis	200,000 *sesterces*
Classis Britannica	100,000 *sesterces*
Classis Germanica	100,000 *sesterces*
Classis Flavia Pannonica	60,000 *sesterces*
Classis Flavia Moesica	60,000 *sesterces*
Classis Pontica	60,000 *sesterces*
Classis Syriaca	60,000 *sesterces*
Classis Nova Lybica	60,000 *sesterces*
Classis Alexandrina	60,000 *sesterces*

After Ellis Jones, J. 2012. *The Maritime Landscape of Roman Britain*. Oxford: BAR/Archaeological and Historical Associates Ltd.

and conical iron helmets. Such troops are well represented in relief on Trajan's Column.

Roman archers fought using a composite bow based on those of the horsemen of the Asian steppe, made from laminated layers of wood, bone, horn and sinew. This gave the weapon much greater penetrating power than the self-bow used by less sophisticated opponents. Further, notched stiffeners at each end of the bow, and its handgrip, gave the bowstring greater leverage. This kept the weapon from bucking when fired, which increased accuracy.

Roman arrows also featured sophisticated technology, with different arrowheads used depending on the opponent engaged. Against unarmoured enemies, for example the majority of German and Gothic foot troops, a broad arrowhead was used to maximise damage to the opponent's body. Meanwhile, against more heavily armoured troops such as Sarmatian lancers and Parthian cataphracts, a much narrower bodkin point arrowhead was used, this causing less damage but able to penetrate armour. Other specialist arrowheads included those designed for use in a siege which featured an iron basket behind the arrow tip, this designed to carry lit inflammable material.

Roman arrow shafts were made of wood, reed or cane depending on where they were manufactured. The arrowhead was set in place with a wooden pile to ensure the arrowhead didn't shatter on impact. The arrows were carried in a pharetra (quiver) held between the shoulder blades by leather straps. Auxiliary archers also had bracers on their left wrists to protect them from the kick of the bowstring when firing. They also had either leather finger guards or a metal thumb ring to enable them to pull the bowstring rapidly. For self-defence they carried a standard auxiliary sword.

Auxilia units could also be fielded in combined formations that featured both infantry and mounted troops, their organisation being less well understood. Such infantry cohorts, cavalry *alae* and combined units were very flexible and could easily be moved around the Empire as needed in the same manner as *vexillationes* of legionaries.

Naval *milites* crewing a monoreme Roman galley, from Sicily. (depositphotos/mountainpix)

The Regional Fleets

The regional navies of the Principate Empire were also the result of the military reforms of Augustus. Before this date the fleets of the Republic were ad hoc in nature, designed to fight symmetrical engagements against opponents including Carthage, the Hellenistic kingdoms and in the Roman civil war rivals across the Mediterranean, all detailed in Chapters 1 and 2. Augustus rationalised this system, recreating the various fleets he inherited into regional navies that reflected the Empire's expanding geographical reach. By the end of the 1st century AD there were 10 such fleets, each with a specific area of territorial responsibility. These are detailed in the below table which also shows the annual stipend of each fleet's *praefectus classis*, reflecting its status.

The *Classis Britannica* in Britain provides a good example of one of the larger Principate regional fleets. This featured 900 ships and 7,000 crew,

including sailors, marines and support personnel. Each regional fleet had an origin specific to its region of operations, with that in Britain dating to the original 900 vessels built by Caligula for his abortive AD 40 invasion. These were later used by Claudius for his AD 43 invasion. Though this fleet took part in every aspect of the campaigns of conquest in Britain from that point, it was actually first called the *Classis Britannica* by Tacitus in the context of the Batavian uprising in Germania Inferior in AD 70 (*Histories*, 4.79.3).

All regional fleets performed both military and civilian roles. In the former context the *Classis Britannica* had responsibility for the North Sea, English Channel, Atlantic approaches, Bristol Channel and Irish Sea, the east and west coasts of the main island of Britain, the river systems of Britain and the continental coast up to the Rhine Delta. The latter reflected the way the Romans viewed *Oceanus* separating Britain from the continent, not as a barrier as we do today in the context of recent military history, but as a point of connectivity linking Britain physically with the rest of the Empire. This is reflected in the fact that the *Classis Britannica*'s headquarters were in Boulogne-sur-Mer in north-western Gaul, as detailed in Chapter 3.

Meanwhile, in its civilian activities the *Classis Britannica* was used in a variety of roles. This included administration, engineering and construction, and running industry and agriculture. These are detailed in full in Chapter 6.

The principal warship of the *Classis Britannica* was the small and mobile *liburnian bireme* galley, a vessel type used in all the regional fleets of the Principate Empire. These had replaced the large polyreme galleys of the republican civil wars by the end of the 1st century BC given the lack of any symmetrical enemy threat at sea in either the Mediterranean or northern waters from that time. The name originates from the Liburni tribe in Dalmatia whose fast *biremes* were renowned in the Roman world for their feats of piracy. Such ships are the most common type depicted on Trajan's Column in the context of the conquest of Dacia. The commonality of *liburnae*, certainly in northern waters, is testified by an analysis of Roman ship fittings found at Richborough using data from the 1922–1938 excavations that shows such vessels were the most common type present.

The *liburnae* of the regional fleets carried the same suite of weapons as their republican polyreme forbears. In naval engagements the principal weapon was a large bronze or iron ram designed to punch a hole in an opposing vessel's hull below the waterline, or alternatively to run down the length of a target vessel aiming to disable it by destroying the oars (and oarsmen) on the given side. Meanwhile artillery was also a common feature on regional fleet *liburnae*, these either bolt-shooting or stone-throwing ballista, or larger stone-throwing *onagers*. These weapons could be used in direct ship-to-ship engagements with standard ammunition, or more problematically with ammunition set alight designed to set their opponents afire. Additionally, the sickle-shaped hooks on the end of long poles detailed by Caesar that were used to cut the rigging of enemy vessels were also still in use, while

another late republican innovation called the *harpax* (harpoon) also featured. This was a simple grapnel attached to a 2.3m shaft trailing a line. It was designed to be fired from a ballista. Metal strips were often attached to the line to prevent it being cut, and once ensnared the opposing vessel was then reeled in and the opponent boarded. The mid-republican *corvus* was also still in use, though not all *liburnae* were equipped with it.

A final point of interest here regarding the *liburnae* of the regional fleets is that they seem to have been individually named. An example is provided by the grave stele of a junior officer of the Classis Ravennate that describes him as the captain of the liburna Aurata (meaning golden).

In terms of other vessel types, and using the *Classis Britannica* again for our examples, we know of at least one larger *trireme* that served in the fleet based on an inscription from Boulogne that mentions such a vessel in the service of the regional fleet. However, for the most part the vessels carrying out the majority of military activity in the waters around Britain remained the *liburnae* throughout the Principate. They were supported, especially around the coastal littoral and along river systems, by a variety of *myoparo* (cutters) and *scapha* (skiffs). Meanwhile merchant vessels based on Romano-Celtic designs with high freeboards and shallow drafts provided much of the fleet's maritime transport capability.

Each regional fleet was commanded by an equestrian-level *praefectus classis* (fleet admiral) appointed directly by the emperor. He reported to a province's *procurator* rather than governor given each fleet's civilian activities, though clearly he fell under the latter's command when on military duty. Over time the position of *praefectus classis* grew into a very senior position on the equestrian career path, with the commanders of the Classis Ravennate and *Classis Misinensis* having the same status as the head of the Praetorian Guard in Rome. However, the most successful *praefectus classis* was Publius Helvius Pertinax, the one-time commander of the *Classis Germanica* in the later 2nd century AD who became the first emperor in the 'Year of the Five Emperors' in AD 193, before his assassination by the Praetorian Guard.

The *praefectus classis* of the first regional fleets was initially a former legionary tribune, and later *legate*. It is clear from epigraphic data that it was common for the fleet admirals to switch between legionary and classis command, and indeed between both and senior civilian positions. Later, after Claudius's integration of the civil and military branches of the imperial administration, the post of *praefectus classis* was opened up to freedmen of the imperial household. This changed back after the 'Year of Four Emperors' in AD 69 when sea power was one of the keys to the eventual victory of Vespasian, and after this time the post reverted back to be an equestrian only position. One can judge from the table above listing the pay of the *praefectus classis* of each of the regional fleets their order of seniority. Additionally, as the Principate phase of Empire progressed, new titles also began to be added to those of the *praefectus classis*, further indicating levels of importance. Thus the commanders of the two senior fleets received the title of praetor to add to the praefectus for their commanders, leading to the titles *praefectus classis praetorii Ravennate* and *praefectus classis praetorii Misinensis*. Similarly, the commanders of the Pannonian and Moesian regional navies gained the title *flavia*, while the commanders of the German and Egyptian regional fleets were later called *Augusta*. We don't know of any added title for the commander of the *Classis Britannica*, but analogy may shed some light here given that the *procurator* in Britain also carried the title *Augusta*.

Using the *Classis Britannica* again as our example, through epigraphy we know of specific individuals who held the post of *praefectus classis* in this regional fleet. These included Q. Baienus Blassianus, named in the role in an inscription from Ostia, Lucius Aufidius Pantera who is named on an alter found re-used in the later 3rd century AD Saxon Shore fort at Lympne, and Marcus Maenius Agrippa who appears on an inscription from Camerinum in Umbria.

As part of his headquarters operation the *praefectus classis* had a specialist staff. This included a *subpraefectus* (executive officer) and aide-de-camp, *cornicularius* (chief of staff), *actuarii* (clerks), *scribae* (scribes) and seconded

dupliarii (ratings) attached from the fleet. Below the headquarters staff the fleets relied heavily on Hellenistic nomenclature in terms of command structure. The commander of a squadron of ships was called a *navarchus* (the most senior the *navarchus principes*), and the captain of an individual vessel a *trierarchus*. Aboard ship the *trierarchus*'s executive team including a *gubernator* (senior officer) responsible for the steering oars, a *proretus* (second lieutenant) and the *pausarius* (rowing master). Other junior officers included the *secutor* (master at arms), *nauphylax* (officers of the watch) and specialists including the *velarii* with responsibility for the sails and *fabri* (ships' carpenters).

Below this level the ship's company was based on the military organization of their land-based counterparts, with the basic unit called a century. This reflected the preference for close action when engaged in naval combat. The century was commanded by a centurion, he assisted by an *optio* (second-in-command), a *suboptio* (junior assistant), a *bucinator* (bugler) or *cornicen* (horn player), and finally an *armorum custos* (armourer). The rest of the ship's complement was comprised of marines (*ballistarii* (artillery crew), *sagittarii* (archers) and *propugnatores* (deck soldiers)), *velarius* (sailors), and plenty of *remiges* (oarsmen). The latter were always professional rather than the slaves often depicted in popular culture, the whole company being styled *milites* (soldiers, the singular being *miles*) as opposed to *nautae* (sailors). This again reflected the Roman preference for maritime close action.

In the Principate, service as a naval *milite* was regarded in the same way as being an *auxilia*. Those in the *Classis Britannica* were often recruited from the former tribes of the coastal regions in north-western Gaul. Terms of service for all ranks was 26 years, a year longer than their auxiliary counterparts, the reward on completion being Roman citizenship. We have unique insight into this in the form of a recent archaeological discovery. This was the finding of the copper alloy military diploma of one Tigernos, a sailor of the Classis Germanica, granting his citizenship after completing his service. Interestingly, he may prove to be Britain's first named sailor as, despite his service on the Rhine, the diploma was found broken into eight pieces at the Roman fort in Lanchester (*Longuvicium*), County Durham.

Each naval *miles* received three gold pieces or 75 *denarii* upon enlistment, with their basic annual pay at the beginning of the Principate being 100 *denarii* for the lower ranks. Crewmembers given greater responsibilities were paid an additional bonus on top, with those paid 1.5 times the basic salary called *sesquiplicarii* and those paid double called *duplicarii*. From this annual salary, as with their land-based equivalents, the *milites* would have had deducted a certain amount to cover the cost of arms, equipment and food, and an additional amount which would be paid into the squadron's savings bank for their retirement fund.

Clothing for the naval *milites* differed between the regional fleets. This reflected differing climatic and operational conditions. Again, using the *Classis Britannica* as an example, an essential item of clothing in the northern waters would have been the *birrus* (rain-proofed hooded cloak) detailed in Chapter 3. Other key items of clothing for the *milites* of this regional fleet would have been the *pilos* (conical felt hat), belted tunic with trousers, and sandals or felt stockings with low-cut leather boots rather than *caligae*. The short *sagum* (cloak) was worn when on formal duty.

For weaponry the marines of the regional fleets' navies were armed in a similar manner to the land-based *auxilia*. Principal missile weapons, in addition to artillery, included bows, slings, javelins and darts. For hand-to-hand work the marines also carried boarding pikes, the *hasta navalis* (naval spear), various types of sword and the *dolabra* (boarding axe).

The Praetorian Guard

The Praetorian Guard was an elite Roman military unit, permanently based in Rome at their *Castra Praetoria* barracks built on the eastern slopes of the Quirinal Hill outside of the Servian Walls. From here they served as the personal bodyguard of the Roman emperors.

The guard had its origins in the Roman Republic. Various commanders of the time were well known for assigning crack troops to be their personal bodyguards, for example Sulla and Mark Antony. Caesar himself used his own legion, *legio X equestris*, as his personal guard. However, the term Praetorian in the later Republic specifically related to a small escort for high-ranking officials including leading senators, governors, proconsuls and *procuratores*.

It was the first emperor, Augustus, who actually created the select force he styled the Praetorian Guard for his own personal protection, sometime after 27 BC. This comprised nine cohorts of 500 men each, these later being increased to 1,000 men. He also added a small number of *equitatae* Praetorian cavalry, these later replaced by the *equites singulares Augusti* (imperial guard cavalry). Claudius increased the number of foot guard cohorts to 12, and Vitellius (April to September AD 69) increased this again to 16 in AD 69 during the 'Year of the Four Emperors' after disbanding the original nine. However, the ultimate victor Vespasian decreased this to nine again.

Praetorian Guard cohorts rotated duty in the imperial palace on the Palatine Hill, with three on guard at any one time. As with the legions, the Praetorian Guard cohorts also included specialists who were able to perform a wide variety of tasks when on campaign. A good example can be found on the tombstone of guardsman Caius Caristicus Redemtus from Brescel (*Brixellus*) in Cisalpine Gaul who is described as a *plumba(rius) ordina(rius/yus)* centurion-ranked lead worker.

The Praetorian guardsmen were well rewarded for their loyalty to the emperor. Augustus ensured the Senate passed a law allowing him to pay them at least twice a legionary's salary. This was increased again by Domitian and later by Septimius Severus (see below). They also had better terms of service, this only 16 years compared to the legionaries' 25. On retirement they were paid a huge gratuity of 20,000 sestertii, though given the many benefits of being a guardsman many reenlisted. Such troopers were known as *evocatii Augusti*.

Early guardsmen, particularly in the reigns of Augustus and Tiberius, were recruited from existing legions and were experienced warriors, though as the Principate progressed this changed and they were increasingly recruited straight into the guard from civilian life. These later Principate guardsmen developed a reputation for being more interested in fine living than soldiering, and interfering in imperial succession, and when Septimius Severus became the ultimate victor of the 'Year of the Five Emperors' in AD 193 he immediately disbanded them and replaced them with his own Danubian veterans, doubling the size of the guard at the same time (he also doubling the size of the *equites singulares Augusti*). At all times the guard only left Rome when on campaign with the emperor, which was more common at the beginning and end of the Principate.

The Praetorian Guard were the only soldiers allowed in the *pomerium* (sacred centre) of ancient Rome while bearing arms. This put them in a powerful position, particularly at times of imperial succession when they often played the decisive role if the imperial throne was contested. The ultimate and most shaming example was when they held an auction for the imperial throne in March AD 193 at the *Castra Praetoria* after a party of 300 of them assassinated Pertinax whom they had elevated to the throne on New Year's Day that year, his crime being to refuse to pay them a huge donative given the *fiscus* at the time was almost bankrupt. Two candidates, the city prefect (and confusingly Pertinax's father-in-law) Titus Flavius Claudius Sulpicianus and the ambitious leading Senator Didius Julianus bid against each other, the former within the camp and the latter standing on its walls. Ultimately the latter outbid the former, but was soon deposed and later killed, with Septimius Severus arriving in Rome to seize the throne and avenge the death of his former mentor Pertinax. It was the guard's role in the fall of the latter that drove him to sort out the Praetorians once and for all, he parading them naked in the *Forum Romanum* before banishing them from the imperial capital, and then replacing them with his own men as detailed above.

Praetorians also had other responsibilities in the imperial capital, including crowd control during the games in the Colosseum and elsewhere. Here they sometimes went a step further, participating in wild beast hunts and similar as part of the entertainment, as under the mad and bad Commodus (AD 180–193), himself a frequent participant in the arena.

The Praetorian Guard was commanded by two Praetorian prefects, the first office holders being Quintus Ostorius Scapula and Publius Salvius Aper from 2 BC. From the reign of Vespasian these prefects were always equestrians, the appointment a serious career advancement. Many chose to monumentalise their success through public building works. A fine example can be seen today in Ostia Antica, the former port of ancient Rome.

Here the forum bath complex was built at the expense of the prefect Marcus Gavius Maximus.

When on campaign with the emperor foot guardsmen were equipped in the same way as the better armed legionaries of the day. At the height of the Principate this would have been with *pilum, gladius, pugio, scutum* (this often featuring an image of winged victory, scorpions and crescents) and *lorica segmentata*, though in the case of the latter *lorica squamata* had begun to feature on images of guardsmen in contemporary sculpture. By the mid-3rd century AD this was the predominant type of Praetorian armour. One point of the difference in the defensive panoply at the time of Pertinax was the helmet, with particularly fine examples being worn. These included exquisitely detailed 'imperial' Gallic types, as seen on a number of guardsmen on Trajan's Column, and also designs referencing the classical past. In that regard, Greek Attic helmets were a common type worn by Praetorians. The base uniform colour was red, with large white helmet plumes (red in the case of centurions and officers). When in Rome on escort duty, smaller oval shields and *lancea* (light spears) were carried, with the suit of armour replaced by a fine quality light toga.

The Praetorian Guard remained a potential source of instability in the imperial capital, even after the changes made by Septimius Severus, and were finally abolished by Constantine I (AD 306–324) in AD 312 after the defeat of his rival Maxentius (AD 306–312) at the Battle of the Milvian Bridge. The victor then declared a *damnatio memoriae* against them, officially removing the guard from imperial history, with the *Castra Praetoria* being publicly dismantled. The imperial guardsmen of the later Dominate are considered in the next chapter.

CHAPTER 5 †
THE DOMINATE MILITARY

Late Dominate Roman
infantry. A legionary
wearing long *lorica hamata*.
Note the long spear, *angon*
(heavy throwing weapon)
and long *spatha*. Meanwhile
the officer is dressed in
a typical late Roman
decorated tunic. (Graham
Sumner)

The origins of the late Roman army in the Dominate phase of Empire actually date back to the beginning of the 3rd century AD. Here, Septimius Severus was the first emperor to create a field army when he invaded Scotland in AD 209 and AD 210. This enormous force of 50,000 men (see Chapter 6 for detail of the campaigns) was built around the Praetorian Guard, *equites singulares Augusti* and one of his own legionary foundings, *legio II Parthica*. The latter was normally based at Albanum, only 34km from Rome, there to put the stamp of his authority on the political classes in the imperial capital. It now formed the core of his new field army. This pattern of basing the legions away from the borders of the Empire – in depth as it were, better able to respond to deep strikes into imperial territory by ever larger 'barbarian' groupings – became more common as the 3rd century AD progressed given the multiple threats faced by the Empire along the Rhine and Danube, and in the east. It was then formalised first by Diocletian, and later by Constantine I when the latter became sole emperor from AD 324. From that time the change from the Principate military establishment to the new Dominate structure was striking, with the legionaries and auxiliaries of the earlier phase of Empire now divided into *comitatenses* (field army troops) (featuring a much larger proportion of mounted troops than previously) and *limitanei* (border troops).

In this chapter I first consider the military reforms of Diocletian and Constantine I, and then sequentially review late Roman infantry, cavalry, naval power and guard troops.

The Military Reforms of Diocletian and Constantine I

As noted in Chapter 4 the Roman Principate army most familiar to the general reader had begun a process of change during the reign of Septimius Severus. Before this time, broadly, most Roman legions and *auxilia* units were based within easy reach of the borders of the Empire. However, as detailed above, Severus created the first Roman field army for his *expeditio felicissima Britannica* which set a precedent that was accelerated by the challenges of the 'Crisis of the 3rd Century.' Far from declining after the accession of Diocletian and the onset of the Dominate Empire, these challenges then continued to increase. The major threats from that time were mass migration attempts into Roman territory by Germanic and Gothic confederations, the growing power of Sassanid Persia in the east, and later the predations of the Huns deep into imperial territory in both the west and east. Such trauma necessitated the radical changes instituted in the Roman military by Diocletian and later Constantine I. By the end of the latter's reign in AD 337 these changes were manifest in six broad ways, these being:

- A general levelling of the difference between the legionaries and auxiliaries in terms of their equipment, roles on campaign and in battle, and standing within the Roman military establishment.
- Military units in general being smaller (sometimes much smaller), with an emphasis on creating brigades of differing troop types (and ultimately field armies) appropriate to a given task rather than having a single type of homogenous force.
- From the time of Constantine I, a clear distinction between *comitatenses* and *limitanei*. This followed the adoption of a defence-in-depth strategy as the imperial experience transitioned from offence to defence, with the latter acting in a policing and 'trip wire' role on the borders of the Empire, and the former deployed far back to counter any significant incursion into imperial territory.
- A much larger mounted component within the field armies, with a greater range of specialist types.
- The gradual disappearance of the Principate regional fleets, with a reversion to the republican concept of ad hoc fleets created as required.
- Again reflecting earlier republican practice, the increasingly widespread use of *foederate* irregular troops, initially armed in their own fashion but under Roman officers, and later under their own officers.

Diocletian made the first great reforms of the military in the Dominate phase of Empire. Firstly, through the creation of the tetrarchy with its two *Augusti* and two *Caesares*, he set in place a command structure at the top of the Roman military that was far more adept at concentrating military force where necessary across the Empire, in both west and east. A prime example are the campaigns of the western Caesar Constantius Chlorus (Caesar in the west AD 293–305, Augustus in the west AD 305–306, and father of Constantine I) in defeating the breakaway North Sea Empire of the 'pirate king' Marcus Aurelius

Mausaeus Valerius Carausius and his successor Allectus in the late 3rd century AD, at the very beginning of the Dominate phase of empire.

The background to Carausius's rise was a crisis on the northern frontiers at the end of the Principate when the Germanic Alamanni burst through the northern frontier in AD 276, penetrating deep into Gaul where they sacked 60 towns. Though Emperor Probus (AD 276–282) restored order, the event destabilised the province of Britannia across the North Sea, with Zosimus saying in his New History (1.68.3) the emperor had to send captured Vandals and Burgundians there under the command of a North African *legate* called Victorinus to help put down a revolt, this an early Dominate use of *foederates*. Whatever form this rebellion took it proved difficult to stamp out, and it wasn't until the later reign of Carus (AD 282–283) that order was finally restored, he taking the title *Britannicus Maximus*.

One outcome of the trouble in Gaul and Britain was a rise in brigandage, with *Bagaudae* (peasant insurgents) plaguing the countryside, particularly on the continent. To tackle this the western Augustus Maximian (Caesar in the west AD 284–286, then Augustus AD 286–310) appointed Carausius, a highly successful regional military leader, to head a special task force designed to defeat the brigands. In this he was quickly victorius. Maximian then turned to him again to defeat yet another serious problem he was facing in the north-west of the Empire. Following the demise of the *Classis Britannica* in the mid-3rd century AD the Romans had lost control of the open ocean in the North Sea. This led directly to a rapid increase in maritime raiding by German and Frankish pirates who targeted the eastern coast of Britain and the Continental coast of Gaul, seriously disrupting the regional economies there. Here Carausius's maritime experience as a young man came to the fore, given he had grown up on coast of Belgica Secunda and served as a river pilot before later joining the military.

Carausius established his headquarters in the old *Classis Britannica* headquarters in Boulogne and quickly got to work, in the first instance building a new fleet to tackle the pirates. His campaign was a great success, with order soon restored in the North Sea. However, from Maximian's perspective he proved too successful, with the emperor accusing Carausius of deliberately intercepting the pirates after the raids rather than before so he could pocket the plunder. The unfortunate Carausius was sentenced to death but was tipped off before the sentence could be carried out. He promptly fled to Britain where in AD 287 he usurped, carving out his North Sea Empire which included north-eastern Gaul and Britain.

Carausius proved a charismatic and popular ruler given his local roots in the region. He also had significant forces at his disposal to maintain him in power, including the three British legions – *legio II Augusta* at Caerleon, *legio XX Valeria Victrix* at Chester and *legio VI Victrix* at York – and the new fleet he had built to defeat the piracy in the North Sea. He was also joined by *legio XXX Ulpia Victrix* in Germania Inferior, where it was based at the legionary fortress at Xanten.

Given this position of strength, Carausius now consolidated. In the first instance he established Britain's first official mint in London, with his coins notably superior to those in circulation when he arrived. Clearly with an eye to public relations, on them he styled himself as 'the saviour of Britain' (*Restitutor Britanniae*). Some of his coins also show that he clearly understood the old Severan maxim about keeping the troops happy, as they bear the legend 'Harmony with the Army' (*Concordia Militum*). It is also likely it was Carausius who completed the construction of the later Saxon Shore forts in Britain, aiming to deter any Roman plans to invade.

Maximian was clearly rattled by Carausius's usurpation and planned to move against him as soon as possible. However, first he had to build his own fleet. This was ready for action by AD 289 when it sailed down the Rhine and into the North Sea. However, the expedition proved an epic failure and an uneasy peace was soon agreed, with Carausius following the age-old plan of claiming legitimacy through association by minting coins featuring himself as an equal with the Maximian and the eastern Augustus Diocletian.

The latter two clearly didn't recognise this picture of brotherly love and before long the newly appointed western Caesar Constantius Chlorus was dispatched westwards with orders to defeat Carausius and return his usurping territories back into the imperial fold. To do this he made full use of the newly created military command structures instituted by Diocletian, gathering a huge field army comprising many of the legions of the west, and *vexillationes* from others, together with an equal number of auxiliary troops. He also built yet another fleet, knowing ultimately he would have to invade Britain.

Constantius Chlorus proved far more capable than Maximian and by AD 293 had defeated Carausius's Frankish allies around the Rhine estuary, he then recapturing Boulogne. These reverses proved the end for Carausius who was assassinated by Allectus, one of his senior officers, who now took over as the ruler of the remaining territories of the breakaway Empire. Confusion surrounds the actual identify of this far less charismatic leader, with some arguing he was Carausius's *procurator*, others his senior military commander, and yet others a Frankish mercenary leader given they increasingly appear in his army from this point. Whatever his origins, he only survived three more years before Constantius Chlorus was ready to assault Britain and claim the diocese back.

In the spring of AD 296 the western Caesar mounted a full invasion of Briton, the fourth Roman invasion of Britain after those of Caesar (twice) and Claudius. For his assault he used a clever stratagem, dividing his force into two. In the first instance he sent his own smaller division down the Thames Estuary to pin Allectus in the diocene capital along with a significant portion of his army. He then sent the larger part of his force to the Solent on the south coast under the Praetorian prefect Asclepiodotus. This slipped past Allectus's fleet in a fog bank and disembarked safely. Heading inland, the army quickly defeated Allectus's land forces, killing the usurper who had travelled south when word reached him of the invasion there. Constantius Chlorus now moved on London, arriving just in time to save it from being sacked by Allectus's remaining Frankish

A late Roman *equites contariorum*, a lance-armed shock cavalryman of the Dominate phase of Empire. Note the rich finery of his armour. (Graham Sumner)

mercenaries. With Britain finally restored to the Empire, the Caesar made a triumphal entry into the diocene capital. This event is commemorated in the gold Arras medallion that carries the legend 'Restorer of the Eternal Light' (*Redditor Lucis Aeterna*). This remarkable large coin shows the first ever depiction of London, with Constantius Chlorus on his charger receiving the thanks of the Londoners. Interestingly, the image also features a *liburnian bireme* galley.

A further reason why Constantius Chlorus was so successful in defeating the North Sea Empire, when Maximian had failed so miserably, was that by the time he became the western Caesar, another of Diocletian's key reforms had been instituted. This was the official separation of the military from the administrative apparatus of the Empire at all levels. At a stroke this freed the military from any form of senatorial oversight, an event as revolutionary as the Marian reforms of the military at the end of the 2nd century BC. No more would senators command Roman armies as they progressed along the *cursus honorum*. From

this time onwards all senior officers in the military were of the equestrian class, building on a trend initiated earlier by Gallienus (AD 253–268). The armies and fleets of the later Empire were now able to coalesce as required much more quickly, without any administrative oversight excepting that of the *Augusti* and *Caesares*. This was a vital reform needed to deal with the multitude of threats the Empire now faced. Constantius Chlorus's defeat of Carausius and Allectus is a supreme example of this. Certainly, in his first campaign against Carausius in AD 293, the usurper was surprised by the speed with which the Caesar was able to gather his army and fleet and move against him.

Meanwhile, Constantine I initiated the final reforms of the Roman military prior to the fall of the Empire in the west in AD 476. He began these after he became the sole emperor in the west following his defeat of Maxentius at the Battle of Milvian Bridge in AD 312. Building on Diocletian's reforms of the apparatus of imperial control, Constantine I left the administrative structures as he found them and concentrated

The Basilica of Maxentius and Constantine in the *Forum Romanum*, Rome. A monumental structure designed to display the power of a Dominate emperor. Inititiated by Maxentius, finished by Constantine.

on a radical overhaul of the military. As noted in Chapter 4, one of his first acts was to disband the troublesome Praetorian Guard after it sided with Maxentius against him. He replaced them and the *equites singulares Augusti* with new units of mounted guardsmen called the *Scholae Palatinae*. Constantine I also formed a separate unit of guardsmen called the *Protectores* who served as his close personal bodyguard and provided his staff officers too. Both are fully detailed later in this chapter.

Reform of the guard completed, the emperor next turned his attention to the wider military. By this time incursions by Germans and Goths over the Rhine and Danube had become frequent events, seriously disrupting the regional economies of the border territories there, while the ever-present threat from Sassanid Persia in the east required a significant commitment from a military establishment frequently beset by civil war. Even taking into account the, by now, common formation of ad hoc field armies to tackle crises as they occurred, Constantine I realised total reform was needed. He therefore restructured the entire military establishment into two completely new types of unit. These were *comitatenses* and *limitanei*. We know the names of many of these units as they are detailed in the late 4th/early 5th century AD *Notitia Dignitatum* list of military units and commands around the Empire.

Comitatenses translates as troops at the emperor's immediate disposal. The term was first recorded in AD 325 when three regional field armies were detailed. Two were based in the west, one in Gaul facing the Rhine and one Illyria facing the Danube, and one was based in the east. Their number had increased dramatically by the time of Theodosius I (AD 379–395) who was able to deploy five field armies in the east alone, with more in the west. Mounted troops in the field armies were commanded by a *magister equitum* and the foot troops a magister peditum, with a *magister militum* in overall command. Sometimes an emperor himself actually commanded a field army, it then being styled a *comitatius praesentalis* ('field army in the imperial presence'). *Comitatenses* troops could also be brigaded together into smaller concentrations

of troops for specific roles. These were commanded by a *comes* (the origin of the title count) or a *dux* (the origin of the title duke). A good example was the force comprising four *comitatenses* units sent to Briton in AD 367 under the *comes* Flavius Theodosius (father of Theodosius I) to counter the 'Great Conspiracy' of Picts, Attecotti, Scots Irish and Germanic raiders who were overwhelming the frontier defences in the diocese.

As can be seen in Julian the Apostate's order of battle at Strasbourg in AD 357 in Chapter 6, the legions and *auxilia* were by this time virtually identical in composition and equipment. Thus, in his front line he fielded the *Moesiaci, Pannoniaci, Iovani* and *Herculiani* legions, flanked by elite auxiliary units now called the *auxilia palatina* (see below for detail, the specific units at Strasbourg being the *Petulantes, Heruli, Cornuti* and *Brachiati*). In his second line he deployed the *Primani* legion, flanked by more *auxilia palatina* troops from the *Celtae, Batavi* and *Regae* units.

Another change in the post-Constantinian reform field armies was the much higher complement of cavalry. This had been a trend in the Roman military since the time of Septimius Severus but was now institutionalised, with mounted troops now making up at least one third of each field army.

One key difference for these *comitatenses* when compared to their Principate forebears was that they weren't based in permanent legionary fortresses on the frontiers of the Empire. Instead, when not on active service they were billeted among local populations deep within imperial territory, available there to form the main strike force in a complex system of defence in depth. From these new locations regional commanders could then gather troops together as required to counter each new incursion into imperial territory.

The time to muster these field armies and then use them operationally was provided by the *limitanei*, a totally different fighting force. These troops were located on the frontiers of the Empire in permanent bases, often the old legionary fortresses and forts of the Principate. Here they were based with their families who lived in the associated *canabae* or *vicus* settlements. Their role, as detailed above, was to act as a localised policing force in times of peace, and a trip wire when major incursions occurred, buying time for the *comitatenses* to arrive. This was often at great personal cost, with for example the *limitanei* in Gaul being totally destroyed by the raiding Alamanni prior to Julian's arrival. One can only guess the fate of their families.

Throughout the Dominate phase of Empire the *limitanei* – both infantry and cavalry – were equipped in a similar manner to less well-armed *comitatenses*. Some were fine military units more than capable of taking their place in the line of battle, and often in times of emergency a number of *limitanei* units were drafted into the field armies. Those so used were called *pseudocomitatenses*. Meanwhile some *limitanei* were specifically equipped to defend the river frontiers of the Empire, they being called *riparienses*. These units contained a significant maritime capability and are also considered later in this chapter.

Finally, irregular troops also increasingly made up a sizeable portion of the late Roman military, particularly in field armies. Most were known as *foederates*, the term originating from the word foederatus used to designate neighbouring states of the Empire who provided military service in return for benefits and payment. An early example was the 8,000 Iazyges lancers who served in the reign of Marcus Aurelius. The term later extended in usage to cover the late Roman practice of subsidising entire German and Gothic confederations, including the Franks, Vandals, Visigoths, Ostrogoths and Huns.

As set out above, while fighting in their own manner and using their own equipment, *foederates* initially served under Roman officers. This changed as the Empire in the west began its terminal decline, with whole bands of *foederate* warriors hired en masse under their own leaders. An early example is provided by Julian the Apostate who, in AD 358 after his success at Strasbourg, hired thousands of Franks to man the Rhine frontier while he rebuilt Roman Gaul following the predations of the Alamanni. Similarly, Valens allowed Fritigern's Goths to settle on the southern bank of the River Danube as *foederates* in AD 376. It is their mistreatment by the regional local government

that prompted the uprising which saw the emperor killed and his combined eastern field armies destroyed at the crucial battle of Adrianople in AD 378. The great Visigothic King Alaric, sacker of Rome in AD 410, also appears in contemporary history for the first time as the leader of his own band of *foederate* troops in Roman service. By the mid-5th century AD, *foederates* made up the bulk of Roman field armies, a prime example being that led by the *magister miletum* Flavius Aetius to defeat Attila the Hun at the battle of the Catalaunian Plains in AD 451. Significantly, this army also included a large number of allied troops, showing the legions of Rome going full circle back to their republican roots in relying on non-Romans to fill out the line of battle and provide specialist troops.

A point to note about *foederates* is the amount of money they could make through their service with the Roman army. After completing their service, this often made them rich men back in their homelands, particularly the foederatus leaders. This often proved a cause of instability, they able to hire their own warbands with which to challenge their own native leaders. The burial of one such leader was found at Fallward in Lower Saxony, providing great insight into the life experiences of this warrior. He was buried around AD 430 in a fine boat with a plank roof, his grave goods including a mixture of Roman and native military equipment, jewelry and furniture.

Two other terms were used in the Dominate phase of Empire to describe irregular troops. First, *buccellarii* (meaning biscuit eater) was a term used to describe the mercenaries who often formed the personal bodyguards of military leaders and members of the aristocracy. They proved highly successful, and by the early 6th century AD had become a formal component of early Byzantine armies where they were styled *boukellarioi*.

Meanwhile, the term *laeti* was used to describe entire communities of Germanic and Gothic warriors allowed to settle within the Empire, this an increasingly common occurrence into the 5th century AD. Many were recruited directly into the ranks of the legions and *auxilia*, or as *foederates* or *bucellari*, with others serving as formal allies.

A closing comment here regarding the reforms

of Constantine I is actually related to his later political reforms when he created his four prefectures which quartered the Empire as detailed in Chapter 3, these being the *Praefectura praetorio Galliarum*, the *Praefectura praetorio Italiae*, the *Praefectura praetorio Illyrici* and *Praefectura praetorio Orientis*. Once the Empire in the west collapsed, that in the east consolidated its position and used the latter two prefectures as the template for the later Roman military in the east. From this point we now refer to the Byzantine Empire, its military forces comprising:

- Two *praesental* (central) field armies deployed with the emperor in times of crisis to frontier hot spots. These were commanded by senior officers called *magister militum praesentalis*.
- Three regional field armies in Thrace, Illyria, and on the eastern front facing Sassanid Persia. These were commanded by *magister militum*.

Late Roman legionaries or *auxilia palatina*. Note ridge helmets, *lorica hamata*, *spatha*, oval shields and *draco*. (Painted by the author)

- As with the late Roman army before the fall of the West, *limitanei* deployed around the imperial frontiers. Regional clusters of these units were commanded by a *dux*.

Late Roman Infantry

The infantry in late Roman armies were still divided into legionaries and auxiliaries as in the Principate. However, as the Dominate progressed the distinction between the two became less and less noticeable, such that by the mid-4th century AD some of the elite formations in the military were actually auxiliaries, and the key distinction in equipment and capability was whether they were *comitatenses* or *limitanei* troop types. Here I consider both legionaries and auxiliaries.

Until the reforms of Constantine I the legions of the early Dominate phase of Empire were still recognizably Principate in size and nature. However, that changed dramatically once the founder of the Constantinian dynasty initiated his great changes in the Roman military. His new legions were now only 1,200 men strong as opposed to the 5,500 men legions of the Principate, with the old cohort system totally abandoned. The new legions were now structured on six *ordines* each with two centuries of legionaries containing 10 *contubernia*, with each *ordo* comprising 200 men. An equestrian-class tribune who had usually served as one of the emperor's *Protectores* commanded them, assisted by a *Primicerius* (second in command), the latter title an evolution of the Principate *Primus Pilus* (senior legionary centurion). Each *ordo* was then commanded by a *Decenarius*. He also directly commanded the first century of each *ordo*, with a *Centenarius* (the equivalent of the old centurion) commanding the second. Each century then had a second-in-command called a *Biarchus* who effectively replaced the *optio* of the former Principate legions, while each *contubernia* was commanded by a *semissalis* (non-commissioned officer).

There has been much speculation as to why Constantine I reduced the size of his legions given they remained much in demand. A key reason would have been administrative given

the difficulties in billeting large numbers of men among civilian population centres deep within the Empire. Another was the difficulty the Empire faced in recruiting new troops after the tribulations of the 'Crisis of the 3rd Century', to the extent that Diocletian had earlier made military professions hereditary (Valentinian I, AD 364 to AD 375, was later forced to reduce the height requirement to join the ranks), with the sons of serving soldiers or veterans required by law to enlist themselves to ensure the complement of troops in legionary and auxiliary units remained stable. However, one key advantage of the new system was that it was now much easier to rapidly brigade the smaller legions into field armies (most late Roman legions were *comitatenses* rather than *limitanei* in nature) to counter the multitude of threats faced by the late Roman army.

Despite their reduction is size the new legions were still based on their Principate predecessors, often initially retaining the same numbering and naming system. However, this did change over time, with the numbering in particular disappearing. For example, the *legio V Iovia* and *legio VI Herculia* founded by Diocletian as his own personal legions to balance the power of the Praetorian Guard later became the *Iovani* and *Herculiani* elite legions detailed above (and in Chapter 6) fighting with Julian the Apostate at Strasbourg in AD 357.

In terms of standards, the broad range used by the Principate legionaries and *auxilia* remained the same in the Dominate phase of Empire. However, one innovation was the replacement of some of the *vexilla* cohort standards by the Sarmatian *draco* standard. The vector of change here was through the cavalry, where this new standard became popular after use by Sarmatian auxiliaries. It featured a large iron or bronze hollow dragonhead with gaping jaws atop a tall pole. A long windsock was then attached to the rear of the head that inflated when held aloft, snapping in the wind. The jaws of the standard also featured several metal

Late Roman legionaries on the march. Note the size of the body shields. (Graham Sumner)

A late Roman legionary showing equipment typical of the early Dominate phase of Empire. Note the round shield, *lorica hamata*, long spear and *spatha*. (Graham Sumner)

tongues designed to make a loud, shrill sound when wind was blowing through it.

A final change with regard to the legions following the reforms of Constantine I was the removal of their integral artillery component, all such weapons and the specialists crewing them now being grouped into specialist artillery units called *ballistarii*.

Turning to the *auxilia*, these troops provided much of the *comitatenses* manpower in the field armies and nearly all the *limitanei*. One new development in the Dominate phase of Empire was the appearance of a new, elite type of auxiliary formation. These were called *auxilia palatina* and were first raised by Constantine I to help bolster the legions in his field armies. Some of the most senior (and probably oldest) were given names, for example the *Petulantes, Heruli, Cornuti* and *Brachiati* who fought with Julian the Apostate at Strasbourg. Many units of *auxilia palatina* were recruited directly from the individual Germanic tribes, each having a strong sense of élan that matched or even bettered those of the legions. Auxiliaries in field armies, including *auxilia*

palatina, were organised in a similar way to the post-Constantinian reform late Roman legions, though at half the strength, with only three *ordines* with two centuries each. They also featured the same command structure. Auxiliary *limitanei* units continued to be organised as in the Principate, maintaining their cohort-based structure and commanded by a tribune. Meanwhile, *foederates* fighting in their own units, rather than those recruited directly into the ranks of the legions and *auxilia*, fought and were equipped in their own native style.

A final development with regard to most legionary and *auxilia* formations took place in AD 395 when, reflecting the by then well-established division of the Empire into western and eastern halves, many were themselves divided into two. However, each pair was then brought back up to full strength, those then deployed in the west being styled *seniores* and those in the east *iuniores*. The aim here was to find a simple means within the existing administrative system of the Dominate military to quickly raise new troops. These were needed to counter the many threats faced across all the Empire's borders. However, the change didn't affect *limitanei* given the local nature of their deployment.

In terms of equipment, from the time of Constantine I the *comitatenses* legionaries and *auxilia* were armed in much the same way. For their defensive panoply they retained the circular or oval body-shield of the late Principate, these often featuring striking coloured imagery. For armour most line-of-battle troops, whether legionaries or *auxilia*, wore the same *lorica hamata* or *lorica squamata* (*lorica segmentata* disappears in the later 3rd century AD), these often much longer than their Principate counterparts and offering even greater protection. Those serving in or near the front rank in battle were also often equipped with additional armour, for example the same *manicae*, thigh guards and greaves as the Principate front rankers. Meanwhile, the muscled cuirass remained a favourite with senior officers, and there is some evidence later Roman *comitatenses* legionaries and *auxilia* also wore such designs made from stiffened leather.

Late Roman *limitanei* foot troops. (Painted by the author)

A major change in the *comitatenses* legionary and *auxilia* panoply was with regard to their helmets. As the Dominate progressed, the 'imperial' Gallic type and its developments all but disappeared, to be replaced broadly by two new mass-produced types made in the imperial *fabricae* (arms factories). These were the ridge helmet and the Spangenhelm, both usually made of iron though sometimes bronze. The former was made by creating a bowl of two or four parts, these designs called 'Intercisa' and 'Berkasovo' types, which were then held together by a central longitudinal ridge. The former had ear holes while the latter didn't. Copied from a Sassanid Persian design, the earliest known example dates to around AD 280 and was found in the Saxon Shore fort at Richborough. Given the simplicity of their construction it proved easy for Roman armourers to add levels of protection to ridge helmets as required, including nose guards, brow ridge, cheek guards and deep neck guards.

Meanwhile the Spangenhelm design originated in the Central Asian steppe, its vector of transfer into the Roman military being the various Sarmatian tribes fighting with and against the Romans from the time of Trajan's campaigns in Dacia in the early 2nd century AD. The basic design featured a framework of metal strips that connect between three and six longitudinal plates, giving a more conical appearance than the more rounded ridge helmet. Again, giving the simplicity of design, it proved easy to add nose guards (sometimes integrally built into Spangenhelms), brow ridges, cheek guards and deep neck guards. Two features unique to this design were the frequent addition of eye protectors resembling modern eyeglass frames, and chainmail aventails to provide neck protection.

For their offensive weaponry the *comitatenses* legionaries and *auxilia* were all now armed with the long spear and *spatha*, with many also equipped with javelins and darts. The javelins came in a variety of types, for example the armour-piercing *spiculum*, this a technological innovation combining the features of the earlier Roman *pilum* with German throwing spears and featuring a characteristically large barbed head. Another armour piercing javelin type was the *angon*, a weapon of Frankish origin featuring a barbed head on a long narrow socket or shank made of iron, this mounted on a wooden haft. Meanwhile *plumbatae* or *martiobarbuli* (lead-weighted darts) were a specific innovation of the Dominate phase of Empire. These were carried in clips on the back of the legionary and auxiliary large oval body shields and could be thrown over-arm for distance or under-arm to give a steep descending trajectory designed to fall on the heads of an approaching enemy.

The *comitatenses* legionaries and *auxilia* armoured and armed in the above fashion fought in deep formations, often with integral bowmen forming the rear ranks to fire over the heads of those in front. Their opponents were therefore faced with the same impenetrable spear wall as those fighting the old Tullian First Class hoplite phalanx. However, the Dominate legionaries and *auxilia* were far better trained, able to rapidly make complex manoeuvres on the battlefield, and to shower their enemies with javelins, darts and their integral bowfire. Infantry armed and fighting in this way were to long serve in the armies of the eastern Empire far beyond the fall of the western Empire, evolving into the *skutatoi* (spear-armed) infantry of the Byzantine Empire, such troops named after their large shields. This was the ultimate evolution of the legionary, these troops continuing to exist into the 11th century AD.

Meanwhile, as detailed above, Dominate *limitanei* infantry were equipped in a similar manner to less well-armed *comitatenses*. While few wore armour, most had helmets and carried the round or oval body shield. For a weapon the long spear was used, together with the *spatha*. However, as the Dominate progressed, particularly in the west, the quality of the *limitanei* fell, and from the beginning of the 5th century AD they should be regarded more as a local genderarmie, excepting the *pseudocomitatenses* units deployed to serve in the field armies.

Late Roman Cavalry

Cavalry units of the Dominate phase of Empire formed a far larger component of the Roman military establishment than in the Principate, particularly in the field armies. The basic unit of organisation was now the *vexillatio* commanded by a tribune, this broadly tracking the administrative structure of auxiliary units, with three *ordines* of two centuries each, given a total complement of

Late Roman legionaries or *auxilia palatina* in defensive formation to receive missile fire. (Graham Sumner)

fighting the Sassanid Persians, and finally *equites scutarii* who may have been regular bodyguard cavalry. Towards the end of the Dominate phase of Empire many standard *equites* also began to carry the bow, a response to conflict with the Huns, as did some units of *equites clibanarii*.

In terms of their defensive panoply, the biggest change when compared to their Principate predecessors followed the similar trend in the infantry, with the widespread use from this time of ridge helmets and Spangenhelms instead of a multitude of earlier helmet types.

Late Roman Navy

One of the results of the economic crash caused by the 'Crisis of the 3rd Century' was the gradual abandonment of the Augustan system of regional fleets across the Empire. This was specifically due to their expense, and from now on there was a gradual change from a system of maritime offence controlling the open ocean to one of defence, with the focus on littoral coastal areas and the riparian control of river systems.

Once more we can turn to Britain to see the broad pattern of what happened following the demise of the Augustan fleets. The last ever mention of the *Classis Britannica* relates to the North African Saturninus, a *trierarchus* of the fleet whose funerary inscription was found at Arles in southern France. This is firmly dated to AD 249, after which the fleet disappears. The outcome was soon evident, with control of the North Sea lost, and by the time of Carausius it was overrun by pirates predating the eastern coast of Britain and the Continental coast up to the Rhine Delta, hence his employment by Maximian to clear them out.

This set a pattern that was to last through to the end of the Empire in the West, with ad hoc fleets created as necessary, but then being disbanded after their use, successful or otherwise. For example, Maximian didn't rebuild his fleet after his failure to defeat Carausius in AD 289, with Constantius Chlorus having to build a totally new one for his AD 296 invasion of Britain. Peaks and troughs in maritime capability were by then the norm, with highpoints in Britain including the deployment

600 horsemen. As with the legions and auxiliaries, from AD 395 many of these regiments were then divided between west and east, though instead of rebuilding their strength to the original most remained at the new 300-trooper level. This required a change in organization, and from that point each *vexillatio* was divided into 10 *turmae* of 30 men. As with the foot troops, once divided the cavalry *vexillationes* were named *seniores* in the west and *iuniores* in the east. Meanwhile, *limitanei* cavalry units retained their Principate command structure as with their infantry counterparts, using the traditional *ala*.

The basic cavalryman remained the *equite*, with the same panoply as their Principate forebears. They were still supported by the specialist types that had originated in the Principate, for example the *equites contariorum* and *equites cataphractarii* (shock cavalry), and *equites illyriciani* and *equites sagittarii* (light cavalry). However, in the Dominate phase of Empire other types now proliferated, including *equites clibanarii* fully armoured lancers, *equites dalmatae* who were armed in a similar way to the *equites illyriciani* (their names indicating where they were initially recruited from), *equites mauri* who were based on their Moorish *symmachiarii* predecessors and who were much in demand when in the early 4th century AD of the *numerous barcariorum Tigrisiensum* detachment of Syrian boatmen who operated on the River Tyne from the fort at South Shields. Another, much greater in scale, was Julian the Apostate building a new fleet to feed his army fighting the Alamanni on the Rhine frontier in AD 356. Here, the Greek sophist and rhetorician Libanius provides a detailed commentary on why this was necessary, saying (*Oratio*, 18.82–3):

> In the past, grain was shipped from Britain and up the Rhine. But after the barbarians took control, they did not let it pass. Most of the ships, dragged onto dry land long before, had rotted. A few did still sail, but these unloaded their cargo in coastal ports, so it was necessary for the grain to be transferred on wagons instead of river, which was very expensive. [Julian] thought that there would be problems if he was not able to restore the traditional means of grain-shipment, so he quickly built more ships than before, and put his mind to how the river could take receipt of wheat...

The fleet Julian built here was enormous. It took him 10 months to construct 400 new vessels to add to the 200 still seaworthy, giving him a total of 600. Zosimus, who says the total was actually 800, adds they were built along the Rhine with timber felled in local forests (New History, 3.5.2). This set a trend for his later campaigning when, as the full Augustus, he built over 1,000 vessels at Samasata on the Euphrates to support his abortive invasion of Sassanid Persia in AD 363, with the campaign costing him his life.

However, the success of Julian's new fleet in Europe was clearly short lived as by AD 367 it was again too small to prevent Pictish and Germanic raiders using the North Sea to attack the east coast of Britain during the so-called 'Great Conspiracy.' Once more a new fleet had to be built as part of the comes Theodosius's campaigns of re-conquest in the diocese. This is the last time Roman naval activity is evident in Britain, with any overt maritime capability disappearing by the mid-AD 390s.

In Britain, the Roman response to the lack of any regular naval presence during the Dominate phase of Empire is writ large across the east and south coast in the form of the Saxon Shore forts there, and the later addition to this new *limes* of a chain of watchtowers along the north-eastern

The substantial town walls of *Venta Icenorum*, the civitates capital of the Iceni, near modern Caistor St Edmund. It was built by the Roman military.

The only remains of
the Saxon Shore fort at
Brancaster in Norfolk, its
defensive boundary ditch.
The fort itself was recycled
to build many of the local
churches.

coast. Regarding the forts, there is a lively and on-going debate about their nature given they were built at different times during the 3rd century AD. While some argue they fulfilled an administrative/ headquartering/harbouring role, to my mind they speak to a militaristic response regarding two existential military threats:

- The onset of Germanic raiding across the North Sea, especially after the disappearance of the *Classis Britannica* in the mid-3rd century AD. The scale of this predation cannot be underestimated, especially into the later 4th century AD when it led to major depopulation along the east coast of Britain.

- The Roman Empire itself. This is in the context of Carausius and Allectus and their plans to defend their North Sea Empire from attempts to reconquer it by Maximian and Constantius Chlorus. Certainly, some of the later forts in the chain date to this time.

In both cases the *limes* clearly proved a failure, showing the false economy of switching from offence with an active fleet to a passive defence with little deterrent value given that, more often than not, the raiders in the first bullet above would

have departed before any defence could be enacted, while Constantius Chlorus was able to effect not one but two landings in Britain.

The name Saxon Shore fort is derived from a single reference, this in the *Notitia Dignitatum*. There, one of the key military posts in Britain is that of the *Comes Litoris Saxonici per Britanniam* (Count of the Saxon Shore). However, it seems unlikely there was an initial set plan for a region-wide defensive network of coastal forts. Rather, it seems the early ones were an attempt to control sea access to The Wash, the Great Estuary (a now silted up major estuary giving access to the civitates capital of *Venta Icenorum* in north Norfolk) and the Thames Estuary. This is evidenced by the fact that the first three, built between AD 220 and AD 230, are located at Brancaster (*Branodunum*) on the northern coast of Norfolk, Caister-on-Sea (thought to be Roman *Gariannonum*) further along the coast, and Reculver (*Regulbium*) on the north Kent coast. These three forts are different in design from the earlier small *Classis Britannica* forts in Britain, being square in plan with very substantial perimeter walls, this again emphasising their military nature.

As the century progressed further forts in the chain were built, even more substantial in nature, at sites such as Richborough, Dover, Lympne and Pevensey, each incorporating the latest military construction technology at the time of its building. For example, the very late ones feature bastions standing proud of their walls allowing enfilading fields of fire. It was the building of these later forts that allowed the creation of this new holistic *limes* to protect the south and east coast of Britain and northern Gaul (where other forts were built too). One factor in building some of the later forts was an evident desire to further control sea access either side of a major waterway, with for example Burgh Castle being paired with Caistor-on-Sea, and similarly Richborough controlling the southern access to the Wantsum Channel in Kent when paired with Reculver. The immense cost, both economically and in terms of manpower, of building these forts is evident in the construction techniques used. All were constructed in roughly the same way, despite the differentials in building date and design. For the walls, first a foundation trench was dug, between 0.7 and 1.7m wide, into which foundation materials such as chalk, flint and clay were laid. *Opus caementicium* concrete was also used in this regard at Brancaster and Pevensey,

while timber piles were also used to provide additional stability at Richborough, Lympne and Pevensey. The superstructure of the fortification was then built from just below ground level, using a plinth of large ashlars that were stepped out on one or both faces of the wall as the first stage. The walls were then built upwards in stages, with the inner and outer facing constructed first and then being in-filled before the next stage was built and so on. Some of the forts also feature tile bonding layers.

Materials used to build the walls of the Saxon Shore forts were dependent on regional availability (not necessarily the most local), though many made extensive use of re-used materials from earlier structures, with Richborough the best example. In terms of newly quarried materials used in the construction of the forts, that at Bradwell in Norfolk helpfully shows the scale of commitment required to build them, the stone used there including:

- Locally sourced Septarian cementstone

Building the Saxon Shore Forts

Location	Boat Loads	Local Cart Loads
Brancaster	560	0
Caister-on-Sea	520	0
Burgh Castle	620	0
Walton Castle	470	0
Bradwell	870	0
Reculver	530	0
Richborough	960	0
Dover	0	13,540
Lympne	220	21,980
Pevensey	1,580	660
Portchester	240	15,530
Total	**6,570**	**51,710**

After Pearson, A. F. 2002a. *The Roman Shore Forts*. Stroud: Tempus Publishing. Oxford: BAR/ Archaeological and Historical Associates Ltd.

- Kentish ragstone from the Medway Valley
- Lincolnshire limestone
- Tufa from the Dour Valley in Kent
- Imported Niedermendig lava from the Rhineland

These materials, unless sourced very locally, would have been transported to their place of use by sea and river, often some distance for the more in-demand stone. Kentish ragstone, a fine limestone found sitting in the Hythe Beds of the lower Greensand formation, provides a good example. It was used in many of the forts, with that used in the fort at Reculver carried 50km further than any other material used there. Meanwhile, Greensands of Folkestone origin travelled even further, for example 175km to Caistor-by-Sea in northern Norfolk, while the Niedermendig lava used at Bradwell travelled even further.

The sheer scale of these enterprises on the part of the Roman military who carried out the construction (see Chapter 7) is illustrated by Table 5 showing the estimated number of boat and cart journeys required to build some of the forts (this excluding the additional re-use of materials from earlier structures).

Utilising these huge quantities of building materials required a major commitment in terms of manpower to build the forts, with 100,000 man-days required to build that at Pevensey alone.

Meanwhile, as the predatory Germanic raiding increased in the later 4th century AD, a final series of fortifications was built to protect the fertile East Riding of Yorkshire. This was a series of defended watchtowers that acted as signal stations to alert land troops deployed inland that a seaborne raid was on the way. These watchtowers were located at Huntcliff, Goldsborough, Ravenscar, Scarborough and Filey. Given the major depopulation event detailed earlier along the east coast, they proved equally as ineffective as the earlier Saxon Shore forts.

Meanwhile, with regard to the vessel types used by the ad hoc fleets of the Dominate phase of Empire, the Principate *liburnae bireme* war galley remained the standard war fighting vessel, supported by the same range of vessels of all sizes including *myoparo* and *scapha* (cutters and skiffs, particularly favoured by the *riparienses* auxiliaries defending the riverine frontiers of the Empire), and all kinds of merchant transports.

Late Roman Guard Troops

As detailed at the beginning of this chapter, Constantine I disbanded the Praetorian Guard and the *equites singulares Augusti* and replaced them with new units of mounted guardsmen that he called the *Scholae Palatinae*. The term schola had formerly been used to indicate members of the imperial retinue, especially when the emperor was on the move. It now gave its name to the new, highly mobile units of guardsmen who always accompanied the emperor.

Each *Scholae Palatinae* unit was formed into a *vexillatio*, just as with other late Roman cavalry units, and shared the same organisational structure. They were commanded by a *tribunus militum*. However, unlike the troublesome Praetorian Guard, the new overall mounted guard had no single independent commander, with the emperor himself holding the post instead.

There were initially five *Scholae Palatinae* units under Constantine I, this increasing to 10 on his death, with five in the western half of the Empire and five in the east. From that time, those in the west were styled *seniores* and those in the east *iuniores*, this perhaps the basis for the naming of other units so divided after AD 395 as detailed above. The number of guard units continued to increase as the Dominate phase of Empire progressed and by the time the *Notitia Dignitatum* was compiled in the late 4th/early 5th century AD there were eight in the west and seven in the east.

In all phases of their existence the *Scholae Palatinae* provided the emperor's close bodyguard. These totalled 40 men chosen for their extreme loyalty who were named *Candidati* after their bright white uniforms.

Members of the *Scholae Palatinae* received benefits similar to their Praetorian Guard predecessors, including improved pay and conditions. They were equipped as standard *equites*

The Roman Saxon Shore fort at Burgh Castle, Norfolk. Part of the late Roman series of forts along the east and south coasts of Britain.

(*opposite*)
A Parthian mounted archer.
Such eastern horse archers
were the bane of many
Roman campaigns against
Parthia and later Sassanid
Persia.
(Livius.org/Jona Lendering)

but, given they were the elite cavalry of the late Roman army, with the finest possible armour and weaponry. However, just as with the Praetorian Guard, over time the *Scholae Palatinae* developed a reputation for enjoying life in the imperial capitals too much, particularly in the east. There, Emperor Leo I (AD 457–474) eventually replaced them with a new guard unit called the Excubitores (derived from the Latin term for sentinel) who were formed into a single unit 300 strong. However, in the west the *Scholae Palatinae* outlived the Empire itself, being retained by Odoacer after he deposed Romulus Augustulus.

Meanwhile, as also detailed, Constantine I additionally formed a separate unit of guardsmen that he called the *Protectores* who served as his close personal bodyguard alongside the *Candidati* (the relationship between the two is unclear), and provided the pool of staff officers for the wider military.

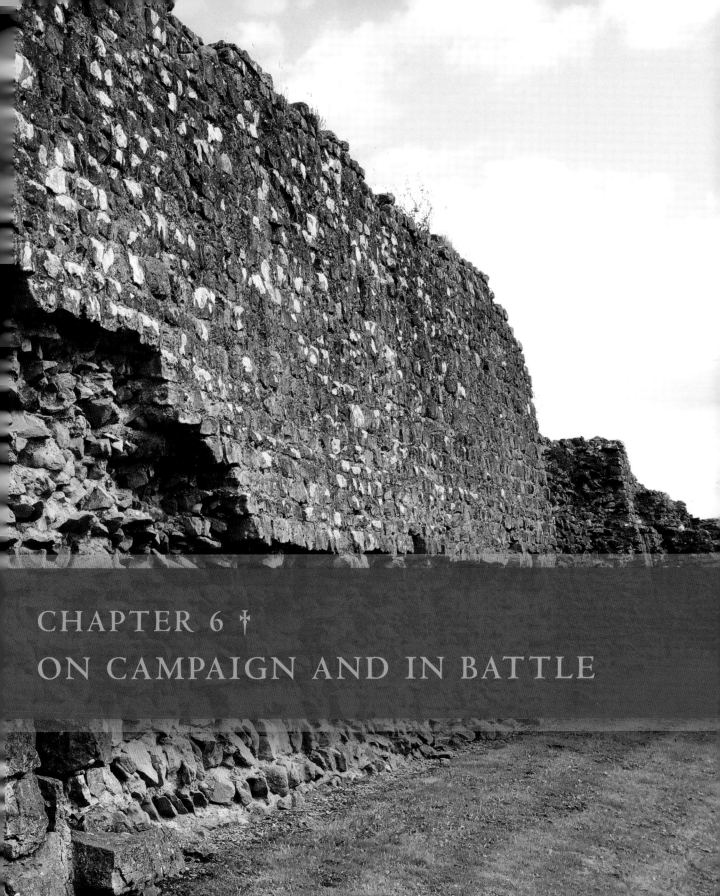

CHAPTER 6 ✝
ON CAMPAIGN AND IN BATTLE

H aving detailed the Roman military in both Republic and Empire, I now turn to its specific activities on campaign and in battle. To do that, this chapter first reviews a number of examples of the Roman military on campaign, then a similar number of examples of the military in battle. I then close the chapter with a short review of the Roman military taking part in less formal operations, for instance when fighting opponents mounting guerrilla warfare-style operations.

On Campaign

The Roman legions of the Republic and Empire, together with their supporting troops, were dynamic, flexible and highly efficient, in the most brutal sense. Well organised and motivated, they won their campaign objectives through the total subjugation of their opponents. Even in loss, they most often returned to hammer away until final victory. Varus's loss of three legions in the Teutoburg Forest in AD 9 is the only notable exception during the Principate, when Augustus refused to reform *legio XVII, legio XVIII* and *legio XIX* after they lost their *aquila* (eagle standards) to Arminius's Germans. Even in Scotland, the darkest and dimmest corner on the north-west border of the Empire, Rome kept returning, never satisfied that the far north of the province of Britannia remained elusive. The secret to the success of the legions on campaign was twofold:

- Dynamism: The legions as envisaged by Marius during his reforms (and later by Augustus) were to be autonomous formations able to operate alone or in groups in enemy territory. As such, they formed legionary spearheads which powered through the battle space, always keeping the enemy on the back foot until victory was achieved. The main objective here, more often than not, was to force a meeting engagement in the form of a major battle. A decisive victory would then be

followed by a swift peace, on terms always agreeable to Rome.
- Logistics: The Romans were masters at ensuring a secure supply chain for their legions and supporting troops when on campaign, making maximum use of marine transport when necessary (both along the coast and up river systems).

To illustrate the nature of this successful campaigning strategy, of which the legions and later auxiliaries were the focal point, I use four examples. The first features Julius Caesar immediately prior to the Principate with his 55 BC and 54 BC incursions into Britain, and his later siege of Alesia. The latter completed his conquest of Gaul. Together these show the value placed by the Romans on combined arms operations and siege warfare. Next, I consider the 1st century AD initial campaign of conquest in Britain by Claudius in AD 43, he succeeding where Caesar arguably failed. Then I turn to the diarchy of Marcus Aurelius and Lucius Verus and their Marcomannic Wars on the Danube. Finally, I consider the campaigns of Septimius Severus to conquer Scotland, these showing how the Romans were able to gather and keep an enormous force of legionaries and auxiliaries in the field, and in the most difficult of conditions.

Caesar in Britain and Gaul

Caesar's landings in Britain were in effect large-scale armed reconnaissances and show the legions

(previous pages)
Section of the town wall, Caerwent, showing how it was constructed with well worked facing stone on the outside and a rubble core.

(opposite)
Arch of Septimius Severus in Rome celebrating his victories in the east. In this chapter his campaigns in Scotland and earlier against the usurper Clodius Albinus are considered.

A typical 'glenblocker' fort as used by the Romans campaigning in the far north of Britain when isolating what are now the Scottish Highlands from the Midland Valley. (Graham Sumner)

of the late Republic in close detail. They took place as his campaigns to conquer Gaul were almost complete. He was keenly aware of the support being given to remaining Gallic resistance from Britain, and knew it was here that the Gallic elites who refused to bow to the might of Rome were fleeing. He therefore decided to act, and decisively.

For his first attempt in 55 BC Caesar marched his legionaries from *legio VII* and *legio X* (around 12,000 men) north to the territory of the Morini opposite Kent. Here he gathered 80 transports and 18 additional vessels modified to carry horses, together with war galleys from the Mediterranean. Knowing the value of scouting, he then sent his tribune Caius Volusenus in a *trireme* to identify a safe landing area on the east Kent coast. Caesar then waited for favourable conditions before crossing the Channel, arriving in late August off Dover, though his cavalry transports missed the tide and were never to arrive. Here he found native British troops massed on the coast awaiting his arrival, no doubt bolstered by Gallic refugees, and so he headed north. His fleet eventually weighed anchor between Walmer and Pegwell bays, below Ramsgate. However, the Briton's had tracked his fleet and were once again arrayed along the shore. He therefore carried out an amphibious assault, with the fleet and the legions working closely together. War galleys were driven hard ashore to the north of Caesar's chosen landing area, the aim being to turn the Britons' right flank. From this position the *quinqeremes, quadiremes* and *trireme*s were able to enfilade the landing area using ballista and hand-held missile weapons. However, even then the legionaries were reluctant to land as the Britons held their ground. An incident now occurred which shows the importance of the sense of identity and honour within the legions. This was when the *aquilifer* of *legio X*, sensing the reticence of his colleagues to disembark, leapt into the shallows and declared 'Leap, fellow soldiers, unless you wish to betray your eagle to the enemy. I, for my part, will perform my duty to the Republic and to my general.' (Julius Caesar, *Conquest of Gaul*, 4.25). This worked, the shamed legionaries swarming ashore, even though the larger transports struggled to get close to the beach

as their design proved unsuitable for northern waters. A ferrying operation therefore seems likely from the transports to smaller ships. Once engaged in hand-to-hand combat the legionaries were quickly successful and the defeated leaders of the Britons sued for peace. However, bad weather later damaged many of Caesar's ships and, after some regional campaigning, the Romans returned to the Continent using the remaining serviceable ships.

Showing typical Roman grit, Caesar determined the next year to return once more, and in much greater force. Thus in 54 BC he gathered five legions and 2,000 cavalry. Learning from his experiences the previous year regarding the type of vessel best suited for amphibious operations in Britain, he also ordered the construction of 600 specially built ships. As detailed in Chapter 2, these featured lower freeboards than his Mediterranean designs to enable easier disembarkation, and wider beams to carry bulkier loads. To these vessels Caesar added 200 locally chartered transports, a further 80 ships which had survived the previous year's incursion, and 28 war galleys (again a mix of *quinqeremes, quadiremes* and *trireme*s from the Mediterranean).

The size of Caesar's force clearly intimidated the Britons as the landing on the east coast of Kent was this time unopposed. Just as in 55 BC however, bad weather intervened again. While Caesar was campaigning inland against a large British force that had eventually gathered to confront him, a storm badly damaged many of his transports anchored off the coast of Kent. Realising the vulnerability to his rear he quickly returned to the landing area and initiated an urgent repair operation (with many of the vessels dragged onto the beach to prevent further damage in the bad weather). The legions then renewed their campaign against the Britons, with the spearheads of legionaries forcing a crossing of the Thames (supported by his war galleys, again showing combined arms in action) and capturing the main base of the British leader Cassivellaunus who then sued for peace. Honour satisfied, Caesar returned to the landing area in Kent and re-embarked his forces for the return journey to north-eastern Gaul, this taking place in two waves given the scale of ship losses in the earlier storm. The first wave travelled to the continent safely, but these vessels were prevented from returning by more bad weather. Caesar then deciding to risk cramming his remaining troops into the few serviceable vessels left in Briton, almost certainly the war galleys. These arrived safely back at the end of September. Thus ended his engagements with Britain.

By 52 BC Caesar's conquest of Gaul was almost complete. However, many of the Gallic tribes remained rebellious. They found a new leader in Vercingetorix of the Averni tribe, around whom resistance coalesced. A mass revolt followed, prompting Caesar to target the Averni capital Gergovia with typical speed. Though repulsed, Roman grit showed through again, the legions fighting a prolonged campaign that forced Vercingetorix and 60,000 of his men to take shelter in the fortified hilltop town of Alesia. Here Caesar determined to starve Vercingetorix into surrender, and we see Roman siege warfare at its best. He ordered his men to construct ditches and an earthen bank topped by a palisade, just as with the marching camps but far grander in scale, an

astonishing 18 km long. This wall was interspersed with timber towers, enabling legionaries and archers to enfilade any attackers to the front or rear. It enclosed the town in a circumvallation. We have great insight here into the sophistication of this fortification thanks to Caesar's detailed description. The bank and palisade were 3.6m high, with sharpened forked branches projecting outwards towards Alesia. Beyond this, two ditches were dug, each 4.4m wide and 2.4m deep. The one nearest the bank and palisade featured an 'ankle breaker' in the bottom, a step cut into its base designed to trap the feet of those scrambling to get up the other side which would snap ankle bones if due care wasn't taken. The ditch further out was filled with water wherever possible,

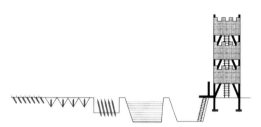

Cross section of Caesar's siege lines at Alesia. (Paul Baker)

Plan view of Caesar's siege lines at Alesia. (Paul Baker)

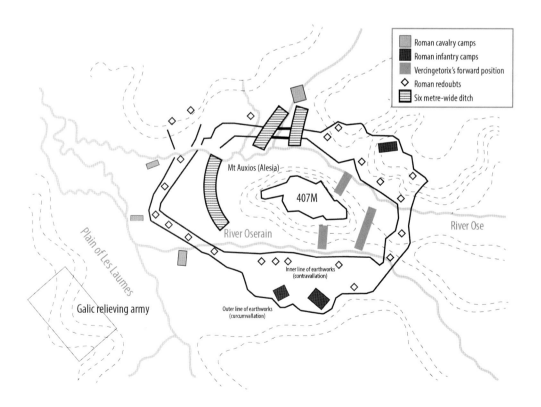

A coin of Caesar minted to celebrate his victories in his conquest of Gaul. Venus is portrayed on one side, who Caesar's family claimed descent from, while the other side shows two captive Gauls flanking a victory trophy.

(right)
A 'lilly', as used in Caesar's siege lines at Alesia.
(Paul Baker)

(far right)
A 'stimuli', as used in Caesar's siege lines at Alesia.
(Paul Baker)

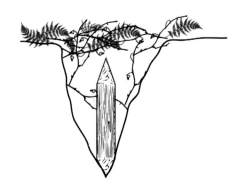
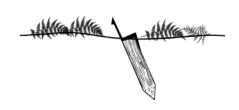

requiring the Roman engineers to line it with clay. Further out from the bank and palisade another, shallower trench 1.5m deep was dug, into which were placed five rows of sharpened stakes. Beyond these were formations of pits up to 1m wide in repeating *quincunx* formation (four in the corners of a square and one in the centre) featuring more stakes, this time concealed. These were nicknamed lilies. Finally, even further out, there was a band of *stimuli*, wooden blocks embedded in the ground into which iron barbs had been placed.

The Gauls responded with constant raids against the building works but failed to slow progress. Then, as construction neared completion, a large force of Gallic cavalry burst through and made off. Caesar, guessing they had been sent to fetch assistance, began a second ditch, bank and palisade fortification to the rear of the first, matching the one facing Alesia. At 22km long this wall was even grander, facing outward to cover his rear and

forming a contravallation. There was only one area of weakness in this outer wall, a section where large boulders and a deep ravine made it impossible to build a continuous fortification. Caesar decided to mask the spot with a kink in the wall.

An incident next occurred which showed the Romans at their most brutal and determined. Vercingetorix, to save whatever food remained for his warriors, forced all the women and children out of the gates of Alesia. He hoped the Romans would let them pass through Roman lines. However, Caesar refused, and they had no choice but to camp between the town and the fortifications. Here they slowly starved.

In late September a Gallic relief army arrived. It quickly launched an attack on the contravallation outer wall. Vercingetorix then also attacked from Alesia against the circumvallation inner wall. The legionaries fought off both attacks, but the assaults were renewed the following night and continued over the next few days. The Roman besiegers thus found themselves the besieged, between their two siege lines. Then, on 2 October, the Gauls attacked the weak spot in the Roman outer wall, with Vercingetorix again coordinating his assault against the inner wall. Caesar quickly realised the attack would be difficult to defend and poured in reinforcements, while distracting Vercingetorix against the inner wall by sallying legionaries out into the open. Despite valiant efforts in both areas Caesar now saw both of his lines were in danger of breaking. To save the day he personally led 6,000 cavalry from the outer walls. These rode to the rear of the Gauls there, attacking them as they assaulted the palisade. The Gauls were butchered, the survivors breaking and routing. The Roman cavalry pursued them closely, causing more slaughter, eventually overrunning the Gallic camp.

Vercingetorix now knew he was defeated and began negotiating with Caesar who agreed to spare the lives of his men, though the Gallic leader was sent to Rome in chains. It was to be a dramatic fall from grace, the one-time king held captive for five years before forming the centrepiece of

A Principate *scorpio* (bolt thrower). These played a major role in the Roman invasion of Britain in AD 43. (Graham Sumner)

Caesar's triumphal parade where he was executed by strangulation. Such was the lot of those who opposed Rome and lost.

The Claudian Invasion of Britain

While Caesar can be credited with the first and second Roman invasions of Britain, it was the third that successfully set up the province of Britannia, changing the history of the islands forever. This was that of Claudius in AD 43, which showed the Principate legionaries and *auxilia* at their most resilient as they campaigned in the almost mythical land, across *Oceanus* (as the Romans styled the seas outside of the Mediterranean) and far from their Mediterranean homes.

The Claudian invasion had its origins in the earlier and farcical attempt by Caligula to mount an expedition to conquer Britain in AD 40. For this cancelled operation detailed planning had taken place, including the building at Boulogne of a lighthouse, extensive harbour works, wharfing, fully stocked warehouses and 900 ships. These were all still in place when the ill-favoured Claudius turned his attention to Britain in AD 43, determined to make his name through conquest.

Opportunity was provided by the death of Cunobelinus, king of the Catuvellauni, whose territory covered much of the south-east above today's London. He was succeeded by Caratacus and Togodumnus, his two sons, who launched an offensive against their Atrebates neighbours in the Thames Valley. These were Roman allies. The Catuvellauni were victorious, with the Atrebatian King Verica fleeing to Rome. Here he sought an audience with Claudius. Caratacus and Togodumnus now overplayed their hand,

The River Medway, looking south from Rochester Bridge. The original Roman bridge was immediately in front of this one. Meanwhile, if Plautius' river crossing battle did take place at Aylesford further south, the Batavian auxiliaries' night crossing after day one of the battle would have taken place in view too.

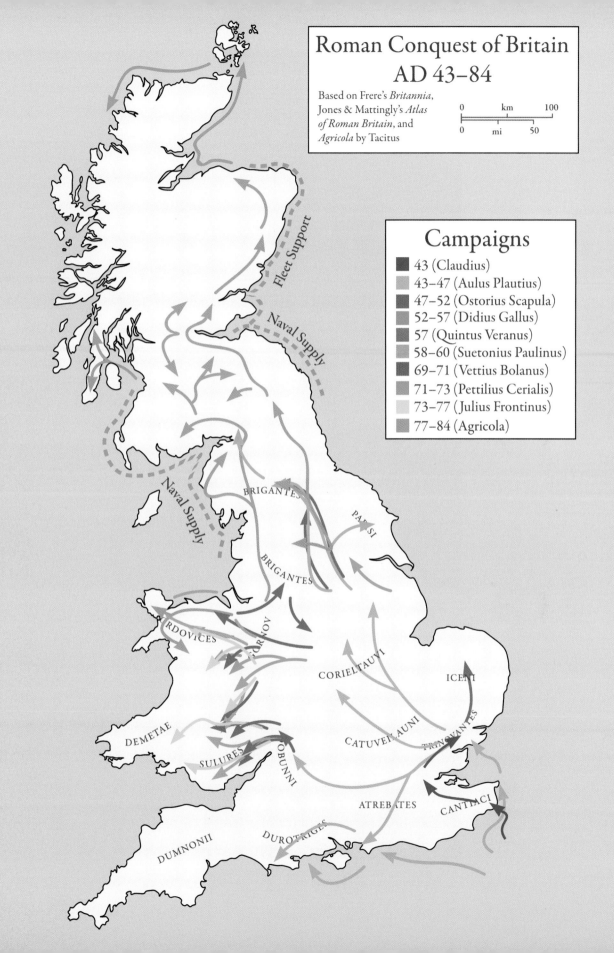

Roman Conquest of Britain
AD 43–84

Based on Frere's *Britannia*,
Jones & Mattingly's *Atlas
of Roman Britain*, and
Agricola by Tacitus

0   km   100
0   mi   50

Campaigns

- 43 (Claudius)
- 43–47 (Aulus Plautius)
- 47–52 (Ostorius Scapula)
- 52–57 (Didius Gallus)
- 57 (Quintus Veranus)
- 58–60 (Suetonius Paulinus)
- 69–71 (Vettius Bolanus)
- 71–73 (Pettilius Cerialis)
- 73–77 (Julius Frontinus)
- 77–84 (Agricola)

Fleet Support

Naval Supply

Naval Supply

BRIGANTES

PARSI

BRIGANTES

RDOVICES

ORNOV

CORIELTAUVI

ICENI

DEMETAE

SULURES

OBUNNI

CATUVELAUNI

TRINOVANTES

ATREBATES

CANTIACI

DUMNONII

DUROTRIGES

The Medway Gap seen from Bluebell Hill on the North Downs. Likely the view Aulus Plautius would have seen as he approached his AD 43 invasion river-crossing battle site.

The likely site of the Claudian AD 43 invasion river-crossing battle at Aylesford. The houses at left are on the far side of the River Medway.

The view of the Britons at Aylesford. Seen from the river with Bluebell Hill in the background.

A typical Roman auxiliary infantryman of the Principate phase of Empire. This ubiquitous troop type would have made up at least half of the foot component of Roman armies of this period when on campaign or in battle.
(Graham Sumner)

demanding Verica's extradition. Claudius rebuffed them, with disturbances following in Britain against Roman merchants already embedded in the future Province. With the means already available thanks to Caligula, and now the opportunity, Claudius decided to invade. The scene was set for one of the greatest amphibious operations in the pre-modern world.

Claudius took no chances. He gathered his army of conquest under the highly experienced Pannonian Governor Aulus Plautius, with another seasoned warrior in future Emperor Vespasian being appointed as one of the legionary *legates*. The invasion force comprised four legions (*legio II Augusta, legio IX Hispana, legio XIV Gemina* and *legio XX Valeria Victrix*) together with auxiliaries, totaling 40,000 men. The 900 ships were also loaded with 3,000 tonnes of grain to feed the invasion force for at least three months after arrival.

As detailed in Chapter 3, a controversy now occurred. The legionaries, superstitious of *Oceanus* and mysterious Britain, refused to board their ships. At the last minute the day was saved by Claudius' freedman Narcissus who boarded a vessel and shamed the soldiery into following him. The huge force then set sail in three divisions, arriving unopposed in mid-to-late summer, the British warriors having dispersed to gather the harvest. The landing place was again on the east Kent coast. Once ashore Plautius secured his beachhead by building a huge 57ha marching camp, the remains of which can still be seen today at the site of the later Saxon Shore fort of Richborough. Some 640m of the defensive ditch have been revealed to date. The sophistication of this fortification is indicated by the presence of a gate tower found by archaeologists on the western side.

Plautius now began his breakout, his 40,000 men snaking along the south side of the North Downs where he could expect the most sunlight during the day. This was also the most fertile and heavily populated part of LIA Kent, with the newly gathered harvest available to plunder. His huge column featured the baggage train in the centre, with the legionaries and *auxilia* on the flanks, front and rear. Meanwhile his *equites alae* scouted ahead, ranging far and wide,

ensuring there were no ambushes and raiding local settlements whenever the opportunity presented itself.

Finally he tracked down his elusive foe, defeating Caratacus and Togodumnus separately in two small engagements in eastern Kent, after which the Dobunni (a tribe based in the Welsh Marches who supplied troops to support the Catuvellauni) became the first of the British Kingdoms to sue for peace. Plautius then continued his advance, arriving on the eastern bank of the River Medway at Aylesford where he found a much larger force of Britons on the far shore ready to block his advance. This was the lowest fordable point on the river and here he fought the 'river crossing battle' referenced by the primary sources. A close-run thing it was too.

This battle is interesting in that as it shows the legionaries were often not enough to secure victory on their own, relying particularly on the *auxilia* for support. At first Plautius tried to force the ford, but his legionaries were repulsed with heavy losses, despite pouring volleys of *pila* into the Britons and closing with *scutum* and *gladius*. Repeated attempts were made but failed, and at the end of the day he withdrew his troops to build a marching camp. British chariots and cavalry pursued them the whole way.

Plautius knew a change of plan was needed and came up with a clever stratagem to turn the flank of the Britons the following day. In the ranks of his auxiliaries he had some native Batavians from the Rhine Delta, famous for being able to swim in full armour. Before dawn he ordered these to cross the Medway north of the battle site using inflated pigskins as floats. Once on the western bank they marched upriver and attacked the British chariot and cavalry horses in their corrals in a surprise assault. Then, with panic spreading through the British ranks, Plautius ordered his legionaries forward yet again to force a river crossing. This time they were triumphant and the Britons broke, the survivors bolting north along the Medway, heading for the River Thames. This they reached near modern Higham, crossing over into Essex near modern East Tilbury, making use of islands and marshes in the river. The Britons then drew up on the north bank to contest any crossing of the Thames, given the Catuvellauni capital of Camulodunum (modern Colchester) was only 60km to the north.

Plautius was hot on their heels, his *alae* of cavalry maintaining contact. In short order he too was on the Thames and once more deployed his troops to force a river crossing. He'd learned from the first crossing battle though and was determined to make good use of all of the forces at his disposal. First, he deployed the legionaries immediately opposite the Britons to pin them in place. Next, he used the war galleys and transports for the first time on campaign – the Medway crossing battle had been above the tidal reach of that river, with his ships unable to help there. In the first instance he used the ships to ferry *auxilia* to the north bank of the Thames, downriver of the Britons. He then used his engineers to build a bridge of boats upriver of the Britons. Legionaries from one of the legions then

quickly crossed over there. Finally, with legionaries to the west of the Britons and *auxilia* to the east, Plautius launched the assault with his main force directly across the river. Supported by ballista and missile-armed marines on his war galleys, victory was swift and brutal, the broken Britons again fleeing north, this time for their capital. The Romans once more pursued vigorously, though the primary sources say that many of the fleeing Britons used their knowledge of the local marshy terrain to make good their escape. In their eagerness many of the pursuing Romans got into difficulty, some being ambushed and killed.

Plautius' now paused and consolidated his position, having learned that Togodumnus was dead and Caratacus had fled to the west to find sanctuary with the Silures and Ordovices tribes in Wales. He was weary of over-extending his lines of supply and so built another huge marching camp before re-supplying his army using the fleet. At

The Principate military combined arms in action in the Marcomannic Wars. A panel on the Column of Marcus Aurelius in Rome showing auxiliary cavalry and infantry at bottom, a legionary *testudo* centre and regional fleet transport vessels at top.

Roman auxiliaries on the Column of Marcus Aurelius wearing *lorica squamata* armour.

the same time, he sent for Claudius to join him to share the final victory. The emperor, waiting near Boulogne, crossed the Channel quickly and arrived at Plautius camp with elephants (see Chapter 2 for detail) and camels to intimidate the native Britons. The force then broke camp and headed north at speed for Camulodunum, arriving in late October. The lightning strike smashed all before it and the Catuvellauni quickly sued for peace, eleven other British tribes also submitting to Roman rule. Claudius then declared the province of Britain founded, established Camulodunum as its capital and appointed Plautius its first governor. He then left, never to return, having stayed just 16 days.

This campaign is illustrative for a number of reasons in the context of the legionaries and *auxilia* on campaign. Firstly, given Caesar's evident failures in the 1st century BC and the known jeopardy of tackling not only *Oceanus* but mythical Britain,

the Romans again showed true grit in their desire for imperial success at this most north-westerly tip of the known world. Such grit was again on display at the river crossing battle on the Medway when, rebuffed on day one, Plautius used his clever stratagem to seize the initiative on day two. That in itself also presents a lesson, with the legionaries unable to win such a crucial battle on their own and having to rely on the support of the *auxilia*. This was also the case at the contested crossing of the Thames, where the fleet also played a major role. Such examples show that the Roman military was at its best when all the various arms of the military were combined. Finally, logistics was vital to the success of the Roman legionary and *auxilia* blitzkrieg in Britain. In that regard we see Plautius pausing after crossing the Thames to resupply by sea, ensuring there would be no pause once he launched his legionaries northwards once again.

The Marcomannic Wars

After the imperial conquests of Trajan's reign, when the Principate Empire expanded to its greatest extent, most of the Roman world experienced a long peace in the reigns of Hadrian and, especially, Antoninus Pius. This came to a shattering end almost as soon as Marcus Aurelius and Lucius Verus became joint emperors in AD 161. In the first instance, trouble broke out in the east with the start of the Roman–Parthian War which lasted until AD 165. However, a far more dangerous war then broke out in the mid-AD 160s, with the start of the Marcomannic Wars along the Danube. Now, for the first time since the Cimbrian wars, Italy itself was threatened as 'barbarian' invaders penetrated deep into the imperial centre.

The principal opponents in these wars were the Germanic Marcomanni, Juthungi and Quadi in Germania Magna, as the unconquered lands north of the Danube were known, and their Sarmatian Iazyges allies. All were being driven hard against Rome's Dacian and Danubian frontiers by the westward expansion of the Visigoths and Ostrogoths to their east, who themselves were being driven westwards by the initial expansion of the Huns out of the Central Asian steppe.

The Marcomanni were descendants of the Suebi who'd fought Julius Caesar in his Gallic campaigns. By the AD 160s they had long migrated away from Roman Gaul to settle in the region of modern Bohemia. The Juthungi were also of Suebi descent, though resided nearer their original homelands in modern Bavaria, while the Quadi (again with Suebi ancestry) were located further east in modern Moravia.

Their armies largely comprised of part-time foot warriors led by an aristocrat elite, all relying

Roman auxiliary cavalry at the charge on the Column of Marcus Aurelius.

The 'miracle of rain' incident recorded on the Column of Marcus Aurelius in Rome where a surrounded and parched Roman force was saved by a sudden thunderstorm.

on a fierce charge to break the enemies battle line using short spears and long iron swords. Only the nobility wore armour, usually chainmail hauberks, though most were equipped with various types of shield and many wore helmets of various kinds.

The fearsome Iazyges were a different matter entirely. These mounted warriors originally came from the Pontic steppe. They began their migration west around 200 BC and by the later 2nd century AD had settled in the region of modern Hungary and Serbia. They were predominantly shock cavalry charging to contact with a 3.5m long *contos* held two-handed and braced across the thighs. Also armed with a bow, many were armoured, often with horn scales attached to a leather jerkin. The nobility were even better equipped, wearing fine chainmail hauberks and iron helmets.

The wars on Rome's northern frontier had actually begun slightly earlier, with invasions across the upper reaches of the Rhine and Danube into Germania Superior and Raetia by the Germanic Chatti and Chauci who took advantage of Rome's distraction while campaigning in the east against Parthia. These disruptive incursions lasted from AD 162 to AD 165. Both were eventually repulsed. The Marcomannic Wars proper then began in AD 166 when 6,000 Germanic Langobard and Lacringli warriors fought their way over the Danube into Pannonia Superior. Though soon defeated by *vexillationes* from *legio I Adiutrix pia fidelis* under a *legate* called Candidus and the auxiliary cavalry *ala Ulpia Contariorum* under the Senator Marcus Macrinius Avitus Catonius Vindex (a veteran of the *legio VI Victrix* in York), this set a trend that lasted for the next 14 years.

After these initial incursions the Romans at first tried to buy off the German tribes causing trouble along the Danube. Marcus Iallius Bassus, governor of Pannonia Superior (a noted literary figure and adopted member of Marcus Aurelius's family) started negotiations with the 11 most aggressive tribes. A truce was soon agreed with the help of the Marcomanni overking Ballomar, after which any Germans remaining on the south side of the Danube withdrew.

However, no permanent peace deal was reached and later in AD 166 the frontier was tested again when the Sarmatian Iazyges and their Germanic Vandal allies invaded the province of Dacia in force. Here the frontier defences failed, with the governor Calpurnius Proculus killed leading a hastily assembled army trying to stem the incoming tide of invaders. These then penetrated deep into the provincial interior, with the emperor forced to deploy the veteran *legio IV Macedonia* from Moesia Inferior to drive them out of Dacia. An uneasy peace then settled on the region.

Marcus Aurelius and Lucius Verus clearly viewed the ongoing threat from north of the Danube as serious and determined to carry out a major punitive expedition against the Iazyges and their German allies. It is unclear if they intended to conquer new territory, particularly in *Magna Germania* (with the subsequent creation of new provinces), or whether their main aim was a punitive expedition on a grand scale. Whichever, it was not to be in AD 167. A serious outbreak of plague across the Mediterranean put their plans on hold for that year. This was so serious that they were forced to recruit gladiators, bandits and Germans to fill the depleted ranks of the Roman military (*Historia Augusta*, Marcus Aurelius, 21.6).

By AD 168 things had stabilised in the imperial capital and the emperors headed north to Aquileia on the north-eastern Adriatic coast where they established their forward headquarters. Orders were then dispatched along the northern frontiers to gather an enormous force to campaign across the Danube that they planned to lead in person.

This included two newly raised legions, *legio II Italica* and *legio III Italica*. Their first targets were marauding Marcomanni, Quadi and Victohali tribesmen who'd taken advantage of the disruption caused by the plague in AD 167 to attack Pannonia Superior. However, as the imperial force approached the key legionary fortress of *Carnuntum* (also headquarters of the *Classis Flavia Pannonica*) the Germans withdrew, giving assurances of their future good conduct. The emperors then returned to Aquileia for the winter, leaving the army poised for further campaigning in AD 169. However, the death of Lucius Verus in January that year set back military operations again, with Marcus Aurelius returning to Rome to supervise his funeral.

The now sole emperor returned to the offensive in the autumn of AD 169. His first target were the Iazyges, though the war at first went badly. The Sarmatians struck first, targeting the Roman gold mines at Alburnum in Dacia. The emperor ordered Claudius Fronto, the governor of Moesia Inferior and an imperial favourite, to gather a local force and intercept them. In the ensuing battle the governor was killed and his force scattered. Meanwhile, with the emperor's attention focused on this crisis, several German tribes along the Danube used the opportunity to launch their own raids deep into Roman territory. In the east, these included the Costoboci who, from their Carpathian mountain homelands, struck the province of Thracia with savage ferocity. Pillaging all before them, they soon reached Greece proper where they destroyed the ancient Temple of the Eleusinian Mysteries near Athens.

However, this wasn't the emperor's biggest problem. Across the Danube the one-time mediator Ballomar now seized his chance to launch a strike deep into Pannonia Superior. Gathering his own Marcomanni warriors and Quadi allies, he headed directly for *Carnuntum* to force a decisive meeting engagement. This he got in AD 170, mauling a Roman force there comprising *legio XIV Gemina Martia Victrix* and 14,000 auxiliaries. This was Rome's biggest military defeat for a century. Ballomar's army then split into two, one column heading west to ravage the province of

Noricum, while the other continued south, razing the city of Oderzo (*Opitergium*) in north-eastern Italy and then besieging Aquileia. This sent shock waves through the Roman world of a kind last experienced in the Cimbrian Wars. The emperor, still on the Danube in the north, quickly ordered the Praetorian prefect Titus Furius Victorinus to lead a hastily gathered force to repel them, but his army was promptly defeated and he was killed, the third senior leader to die since the troubles had begun.

Realising the serious position now faced by Rome, Marcus Aurelius turned to the up-and-coming troubleshooter Pertinax, who was briefly emperor in AD 193, promoting him to the post of *procurator* in both Dacia and Moesia Superior. The timing of his move couldn't have been better given the shambles elsewhere in the region. Pertinax immediately set to work reordering the economy of Dacia. This had been severely dislocated by the earlier incursion of the Iazyges. With taxes from the region's industry, agriculture and population once more flowing into the imperial *fiscus*, new troops were raised and the frontiers and fortifications there strengthened. Then, in the spring of AD 171, Marcus Aurelius was at last ready to strike back against the Marcomanni and Quadi. First, he quickly redeployed the legions from the border to the imperial interior to challenge the raiding Germans who by this time were running out of provisions. He then appointed the highly experienced Tiberius Claudius Pompeianus commander in chief, who immediately recruited Pertinax to be his aide. Pertinax served with Pompeianus for a short time while preparations were made to go back on the offensive, then was elevated again to become an adlected senator which allowed him to take command of *legio I Adiutrix pia fidelis* in Pannonia Superior as part of Pompeianus's much wider military reorganization in Europe. This included bolstering the *Classis Flavia Moesica* on the lower Danube and the building of a new series of fortifications in northern Italy called the *praetentura Italiae et Alpium*. Pompeianus then divided his force into legionary spearheads, each supported by their own auxiliaries. He himself quickly relieved Aquileia,

routing the Marcomanni and Quadi there who fled back north across the Danube, suffering heavy casualties in the process. Meanwhile, another column under Pertinax struck out for the second German force that was still ravaging Noricum and had even reached Raetia. Total success followed, with this German force also driven beyond the Danube with heavy casualties. Marcus Aurelius himself publicly praised Pompeianus and Pertinax for their service.

The emperor now realised the Romans were still in no position to go on the offensive across the Danube and consolidated his forces along the northern *limes*, rebuilding and reinforcing the defences where they had been overrun. Intense diplomatic activity then followed as he attempted to win over as many of the German and Sarmatian tribes as possible before going back on the counterattack. In particular, peace treaties were signed with the Quadi and the Iazyges, with the Lacringi and Hasdingi Vandals also becoming Roman allies and agreeing to provide warriors for his next campaign.

In the spring of AD 172 Marcus Aurelius was finally ready to go on the offensive and launched a massive assault across the Danube from Pannonia Superior and Noricum against the Marcomanni and any German and Sarmatian tribes still allied with them. Ballomar's loose confederation was shattered and the Marcomanni quickly sued for peace, with the emperor taking the title *Germanicus* and coins being minted featuring the term 'Germania Capta'. Pertinax, leading *legio I Adiutrix pia fidelis*, was again in the vanguard, though another *legate* gained the greatest fame. This was Marcus Valerius Maximianus who, leading the Pannonia Inferior-based *legio II Adiutrix pia fidelis*, killed the chieftain of the German Naristi tribe in single combat. The emperor granted the *legate* the chieftain's fine stallion as a reward.

The Romans again campaigned north of the Danube in AD 173, this time against the Quadi after they predictably broke their earlier treaty commitments. Victory again followed, though the campaign is best known for the 'miracle of rain' incident recorded on the Column of Marcus Aurelius in Rome and on coins. Here, *legio XII*

Fulminata and perhaps Pertinax with his *legio I Adiutrix pia fidelis* had been trapped by a larger force of Quadi and were on the brink of surrendering because of thirst and heat. However, a sudden thunderstorm provided a deluge that refreshed the legionaries and *auxilia*, while a lightning strike on the Quadi camp sent the Germans fleeing in terror.

Roman military attention now switched to the Rhine frontier. Here, future Emperor Didius Julianus (the brief successor to Pertinax in the 'Year of the Five Emperors') had been the governor of Gallia Belgica since AD 170. As detailed above this province, once home to some of Julius Caesar's fiercest Gallic opponents, stood just south of the northern border provinces of Germania Inferior and Germania Superior. In AD 173 it suffered a major incursion from the Germanic Chauci. Taking advantage of the Roman tribulations on the Danube, they smashed through the *limes* along the lower Rhine and penetrated deep into the rich farmlands of modern Flanders. The legions in the two German provinces struggled to contain the threat and Didius Julianus was forced to raise a force of local recruits, probably veterans settled in *coloniae*, which he led to great effect. Soon the Germans had been forced back over the Rhine. The governor then began a programme of fortification along the English Channel coast of his province, before returning triumphant to Rome to celebrate a triumph.

With the *limes* along the Rhine now stabilised, in the spring of AD 174 Marcus Aurelius was now ready to go on the offensive once more. He quickly crossed the Danube with a huge force, targeting any Quadi still holding out against Rome. Over the winter a number of tribes there had deposed the pro-Roman King Furtius and replaced him with his arch-rival Ariogaesus. Marcus Aurelius refused to recognise the latter and forced him to stand down, sending him to Alexandria in exile. By the end of the year the whole of the Quadi were subjugated, with the leading nobles sending hostages to Rome, warriors being recruited into the ranks of the Roman auxiliaries for assimilation, and Roman garrisons being installed in fortified camps throughout their territory.

Marcus Aurelius had one more piece of unfinished business along the Danube, to punish the Iazyges for the death of his friend Fronto in AD 169. In AD 175 he again gathered a mighty force and launched an assault from Pannonia Inferior and Dacia deep into their homelands. For this *expeditio sarmatica* the emperor targeted the plain of the River Tizsa in modern Hungary, winning a number of victories after which the leading Iazyges King Zanticus surrendered and a peace treaty was agreed. Captured Roman prisoners were then returned and the Iazyges supplied Rome with the 8,000 *contos*-armed cavalry mentioned in Chapters 4 and 5. The emperor then took the title '*Sarmaticus*' and once more minted coins to celebrate victory. This brought to an end the First Marcomannic War.

We have remarkable insight here into the true jeopardy faced by the Empire in this conflict through the words of the emperor himself. This is in the form of a series of philosophical, somber observations written down in Greek by Marcus Aurelius when on campaign which he styled 'To Himself'. They have survived to this day as his *Meditations*, and given the unpredictable nature of the first conflict in the Marcomannic Wars, one observation is particularly prescient (5.9):

> Do not be distressed, do not despond or give up in despair, if now and again practice falls short of precept. Return to the attack after each failure and be thankful if on the whole you acquit yourself in the majority of cases as a man should.

Soon the emperor's resolve was tested once more, for early in AD 177 the Quadi reneged on their peace agreements with Rome once more. The Marcomanni soon followed and so began the Second Marcomannic War. This new insurrection spread rapidly along the upper Danube and soon the Germans had penetrated the *limes* and began raiding imperial territory. Marcus Aurelius reacted swiftly, calling his new campaign the *secunda expeditio germanica*. With his army again led by Marcus Valerius Maximianus, the emperor arrived at *Carnuntum* in Pannonia Superior in August AD 178. There the Romans forced a meeting engagement with the Marcomanni who were comprehensively defeated. The Romans then advanced on the Quadi who were almost wiped out at the battle of Laugaricio in modern Slovakia. Maximianus's own *legio II Adiutrix pia fidelis* fought particularly well here. The few German survivors were then chased back north beyond the Danube, where the Praetorian prefect Tarruntenus Paternus then led a punitive campaign against the Quadi in their homeland which he ravaged.

Campaigning along the Danube ended dramatically though on 17 March AD 180 when Marcus Aurelius died of natural causes in Vienna at the age of 58. He was succeeded by his son Commodus. The new emperor had no interest in continuing his father's campaigns along the Danube. Instead, he was keen to return to Rome to secure his position. Commodus quickly established new peace treaties with the Marcomanni and Quadi, against the advice of his senior military commanders. The terms included them providing 20,000 warriors to serve in the Roman army, these being distributed to auxiliary units across the Empire. Those remaining were partially disarmed and forbidden from attacking their Iazyges and Vandal neighbours without permission from Rome. Finally, the Germans were also forbidden from settling along a narrow strip on their own northern bank of the Danube, and also on the various large islands along the river's length. Commodus then left for the imperial capital in early September AD 180 where he celebrated a solo triumph on 22 October. Thus ended the Second Marcomannic War, with the so called 'Peace of Commodus'.

However, trouble north of the Danube continued and soon the Iazyges and a German tribe called the Buri whose homeland was to the north of the Marcomanni and Quadi near the headwaters of the Vistula river rebelled again. Once more the emperor ordered his legions north of the Danube and victories were quickly celebrated by Maximianus again, and also by the leading senators Pescennius Niger and Clodius Albinus, both to play key roles in the 'Year of the Five Emperors.' When a lengthy peace finally descended on the region in AD 182 Commodus celebrated by taking the title Germanicus Maximus. Thus ended the most challenging series of conflicts faced by the Empire for a century and, given the settlement

of many Germans within the Empire afterwards, one that began a process which was to change the very nature of imperial identity. Soon, as detailed in Chapters 4 and 5, German warriors were not just filling the ranks of auxiliary units but joining the legions, while their leaders eventually came to dominate the officer class in the Roman military.

The Severan Campaigns in Scotland

In AD 207 the great warrior Emperor Septimius Severus was bored in Rome. Having hacked his way to power in the 'Year of Five Emperors' in AD 193, fought two campaigns in the east including the sack of the Parthian capital Ctesiphon, seen off the usurpation of the British governor Clodius Albinus, and campaigned in his native North Africa, he was now reduced to fretting about the behaviour of his sons Caracalla and Geta in the imperial capital. Then a golden opportunity presented itself for one final stab at glory.

As detailed in Chapter 3, Britannia was a troubled province. It had suffered periodic unrest along its northern borders throughout the 2nd century AD, with the Maeatae and Caledonian tribal confederations emerging towards its end. In the late AD 190s, with the defences along Hadrian's Wall depleted after Albinus' usurpation attempt, the governor Virius Lupus had been forced to pay huge indemnities to both to prevent further trouble. Such enormous injections of wealth to the northern elites of unconquered Briton, though buying peace in the short term, only further assisted the coalescence of power among their leaders. Trouble again erupted at the beginning of the 3rd century AD though was quickly stamped out, with Lupus and his successor Lucius Alfenus Senecio then beginning the slow process of rebuilding the northern frontier. However, in AD 206/ 207 a disaster of some kind occurred, with Senecio writing an urgent appeal to Severus saying the province was in danger of being overrun. In it he requested either more troops or the emperor himself. He got both.

Severus's response can be best described as 'shock and awe' writ large. For his expeditio *felicissima Britannica* he gathered his wife Julia Domna, the squabbling Caracalla and Geta, key senators, courtiers and advisors, the imperial *fiscus*, the Praetorian Guard, *legio II Parthica* and *vexillationes* from all of the crack legions and auxiliary units along the Rhine and Danubian frontiers. They were all transported to Britain by the *Classis Britannica* in the spring of AD 208. Severus then established York as his imperial capital. There his troops joined the incumbent *legio VI Victrix*, with the *legio II Augusta* from Caerleon and *legio XX Valeria Victrix* from Chester being summoned to join them. In total this gave him an army of 50,000, together with the 7,000 sailors and marines of the regional fleet. As set out in Chapter 5, this was in effect the first Roman field army.

To support this colossal force the fort, harbour and supply base at South Shields was chosen as the main supply depot, with as mentioned earlier the granaries there increased in volume by a factor of 10, with 20 added to the original two. These could now hold 2,500 tonnes of grain, enough to feed the whole force for two months. From here the vessels of the *Classis Britannica* fulfilled their transport role using the Tyne and well-trodden eastern coastal routes to keep the army supplied once the campaign began, making use of the regional river systems wherever possible. The fort at Corbridge on Dere Street just short of Hadrian's Wall was similarly upgraded, with the granaries there rebuilt even before Severus had arrived (showing the degree of logistical planning). Then, in the spring of

AD 209, Severus began the first of his two assaults against the Maeatae and Caledonians to the north. He was joined by Caracalla, leaving Geta behind in York to take charge of the imperial administration supported by Julia Domna.

The huge force marched north from York along Dere Street, crossing Hadrian's Wall and then reaching the Scottish Borders where it destroyed all before it. The whole region was cauterised of any opposition. Notably, at this time the Antonine fort at Vindolanda just south of the wall was demolished, with LIA round houses being laid out on a Roman grid pattern there instead. This has been interpreted as a concentration camp for the displaced local population.

The line of march north along Dere Street through the Scottish Borders can be traced by the sequence of enormous 67 ha marching camps built along its route. These are found at Newstead, St Leonards (the largest at 70 ha), Channelkirk and Pathhead. Once again, just as with Plautius's campaign of conquest with his smaller force in the 1st century AD, the baggage train would have been at the centre of the huge column, with the legionaries and auxiliaries deployed along the flanks and at the front and rear, and with *ala* of cavalry ranging far and wide through the countryside.

Any resistance here would have been in the form of defended settlements such as hillforts, and in that regard one analogy shows the desperate

Dere Street running past the Roman fort site at Newstead. This was the principal invasion route when the Romans headed into the far north of Britain.

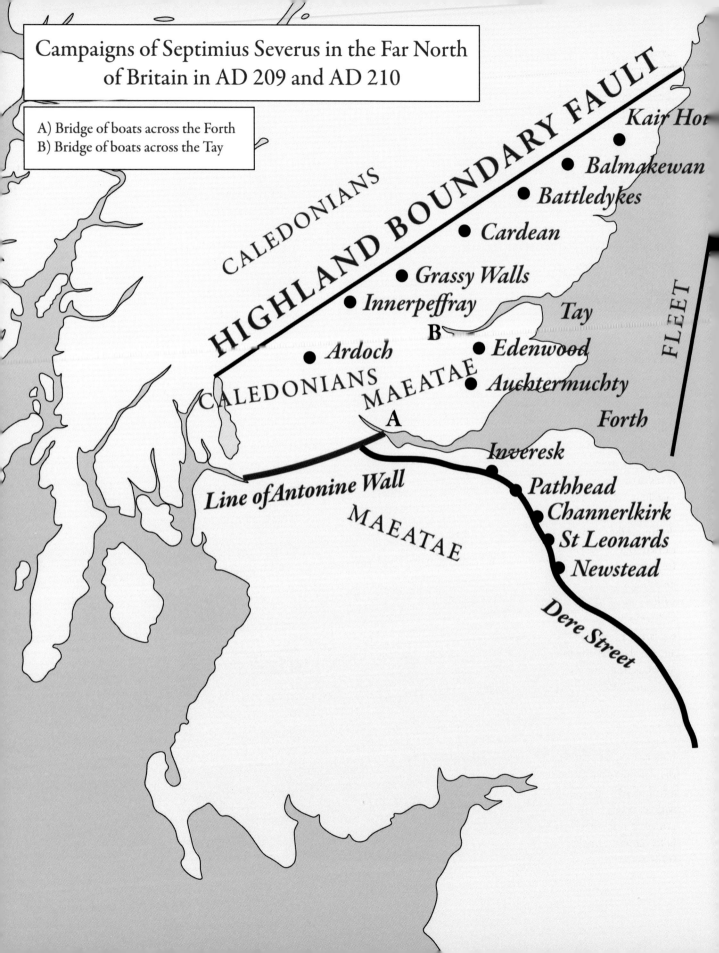

Campaigns of Septimius Severus in the Far North
of Britain in AD 209 and AD 210

A) Bridge of boats across the Forth
B) Bridge of boats across the Tay

HIGHLAND BOUNDARY FAULT

CALEDONIANS

Kair Hot

Balmakewan

Battledykes

Cardean

Grassy Walls

Innerpeffray

Tay

B

Ardoch

Edenwood

CALEDONIANS

MAEATAE

Auchtermuchty

FLEET

Forth

A

Inveresk

Line of Antonine Wall

Pathhead

MAEATAE

Channerlkirk

St Leonards

Newstead

Dere Street

situation the natives found themselves in. This is in the context of recently published research regarding the 7ha hillfort site at Burnswark in Dumfriesshire. Here, a debate has taken place as to whether data previously considered from antiquarian and 1960s archaeological excavations showed an actual Roman siege from the Antonine period, or a Roman siege training exercise. The key items of interest were the north and south Roman marching camps, and also a plethora of ballista bolts/balls and lead slingshots found at the site. To determine the truth the Trimontium Trust recently carried out a review of existing research and fresh data, the latter based on a systematic metal-detecting survey to identify more lead sling shots with a view to plotting their scatter. Experimental archaeology regarding the use of slings in siege warfare was also carried out. The results suggest an actual siege, the two camps seen as a real-world tactical response to the topography and the widespread scatter of sling shots and other missiles (and their quality) suggesting deadly intent. The latter indicates a massive missile barrage, both at the gateways and also along a full half kilometer of hillfort rampart. The simplest explanation is that the defenders on the hilltop were suppressed by a hail of sling bullets, fired by *auxilia* specialists, with an accurate range of 120m and the stopping power of a modern handgun, as well as ballista bolts and arrows. This covered an attacking force of

legionaries in *testudo* formation sweeping out the three huge gateways and storming the hilltop. Such a combination of missile troops and legionaries was brutally effective. Further, one other factor adds even more insight into the awful experience of the native Britons on the receiving end of this devastation. This is because some of slingshots were hollowed out with a 4mm hole through their centre, designed to make a screeching noise when slung. This is an early example of psychological

A classic Principate legionary on the northern borders of the Empire. (Graham Sumner)

warfare on the battlefield, bringing to mind the screaming sirens of diving Junkers Ju-87 Stukas during the Blitzkrieg early in World War II, adding to the misery of those on the receiving end.

The Scottish Borders subdued, Severus reached the Firth of Forth at Inveresk where Dere Street turned west at the River Esk crossing. He then re-established the Antonine fort, supply base and harbour at Cramond and then repaired and re-manned the Antonine Wall to protect his rear. Next, he built a bridge of 900 boats at South Queensferry, before dividing the huge force into two legionary spearheads. The larger comprised two thirds of the troops available (likely with the three British legions, used to campaigning in this theatre) under the fitter Caracalla, and a smaller one featuring the Praetorian Guard, other guard units and *legio II Parthica*, this under the ailing Severus who was suffering from severe gout. The other units in the overall force, for example the *auxilia*, would have been divided between the two as required.

Caracalla now led his larger force in a blitzkrieg lightning strike south-west to north-east along the Highland Boundary Fault, building a sequence of 54 ha marching camps as he went along to seal off the Highlands from the Maeatae and Caledonians living in the central and northern Midland Valley. The camps were at Househill Dunipace near Falkirk (presumably the stopping off point before crossing the Forth), Ardoch at the south-western end of the Gask Ridge (where Antonine watch towers may again have been re-manned), Innerpeffray East, Grassy Walls, Cardean, Battledykes, Balmakewan and Kair House. The latter was only 13km south west of Stonehaven on the coast, with the Highland line visibly converging with the sea.

The plan was to turn these camps into Glenblocker forts to prevent any Caledonian reserves from emerging into the campaigning theatre from the Highlands. As such, each would have deliberately cut off the glens leading into the Highlands.

With the Highlands and the route northwards to the Moray and Buchan Lowlands beneath the Moray Firth now sealed off, Severus next sent the *Classis Britannica* along the coast to seal that off also. This left the Maeatae and Caledonians in the central and northern Midland Valley in a perilous position, with nowhere to flee. Severus took full advantage, leading a second legionary spearhead with the remaining one third of his force across the bridge of boats on the Firth of Forth again, but this time heading directly north across Fife to the River Tay. This was a region heavily settled by the Maeatae in particular, and to secure it he built two further marching camps, 25ha in size, at Auchtermuchty and Edenwood. Reaching the Tay at Carpow he then rebuilt and re-manned the Flavian and Antonine fort, supply base and harbour there. This completed his east coast supply route to keep the huge army in the field, featuring South Shields, Cramond and Carpow. He then built another bridge of boats, this time across the Tay, and hammered north into the northern Midland Valley below the Highland line, his legionaries smashing all before them. The conflict there was particularly brutal as the natives refused to gather to allow a definitive set piece battle to take place (either for tactical reasons, or because they had no chance to coalesce). The campaign therefore became a grinding guerrilla war in the most horrific conditions, with the weather even worse than usual. Both of the key primary sources, Cassius Dio and Herodian, graphically describe the campaign: The former, in his *Roman History*, says (76.13):

> ... as he [Severus] advanced through the country he experienced countless hardships in cutting down the forests, levelling the heights, filling up the swamps, and bridging the rivers; but he fought no battle and beheld no enemy in battle array. The enemy purposely put sheep and cattle in front of the soldiers for them to seize, in order that they might be lured on still further until they were worn out; for in fact the water caused great suffering to the Romans, and when they became scattered, they would be attacked. Then, unable to walk, they would be slain by their own men, in order to avoid capture, so that a full fifty thousand died [clearly a massive exaggeration, but indicative of the difficulties the Romans faced]. But Severus did not desist until he approached the extremity of the island.

Meanwhile Herodian, in his *History of the Roman Empire*, says (3.14):

> ... frequent battles and skirmishes occurred, and in these the Romans were victorious. But it was easy for the Britons to slip away; putting their knowledge of the surrounding area to good use, they disappeared in the woods and marshes. The Romans' unfamiliarity with the terrain prolonged the war.

Eventually the weight of numbers told and, with the entire regional economy destroyed, the Maetae and Caledonians sued for peace. The resulting treaty was very one sided in favour of Rome. Severus then proclaimed a famous victory, with he and his two sons being given the title Britannicus and celebratory coins being struck to commemorate the event. Campaigning, at least in the short term, was over, and to apparent imperial satisfaction. As always in the Roman experience north of the provincial border though, such a state of comparative calm was not to last.

Severus, Caracalla and the military leadership wintered in York and were still there in May AD 210 as a letter sent from there in their names is dated to the 5th of that month. However, clearly the terms which had so satisfied the Romans in AD 209 were not so agreeable to at least the Maeatae

A column from the basilica of the legionary fortress at York, built at the time when Septimius Severus turned it into his imperial capital.

(probably the recipients of the most extreme experiences of the AD 209 campaign) as in AD 210 they revolted again.

The Caledonians predictably joined in, and Severus determined to go north once more. On this occasion though he had clearly had enough of the troublesome Britons in the far north and gave his famous order to kill all the natives the legionaries and *auxilia* came across. The entire campaign was then re-enacted exactly as in AD 210, though wholly under Caracalla as Severus was too ill when the advance began. It was even more brutal than the first, given there was peace along the northern border for four generations afterwards. Archaeological data also shows a major depopulation event took place. This indicates something akin to genocide was committed in the central and upper Midland Valley.

At the end of the campaigning season, whatever was left of the native leadership again sued for peace,

Roman *equites* played a key role in nearly all of the campaigns and battles of both the Principate and Dominate phases of Empire. (Graham Sumner)

on even more onerous terms than previously, and the 'Severan surge' headed south again to winter near York, leaving significant garrisons in place. However, any plans to remain north of the Solway Firth–Tyne line were cut short when Severus died in York in February AD 211 in the freezing cold of a British winter. Caracalla and Geta, far more interested in establishing their own individual power bases in Rome, quickly left and Severus's 50,000 men gradually returned to their own bases. The northern border was then reestablished on the line of Hadrian's Wall once more.

A final point to note here is that the British legions seem to have performed particularly well during the Severan campaigns in Scotland, with for example *legio VI Victrix* being awarded the commemorative title *Britannica Pia Fidelis* (based on tile stamps from Carpow) and *legio XX* being similarly styled *Antoniniana* by Caracalla after the death of his father.

In Battle

Having looked at the legionaries and their supporting troops on campaign to see how the Roman military operated at a strategic level, I now focus on their experiences in battle. This allows their tactical use to be examined in close detail. To provide such an overview I have chosen four specific engagements which book-end the Republic and Empire chronologically, these being Caesar's victory over Pompey at Pharsalus in 48 BC, Gaius Suetonius Paulinus' defeat of Boudicca in AD 61, Severus's defeat of Clodius Albinus at Lugdunum in AD 197, and Julian the Apostate's victory over the Alamanni in AD 357 at Strasbourg. The first, from immediately prior to the Principate Empire, shows how late republican legionaries performed when evenly matched with their opponents given this was legionary versus legionary. The second shows the legionaries and *auxilia* fighting against great odds and still winning through, detailing why this was so often the case. The third is illustrative of how Roman armies of enormous size were commanded and controlled in battle, while the fourth shows the legionaries and *auxilia* performing in a late Roman Dominate context.

The Battle of Pharsalus

Pharsalus, in Thessaly in north-eastern Greece, was the location of the decisive battle in 48 BC between Caesar and Pompey at the height of the civil wars of the 1st century BC. Previous encounters between the two had been indecisive and matters would now come to a head in the largest encounter between Romans armies to that date.

The campaigning theatre was chosen by Pompey who fled Italy in 49 BC rather than confront Caesar, as detailed in Chapter 1. He believed some of the local legions there would side with his younger rival. This reflected the autonomous nature of the Marian legions, each of which had a very distinct sense of identity and loyalty.

Caesar almost caught Pompey as he left Brindisi (*Brundisium*) in Southern Italy but he escaped, heading for Greece where he began to gather his legions. Caesar then targeted Pompey's seven legions in Spain to neutralise the threat to his rear before he looked to Greece. There Pompey had made Beroea his headquarters where he mustered nine legions and many allied troops armed in their native fashion, for example cavalry, archers and slingers. He also gathered a large fleet of 600 ships.

Back in Italy Caesar struggled to get the backing of the ruling classes who made Pompey the commander-in-chief of the Republic's armies. The latter decided to defend the western coast of Greece from any attempt by Caesar to land his army there and moved westwards from Thessaly, establishing a winter camp on arrival. Then, late in the campaigning season, Caesar surprised all. Defying Pompey's naval supremacy, he determined to risk a winter crossing from Italy and mustered as many legionaries as he could, sailing on 4 January. He left his baggage train behind to save time and landed without incident at Palaeste, having avoided Pompey's fleet stationed on Corcyra (modern Corfu). He then drew Pompey out of his winter quarters by sacking the nearby cities nominally under the latter's protection, the two forces facing off either side of the River Apsus in Illyria. There they would remain for four months.

Caesar's second-in-command Mark Antony arrived in April with reinforcements, boosting the number of Caesar's legions to 11. The two forces now broke camp, Pompey heading back to Thessaly and Caesar following. There they faced off again at Asparagium. Despite outnumbering his opponent Pompey still refused to force a meeting engagement, confident he could harass Caesar's lines of supply. He then moved again, this time to the coast at Dyrrachium. Caesar now began an audacious project to build an enclosing wall around Pompey's camp to box it against the sea. Realising the danger Pompey countered quickly by sallying out with his troops, forcing Caesar to retreat. The republican leader then established a new camp south of Caesar's siege fortifications, threatening the latter's rear. However, on 9 July, when Pompey's forces were split between Dyrrachium and the new camp, Caesar attacked the former. Pompey was forced to send five of his legions to extricate the trapped troops. Both sides suffered many losses, particularly Caesar, but the action proved indecisive.

Caesar now abandoned the blockade and withdrew south, concerned at the increasing disparity in numbers as Pompey continued to receive reinforcements from his allies in the east. Pompey's cavalry pursued but Caesar escaped to Thessaly, setting up camp on the north bank of the River Enipeus between Pharsalus and Palaepharsalus. Pompey followed with his whole force and set up his own camp a kilometre to the west. For this he chose a range of low hills, these providing a good strategic position ensuring a safe route for supplies to reach him from the coast. The two armies again faced off.

Both armies featured a core of legions together with allies, though Pompey had the greater force and slightly more allies. By this time Caesar had with him elements of nine of his legions numbering some 23,000 legionaries in 80 cohorts (many of which were understrength). He also had between 5,000 and 10,000 allied foot and around 1,000 Gallic and German cavalry. Pompey had elements of 12 legions together with seven cohorts of legionaries from Spain, in total numbering 50,000. He also had 4,200 allied foot and 7,000 allied horse.

Caesar, clearly outnumbered, was keen to settle the issue immediately. However Pompey, on the range of hills, was unwilling to abandon his advantage of high ground, despite the weight of numbers in his favour. Several days passed before Caesar decided to fall back in the hope of drawing Pompey from his camp. On the morning of 9 August Pompey took the bait and moved his troops out onto the plain. Caesar pounced immediately, abandoning his baggage and even destroying his own field defences to get more of his legionaries onto the battlefield.

Pompey was the first to begin deploying, with 110 cohorts of legionaries plus line-of-battle allies lined up along a 4km front in the *triplica acies* formation. This was a repeating succession of four cohorts in the first line and three in each of the second and third lines. He deployed most of his cavalry, archers and slingers on his left flank hard up against the low hills where his camp was, with a smaller cavalry and light infantry force on the right against the River Enipeus. His veteran legionaries were dispersed throughout his force to support newly recruited troops. Pompey's plan was for his cavalry to circle around Caesar's flanks and attack his rear while his infantry pinned Caesar's centre. Pompey positioned himself at the rear of the left wing.

Meanwhile Caesar, beginning his deployment later, lined up his troops parallel to Pompey's but with his three lines somewhat thinner given his numerical disadvantage. He was keen to avoid a hanging flank that Pompey's legionaries could exploit. Next he positioned himself opposite Pompey, behind the veteran and highly motivated *legio X*, the best legion on the field. He then deployed his cavalry on his right, and to harass the opposing legionaries positioned his light missile troops across his centre. As a precaution against Pompey's superior cavalry numbers he also moved six cohorts of legionaries from his rear line, positioning them as a reserve on his extreme right flank at an oblique angle.

The armies now closed to within 140m and faced off, Pompey then ordering the first attack with his cavalry where he held the numerical advantage. Caesar's cavalry counter-charged and a melee ensued. Meanwhile, Caesar's first two lines of infantry approached Pompey's foot who stood their ground rather than advancing to meet the oncoming enemy. Seeing Pompey's lines were not advancing, Caesar halted his legions just out of range of the legionaries' lighter *pila*. He then redressed his ranks, before ordering a charge by his first two lines (the third being held in reserve). The legionaries surged forward, each unleashing both *pila* before drawing their *gladius* and closing. Pompey's legionaries countered, both sides finally meeting in a savage crescendo.

On the left flank Pompey's cavalry were beginning to make their weight of numbers tell and Caesar ordered his mounted troops to withdraw, leaving Pompey in control of the flank. However Caesar now ordered his right flank reserve of six cohorts forward to engage Pompey's cavalry who were reforming. They charged to close quarters, hurling their *pila* into the faces of their opponents who broke in short order. The republican cavalry fled the field in confusion, leaving Caesar in control of the whole flank.

In the centre Caesar now committed his third line to prevent Pompey from redeploying his own legionaries. He then wheeled the six cohorts on his right into the exposed left flank of Pompey's legionaries. Butchery ensued and Pompey's army broke, the allied troops fleeing first before the legionaries routed. The latter retreated headlong for the hills, with Pompey retreating to his camp before leaving the field completely. The one-time champion of the Republic now rode for Larissa with a small escort, disguising himself as an ordinary soldier.

Caesar was relentless in his pursuit. He wiped out Pompey's camp, causing what was left of Pompey's legions to flee to a hill called the Kaloyiros. This he besieged, and eventually Pompey's remaining legions, leaderless, surrendered. Caesar claimed to have killed 15,000 of his opponents, losing 1,200 himself. Pompey never recovered, fleeing to Egypt where he was beheaded on arrival.

What is clear from the primary sources regarding

this battle is that the élan of Caesar's legions, particularly *legio X*, more than made up for their numerical disadvantage. Pompey, dubbed the Great by contemporaries, was far from it in this campaign and once Caesar had destroyed his rival's left flank, the command and control he excised over his legions ensured Pompey's army was quickly rolled up. Caesar also made much better use of reserves, knowing that with the legionaries of both sides evenly matched (at least in terms of equipment) the ability to exploit success would be vital. So it proved.

The Defeat of Boudicca

The most famous event in the story of the Roman occupation of Britain is the blood-soaked rebellion of Boudicca in AD 60/61. This almost ended the Roman presence in the islands and saw the legionaries fighting in the most extreme of conditions. Defeat would have meant destruction of four whole legions, on a scale even larger than the loss of the three legions in the Teutoburg Forest in AD 9. That the legionaries won is testament to their morale, training and fitness.

By the late AD 50s, through a series of lightning campaigns, the legionary and auxiliary spearheads had defeated all opposition in the south, east and the Midlands of Britain. In the north the Brigantes, allies of Rome, kept the peace. This just left Wales, where the governor Gaius Suetonius Paulinus

was mounting a gruelling campaign in difficult conditions and terrain. His target was the north-west of the peninsula, specifically Anglesey deep in the heart of Deceangli and Ordovices territory. This mysterious island was home to the druids, leaders of LIA religion in pre-Roman Britain and the emotive centre of any remaining resistance to Rome. In AD 60 he made an amphibious assault there. This was a Claudian invasion in miniature, using specially built flat-bottomed transport boats to cope with the treacherous coastal currents and shallows around the island. Though the fighting was desperate, Paulinus was ultimately successful and Anglesey captured.

However, the governor's attempt to consolidate was cut short by the revolt of Boudicca, queen of the Iceni in northern East Anglia. The context behind this dramatic event was the earlier death of the Iceni King Prasutagus, Boudicca's husband. He was an ally of Rome who in his will left his kingdom to both his daughters and Emperor Nero. However, when he died this was ignored and the kingdom annexed by Rome. The primary sources say Boudicca protested but was flogged and her daughters raped for her trouble, though one adds that another factor was Roman financiers calling in their loans to the British elites there.

Whatever the cause, the queen rebelled. Soon Boudicca's incendiary insurrection had ignited most of the south-east above the Thames against

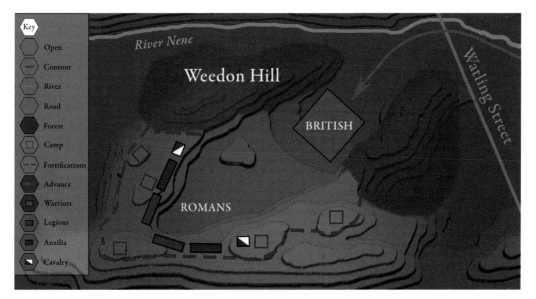

Paulinus' deployment proved crucial in his shattering defeat of Boudicca in AD 60/61. Choosing the battlefield carefully, his heavily outnumbered legionaries and *auxilia* were easily able to contain and then slaughter the Iceni Queen's warriors as they were funnelled into a narrow bowl-shaped valley. It turned into a killing field for the Britons. (Nigel Emsen)

Church Stowe, possible site of Paulinus's defeat of Boudicca. This was the legionaries' view from the head of the bowl-shaped valley described by the primary sources. The Britons would have approached from the funnel at the head of the valley, with Watling Street running left to right behind them.

the Romans. Marching south at the head of an army close to 100,000 strong, she first targeted the then provincial capital at Colchester. The nearest Roman legion was *legio IX Hispana* in the Midlands. Its *legate* Quintus Petilius Cerialis, a future governor of the province, moved quickly to lead a large force comprising *vexillationes* of legionaries and auxiliaries to intercept Boudicca. This arrived too late to save Colchester which by that point had already been torched with great loss of life, a large number burned alive as they sought shelter in the Temple of Claudius there, built to celebrate Plautius' earlier victory. Cerialis' force was then decisively defeated by the main British army, with the *legate* fleeing for his life alongside his cavalry, leaving his legionaries to their fate. They then remained incongruously holed up in a nearby fort until after the insurrection had been defeated.

In Wales, Paulinus had abandoned his assault on the druids as soon as he heard of the revolt. The governor immediately headed south-east along the route of Watling Street, accompanied

by most of *legio XIV Gemina*, some *vexillationes* from *legio XX Valeria Victrix* and a few auxiliary units including two *alae* of cavalry. Reaching High Cross in modern Leicestershire where Watling Street crossed the Fosse Way (the military trunk road linking Lincoln with Exeter) Paulinus then sent for the Exeter-based *legio II Augusta* to join him. However, the unit's *legate* and second-in-command were away, with its *praefectus castrorum* in charge. Called Poenius Postumus, he ignored the call, bringing shame on the legion. Clearly, he thought the province was about to fall and wanted to stay on the River Exe from where he could evacuate his troops if necessary. Meanwhile, some stragglers from *legio IX Hispana* also found their way to Paulinus, giving him a total force of around 6,000 legionaries from the three legions, 4,000 foot auxiliaries and around 1,000 mounted auxiliaries.

At this point Tacitus has Paulinus marching in person to London, the recently founded major trading port on the River Thames, from where the provincial *procurator* Catus Decianus had fled to Gaul as Boudicca and her growing force marched

Boudiccan Revolts AD 60/61

	Primary area of revolt	→	Possible route of Petillius Cerialis
	Secondary area of revolt	⇢	Possible route of Paulinus' cavalry squadron
⇢	Retreat of Decianus Catus	→	Main movements of Roman army
⚜	Town attacked by rebels	→	Rebel forces main movements
♜	Roman forts		

● Civilian site

0   100 km
0   100 miles

VERTURIONES

DAMNONI

EPIDII

SELGOVAE

NOVANTAE

CARVETII

BRIGANTES

PARISI

(Irish Sea)

(North Sea)

SETANTII

BRITANNIA

MONA

Part of Legio XX left in N. Wales

DECEANGLI
Legio XIV and most of Legio XX

GANGANI

♜ Rhyn Park

CORITANI

ICENI

ORDOVICES   Wroxeter ♜

CORNOVII

♜ Mancetter

Part of Legio IX ♜ Longthorpe

Thetford ●

TRINOVANTES

Possible battle site

Great Chesterford

CATUVELLAUNI

Camulodunum (Colchester) ⚜

DEMETAE

DOBUNNI

♜ Kingsholm

Secondary revolt by Trinovantes and other tribes

SILURES Usk ♜

Verulamium ⚜ (St Albans)

Caesaromagus ⚜

Londinium ⚜ (London)

ATREBATES

Flight of Decianus Catus

BELGAE

CANTIACI

● South Cadbury

REGNI

Chichester

GAUL

Legio II

DUROTRIGES

♜ Isca Dumnuniorum (Exeter)

DUMNONII

Lake Farm ♜

Oceanus Britannicus (English Channel)

on the town. It is useful to quote the historian in full at this point given the real sense of jeopardy he presents as the new province fell into chaos (*Annals*, 14.33):

> Paulinus ... with wonderful resolution, marched amidst a hostile population to Londinium, which, though undistinguished by the name of a colony (it was styled by the Romans a municipium mercantile town), was much frequented by several merchants and trading vessels. Uncertain whether he should choose it as a seat of war, as he looked round on his scanty force of soldiers ... he resolved to save the province at the cost of a single town. Nor did the tears and weeping of the people, as they implored his aid, deter him from giving the signal of departure and receiving into his army all who would go with him. Those who were chained to the spot by the weakness of their sex, or the infirmity of age, or the attractions of the place, were cut off by the enemy.

The key reference here is that which describes the local population as hostile when Paulinus was marching down Watling Street through Leicestershire and Hertfordshire, indicating that the Catuvellauni certainly, and perhaps even the Trinovantes to their east, had joined the Iceni in the great revolt. In these circumstances Paulinus' force would have been constructing defended marching camps at the end of each day's march as they travelled south-east. It is therefore unlikely that if Paulinus did indeed travel in person to London, he took his whole army. More likely he would have travelled with a bodyguard of auxiliary cavalrymen, or even more likely have sent an advance guard to assess the situation with authority to order an evacuation if needed.

In the event, when Boudicca did arrive in London, any remaining Romans or Romano-British were butchered, and the town burned to the ground. Boudicca then targeted the new *municipium* of St Albans (*Verulamium*), razing this also. The primary sources say that 80,000 were killed in the three sacking events by this point, indicating the scale of the insurrection and its rank savagery. However, the stage was now set for Roman retribution, and on a devastating scale.

By this point the primary sources say Boudicca's force had grown to 230,000, though only 100,000 were still likely warriors. This was an enormous force to keep in the field and she knew that a meeting engagement with Paulinus would be needed quickly to keep her army and its swelling number of dependent camp followers together. She also knew that if the governor was defeated, the Romans might abandon the province for good. Boudicca therefore advanced north-west along Watling Street to seek out the Roman army. As she progressed, she would also have received intelligence about the size of Paulinus's force, and no doubt felt the outcome of the forthcoming battle was a foregone conclusion.

In that she was wrong, as the wily Paulinus was ready for her and chose the place to make his stand very carefully. This was in a bowl-shaped steep defile, with woods on either side and rear and an open end facing Watling Street, Boudicca's line of advance. The woods protected his flanks and limited the frontage of the line of battle, negating the British superiority in numbers and playing to the martial superiority of his own legionaries. The exact location of the battle is unknown, with leading candidate sites including High Cross where Paulinus had awaited the arrival of *legio II Augusta* in vain, Church Stowe in Northamptonshire and Markyate in Hertfordshire. Interestingly, the latter is between Dunstable, a Roman site not destroyed by Boudicca (indicating she didn't arrive there), and St Albans to its immediate south-east which she did destroy. All three sites also have a significant water source, essential with so many engaged in the battle.

Paulinus deployed his legionaries and *auxilia* uphill of the Britons. He divided his foot troops into four main bodies with a centre, left and right flanks, and with a reserve to the rear of the centre. He then positioned an *ala* of auxiliary cavalry on either extreme flank hard against the woods there, where he finally deployed field defences for additional protection. Boudicca deployed her enormous force opposite, though in much denser formation, with the chariots in front manned by her own elite warriors. So confident were the Britons of victory that the families of the warriors joined the baggage train at the rear of her battle line to watch events unfold.

Boudicca now exhorted her army to more slaughter, then opened the battle with a wild uphill charge with both the chariots and foot warriors. The former rode across the front of the Romans, hurling insults and javelins, before turning square on to close for hand-to-hand combat. The foot troops followed close behind. The discipline of the legionaries now shone through. En masse they released their lighter *pila*, 6,000 iron-barbed javelins arcing high in the air in a steep parabola and then dropping on the heads of the Britons, many without helmets. The auxiliary infantry joined in with their own *lancea*, and with ballista, bows and slings used by specialist missile troops. Then, at point blank range, the legionaries unleashed their second, heavier *pila*. These flew in a flat arc, hammering into the front ranks of Britons who came to a shuddering halt in a tangle of dead horses, overturned chariots, bodies and wounded.

Paulinus saw the British advance had faulted and he seized his chance to take the initiative. He now ordered the legionaries to move forward in a series of *cuneus* (wedge) formations, with centurions and standard bearers to the fore. The auxiliaries followed on the flanks. Swords were drawn and shields set hard forward. The wedges then charged downhill into the dense mass of Britons, causing slaughter everywhere and forcing the natives into a huge, desperate crush where the warriors couldn't use their weapons. A massacre ensued as the Britons broke and tried to run away. However, they were trapped on the field by the surrounding families and baggage train. All were hacked down where they stood, the legionaries giving no quarter.

The result was a mighty victory for Paulinus, with Tacitus saying (*Annals*, 14.35):

The troops gave no quarter even to the women: the baggage animals themselves had been speared and added to the pile of bodies. The glory won in the course of the day was remarkable, and equal to that of our older victories: for, by some accounts, little less than eighty thousand Britons fell, at a cost of some four hundred Romans killed and a not much greater number of wounded. Boudicca ended her days by poison; while ... Postumus, camp prefect of the second legion, informed of the exploits of the men of the fourteenth and twentieth, and conscious that he had cheated his own corps of a share in the

honours and had violated the rules of the service by ignoring the orders of his commander, ran his sword through his body.

The Romans then quickly drafted in 2,000 more legionaries from Germany together with 1,000 auxiliary cavalry and eight units of auxiliary foot to help stamp out the last flames of resistance. This was carried out with such vigor in the Iceni homelands of north Norfolk that the region remained for many years under-developed compared to the rest of the province.

Thus ended the Boudiccan revolt, the province secured for another 340 years. However, Paulinus didn't receive the plaudits he might have expected. This was because the absent *procurator* Decianus hiding in Gaul was quickly replaced by Emperor Nero with a new man named Gaius Julius Alpinus Classicianus. The latter was critical of Paulinus's post-revolt punitive actions against the Britons, fearing it might spark another revolt. He reported this to the emperor who sent his own freedman Polyclitus to conduct an investigation. Though we don't have the full details of its findings, the investigator did report that Paulinus had lost some ships from the regional fleet. This excuse was used to relieve him, and he was replaced by the more conciliatory Publius Petronius Turpilianus as governor. However, Paulinus does not seem to have returned to Rome in disgrace, as a lead tessera found there features both his and Nero's names alongside symbols of victory, and a man with his name was nominated as consul for AD 66. Nevertheless, the Romans had been badly rattled by the rebellion, and in my view if Paulinus had lost his battle Britannia would have fallen, with the Romans perhaps unlikely ever to return.

The Battle of Lugdunum

On 19 February AD 197 a titanic clash of arms took place outside *Colonia Copia Claudia Augusta Lugdunum*, capital of the Roman province of Gallia Lugdunensis as detailed in Chapter 3. Some call it the biggest battle in Roman history. The protagonists were both North African by origin, Emperor Septimius Severus (detailed above in the context of his Scottish campaigns) and the usurping British governor Clodius Albinus. The

Detail of Roman Principate auxiliaries on the Arch of Septimius Severus in Rome. Those which fought at the battle of Lugdunum would have been similarly equipped.

engagement was sanguineous in the extreme, with huge casualties on either side. Yet its origins can be traced back to events four years earlier, when Severus himself was still a governor with no evident designs on the purple.

All of the primary sources begin their tale on New Year's Eve AD 192 when Emperor Commodus was assassinated. This ushered in the 'Year of the Five Emperors.' Severus was governing Pannonia Superior at the time. He fell like a sword of Damocles on Rome after his mentor Pertinax (the first of the five imperial candidates that year) was assassinated by the Praetorian Guard. By the year's end he was the last man standing in the imperial capital, with only two challengers left to his claim on the throne. These were the Syrian governor Pescennius Niger and the British governor Albinus. Prioritising Niger as the bigger threat, Severus proclaimed Albinus his Caesar to secure the west. He then fought a year-long campaign in the east against Niger, finally defeating him at the battle of Issus in May AD 194. Severus then turned his attention to the eastern frontier and the Parthians. However, his plans were curtailed when

news reached him that Albinus had usurped in Britain. Herodian (2.15) is explicit that Severus's earlier appointment of Albinus to be his Caesar was a simple ruse to buy time to defeat Niger. Matters came to a head in autumn of AD 196 when word reached Albinus that Severus now felt secure enough to appoint his elder son Caracalla Caesar, and specifically to be his successor. The British governor saw the writing on the wall and decided to take the initiative, minting his own coins on which he styled himself a full Augustus, and then usurping. The move was popular in Britain, with Herodian (3.7.1) describing scenes of revelry. However, soon sobering news reached him that Severus was on his way to stamp the rebellion out. Albinus moved quickly, gathering his three British legions and a significant number of the auxiliaries from the province. Together they were ferried by the *Classis Britannica* to Gaul. Here Albinus aimed to gather a great army to challenge the emperor.

The *Historia Augusta* (Life of Clodius Albinus, 8.3) details Albinus next survived an assassination attempt by Severus. An experienced soldier who had served in the legions with distinction, the usurper then determined to take the fight to emperor, heading deep into the Gallic interior. After a failed effort to occupy the Rhineland he had the upper hand in a few initial engagements against Severan loyalists, with Herodian (3.7.2) describing minor skirmishers here and there. This rattled Severus who sent his reliable *legate* Virius Lupus, governor of Germania Inferior, with troops from the Rhine to slow Albinus' advance. An engagement took place in central Gaul, with the usurper victorious. Dio says many of Lupus's troops were killed (6.2). Albinus then besieged Trier, though this held out against his hasty attempts to breach its strong walls. He then considered an ambitious plan to force his way into Italy through the Alpine passes, though abandoned this when he learned that Severus had strongly garrisoned them. Albinus now switched targets to one he knew Severus couldn't ignore. This was Lugdunum in the south-west, which had been Severus's provincial capital when governor of Gallia Lugdundensis in the AD 180s.

On arrival Albinus established his capital there, expelling the governor T. Flavius Secundus Philippianus. He then awaited news of Severus, his forces bolstered by the arrival of Lucius Novius Rufus, governor of the Spanish province of Hispania Tarraconensis, together with a legion.

It is at this point we hear the unlikely tale of Numerianus, a former schoolteacher in Rome. For some reason devoted to Severus, unlike much of the Roman political classes who broadly supported Albinus, he set off for Gaul pretending to be a senator on official duty. Gathering a small force on the way he then set about harassing Albinus' army camped around Lugdunum. Dio (76.1) says he achieved some success, killing some of the usurper's cavalry and, more importantly, capturing 70 million *sesterces* (around $210 million in modern money) that he sent to the delighted Severus. The emperor later awarded him a fine country estate and pension for his improbable exploits.

After a short stay in Rome Severus was now ready to advance on Albinus and, sending word to the legions on the Rhine and Danube to join him, chanced a winter passage over the Alpine passes with those troops already with him. He arrived in south-western Gaul in early AD 197 and headed directly for Lugdunum. Matters soon to came to a head.

The size of the armies at Lugdunum has been much debated in recent years. As commonly translated, Dio is very specific here, saying (76.6):

> There were 150,000 soldiers on each side, and both leaders were present in the conflict, since it was a life-and death struggle between them.

That would give an enormous total of 300,000 men engaged. Some have questioned this, arguing that Dio actually meant 150,000 overall but was mistranslated. It is useful here to consider the overall size of the Roman army in the later 2nd century AD. The legions at the time still numbered the 5,500 men each, this established as the norm by Augustus. Under Severus they now totalled 33 after he formed *legios I, II* and *III Parthica* for his first eastern campaign. This would give a normal establishment of 181,500 legionaries. We can add to this a similar number of supporting auxiliaries and naval *milites* to lift the overall military complement at the time of Severus to 363,000 men. Now, given Severus had been campaigning in the east when Albinus usurped and may have drawn troops from each region he passed through on his return, and that Albinus had similarly added troops from Spain to his three British legions, it is feasible that each had an army of 150,000. The truth is we will never know, but even armies of 75,000 each were still huge by ancient world standards.

What we can infer with a degree of certainty is the composition of the two armies, given one was specifically from the east and one west. As detailed, Severus had been campaigning on the eastern frontier when he learned of Albinus' usurpation. The legions there at his disposal included *legio XV Apollinaris* and *legio XII Fulminata* in Cappadocia, *legio IV Scythica*, *legio III Gallica* and *legio XVI Flavia Firm*a in Syria, *legio III Cyrenaica* in Arabia Petraea, and *legio VI Ferrata fidelis constans* and *legio X Fretensis* in Syria Palaestina.

To these we can add his newly formed three *Parthica* legions. It is highly unlikely Severus would have stripped the frontier zone there of his elite troops, so we can expect he instead took *vexillationes* from those not directly engaged on the border, for example those in Syria Palaestina. He also took troops from his three Parthian foundings, perhaps in their entirety.

Travelling east Severus would then have accessed his legions along the Danube, again calling on *vexillationes* if not entire legions to join him. Given his army at Lugdunum is referenced by Herodian as being Illyrian (3.7.3), it seems likely the bulk of his army came from this region. The principal formations here were *legio III Italica concors* in Raetia, *legio II Italica* in Noricum, *legios X Gemina* and XIV *Gemina Martia* in Pannonia Superior (and possibly *legio I Adiutrix pia fidelis*), *legio II Adiutrix pia fidelis* in Pannonia inferior, *legio IV Flavia felix* and *legio VII Claudia pia fidelis* in Moesia Superior, *legio XIII Gemina pia fidelis* in Dacia and *legios I Italica, V Macedonia and XI Claudia pia fidelis* in Moesia Inferior. These were some of the crack legions in the whole Empire, battle hardened in the recent Marcomannic Wars.

A section of the Severan land walls of Roman London, built to remind the elites of the provincial capital who was in charge after the usurpation of Clodius Albinus.

Severus also called on troops from the four legions along the Rhine, these being *legios VIII Augusta* and *XXII Primigenia pia fidelis* in Germania Inferior, and *legios I Minervia pia fidelis* and *XXX Ulpia Victrix* in Germania Superior. As usual, to these legionaries we can add an equivalent numbers of auxiliaries, these also providing the main mounted component of his army. Finally, we know Severus also took the Praetorian Guard with him, these completely reformed by him with Danubian veterans to twice its original size in AD 193, and the imperial guard cavalry.

The *Historia Augusta* calls Albinus' army a 'mighty force' (Life of Clodius Albinus, 8.4). At its core were the three British legions, *legio II Augusta* from Caerleon, *legio XX Valeria Victrix* from Chester and *legio VI Victrix* from York. All were highly experienced, their legionaries frequently campaigning in the unconquered far north of Britain. As detailed above, when he arrived in Gaul Albinus was then joined by a legion from Spain under Rufus, this being *legio VII Gemina*, the only legion stationed in the Iberian Peninsula. This overall force was of legionaries was again joined by an equivalent number of auxiliary foot and horse, the latter numbering 5,000. Albinus may also have called on the urban cohort stationed at Lugdunum, thought to be *cohors 1 Flavia urbana*, where it had earlier been placed by Vespasian to protect the important mint there. The size of Albinus' army is indicated by his first action when arriving in Gaul, ordering the governors of the four Gallic provinces to urgently provide food and money to support his campaign (Herodian, 3.7.1).

The battle of Lugdunum was a two-day affair, with the *Historia Augusta* (Life of Septimius Severus, 11.1) saying that a precursor engagement took place at Tournos (Tinurtium), some 40km north of Lugdunum on the right bank of the River Saône on 18 February. Here Albinus was trying to steer the Severan army away from his new capital but failed. Severus had the better of the engagement, despite falling from his horse. Albinus then withdrew to Lugdunum where Herodian (3.7.2) says the usurper was to remain, leaving his troops to deploy the following day for the main engagement that was fought outside the city walls. Given his

earlier martial prowess, this seems unlikely, and the chances are Albinus led his army in person.

As described by both Dio and Herodian, the main battle was a heavy infantry engagement on a grand scale given a comparative lack of cavalry present, particularly in Albinus' army. The clash was specifically a story of two wings, these dividing the battle line in half rather than it featuring the more traditional centre and two wings.

On his right Severus deployed his more experienced legions and *auxilia*, with the less experienced troops on his left and with the Praetorian Guard and the majority of his cavalry held in reserve under a *legate* called Laetus. Meanwhile Albinus placed the three British legions, his most loyal troops, on his own right. It seems likely his left wing comprised the Spanish legionaries, *auxilia* and the urban cohort.

Severus opened the engagement by advancing his right wing. Soon the legionaries were in light *pilum* range, with volley after volley flying between the two lines, the *auxilia* throwing their *lancea*. Then, as the cohorts closed, the heavier *pila* were thrown at point blank range, clattering against raised scuta. Each legionary now drew his *gladius* and charged

to a shuddering impact. The battle now descended into thousands of individual combats, each warrior seeking a killing blow against his opponent. This was civil war and no quarter was given, the fighting savage and with the *gladii* inflicting fearsome wounds. Eventually the experience and morale of Severus's better troops told, and Albinus' men broke and fled for the safety of Lugdunum. Severus's troops pursued, only stopping when they reached the tents of Albinus' army outside the city walls that they then comprehensively looted.

The battle on Severus's left wing was far different, and almost cost him his life. Here the experienced II *Augusta*, XX *Valeria Victrix* and VI *Victrix* had carefully prepared their position ahead of the battle. Crucially, they had strewn the ground to their front concealed field defences. These included shallow trenches 1.5m deep with rows of sharpened stakes in the bottom, lilies as detailed above for Caesar at Alesia with a sharpened stake in the bottom, and bands of *stimuli* (wooden blocks) embedded in the ground with an iron barb standing proud of the surface.

As Severus's left wing advanced Albinus' legionaries lured them into the trap. Advancing

The Arch of Septimius Severus in the *Forum Romanum* in Rome. Built right next to the *curia* to remind the elites of Rome who the boss was. A contemporary structure with the land walls was built in London for the same reason, to display imperial power.

as far as the field defences, they threw their lighter *pila*. Then, as the Severan troops closed, they pretended to withdraw in disorder. Their opponents broke into a full charge, thinking Albinus' right wing was breaking. The inevitable then occurred, with shocked Severan front rankers falling headlong onto the sharpened stakes and iron barbs amid the concealed field defences. Propelled by the momentum of the charge the second and third ranks followed in short order, adding to the carnage. Stunned rear rankers then shuddered to a halt amid shouts from centurions and *optio*s trying to regain order. Soon the troops on the Severan left wing began to withdraw, but the suddenness of their reverse of fortunes forced those at the very back into a deep defile where many lost their footing. Soon the whole wing was trapped between the field defences to the front and the defile at the back. The British legionaries now crossed their own field defences using pre-layed track ways, reformed on the other side and charged the mass of disordered Severan foot. Heavy *pila* were hurled as they closed, then *gladii* drawn. *Auxilia* archers and slingers joined in, a great slaughter following. Severus, watching in horror from the rear, realised the day might be lost if he didn't act immediately, especially as his victorious wing was still looting the enemy tents. He mounted his charger and personally led the Praetorian Guard to the rescue of his beleaguered left. However, things didn't go according to plan and soon these elite troops found themselves drawn into the maelstrom between the defences and defile. Dio (6.6) says the guard were nearly destroyed, with Severus then losing his horse. The wing broke into full flight, with Herodian (3.7.3) adding the three British legions now began chanting their hymn to victory as they pursued vigorously.

Severus now showed battlefield leadership worthy of Caesar himself. Tearing off his riding cloak, he led his own bodyguard into the mass of routers and slowly, surely started rallying pockets here and there. Dio describes the scene, saying he was (6.7):

... hoping either that they would be ashamed and turn back or that he himself might perish among them. Some indeed did turn back when they saw him in this attitude ....

Eventually he managed to reform a battle line that at last stopped the British legions, now exhausted from their pursuit. Then, slowly but surely, Severus's troops began to push their opponents back.

With its two wings each fighting a separate battle, Lugdunum had to this point many parallels with another decisive encounter of the ancient world, Cynosophelae 197 BC. There Philip V's right wing pushed back Flaminius's left, and the latter's right the Macedonian left. The parallels now continued, with Laetus and his Severan cavalry reserve spotting an opportunity. The Albinian right wing had advanced far proud of where its own now routed left wing had been deployed, and its own left flank and rear were now exposed. Laetus fell on this in a savage charge, butchering the British legions before then could form a defence. The bloody engagement was soon over, with Severus winning a true Pyrrhic victory given the scale of slaughter on both sides. Dio says (7.2):

Many, even the victors, deplored the disaster, for the entire plain was seen to be covered with the bodies of men and horses ... some of them lay there mutilated by many wounds, as if hacked in pieces, and others though unwounded, were piled in heaps, weapons were scattered about, and blood flowed in streams, even pouring into rivers.

Confusion surrounds the fate of Albinus. Dio (7.3) says he sought refuge in a house on the River Rhone where he committed suicide, while the *Historia Augusta* (Life of Clodius Albinus, 9.3) has him either stabbing himself or having a slave do so, but surviving. The usurper, either dead or half alive, was then found by Severus. He was swiftly decapitated, his head sent to Rome and the body ritually desecrated by the emperor who trampled it on his charger. Albinus' family met a similar fate, his sons and mother murdered on Severus's orders, together with any senators unfortunate enough to have chosen the wrong side. Lugdunum itself was sacked and burned, with the Severan dynasty finally secured.

The Battle of Strasbourg

Also known as the battle of Argentoratum, this engagement fought in AD 357 shows the evolution of the legionary into a warrior very different from that of the Principate at its height (this process fully detailed in Chapters 5). Now clad in his thigh-length *lorica hamata* and with flat oval body shield and sturdy ridge helmet or Spangenhelm, he was a spearman fighting in a deep formation not that dissimilar to the Tullian phalanx. He was also joined in the line of battle by new *auxilia* units as good if not better than many of the legionaries, and was also part of a combined arms force, less reliant on heavy foot and with a much larger mounted component.

This battle was the culmination of the war between the western Roman army under the Caesar Julian the Apostate and the Alamanni tribal confederation led their senior king, Chnodomar. The conflict had begun in AD 355 when Julian moved to evict the marauding Germans from Gaul and restore the *limes Germanicus* along the Rhine.

This had been largely destroyed during the civil wars of AD 350–353.

The Alamanni were originally from the Main valley in central Germany. They came into contact with Rome when they colonised the *Agri Decumates* region in modern Baden-Wurttemburg in south-west Germany after this was evacuated by the Romans in the mid-3rd century AD (it had been part of province of Germania Superior for 150 years). In the AD 350s they established a series of cantons on the eastern bank of the Rhine from where they began launching substantial raids across the river into the Empire, taking advantage of the political turmoil there. The level of raiding increased as the decade progressed, and they eventually began to settle on the western side of the river, drawing the attention of the Caesar.

Julian's task was daunting. The preceding civil war had left Gaul in chaos, with many key towns in German hands including Mainz, Worms, Speyer, Saverne, Brumat and Strasbourg. Only Cologne with its massive fortifications, and three other strongpoints on the Rhine, were still under Roman

Elite military technology in the Roman provinces. The Porta Nigra city gate at Trier, note the number of artillery embrasures, built after AD 170.

control. Meanwhile in the interior large bands of Alamanni and other German tribes such as the Franks were roaming the countryside, pillaging at will. Some reached as far as the River Seine.

Julian was ordered to secure the Rhine border by the Augustus Constantius II, his kinsman. The Caesar travelled from Milan where he was given a guard of 300 *Scholae Palatinae* cavalry, a regiment of 600 *equites cataphractarii* (fully armoured lancers), and some bow-armed *equites Sagittarius* (light cavalry). This formed the core of his field army. En route north he then received word that Cologne had fallen, and that all of the regional *limitanei* had been overpowered and destroyed by the Germans.

Julian spent the winter of AD 355/356 in Vienna, in the spring heading north for Reims (*Remi*) where the regional *magister militum* Marcellus had gathered the remaining *comitatenses* units from across Gaul. The Caesar's journey was fraught with danger given it involved a long march through countryside swarming with German raiding parties, all larger than Julian's own mounted escort. He reached Reims though, on the way rescuing Autun from a German force trying to invest the town. This was a particularly important location as it was home to a number of the state-run *fabricae* (manufactories) that made much of the military equipment for the region.

At Reims Julian decided to tackle the Alamanni issue at source by marching north once more, heading directly for the border. He first targeted Alsace, losing one minor engagement on the way and winning another. Reaching the Rhine, he realised his force was too small to take on the main Alamanni force alone. Instead he headed for Cologne to recover it for Rome, finding the town in ruins when he arrived. He set his legionaries and *auxilia* the task of rebuilding the town walls, and then signed a peace treaty with the Franks who had been raiding with the Alamanni. This allowed him to concentrate on the latter.

He spent the winter of AD 356–357 in Sens (*Senones*) near Paris, quartering his troops across the regional towns to spread the burden of their maintenance given the precarious nature of the local economy. The Alamanni heard of this and besieged him in Sens, he only having his cavalry

with him, but they withdrew after a month. He then sacked Marcellus who had failed to come to his aid, replacing him with another senior officer called Severus more favourable to the Caesar.

Constantius, always wary of his cousin, now intervened. A plan was drawn up to trap the Alamanni in eastern Gaul using a pincer movement. In this, Julian would advance eastward from Reims, while a major field army of 25,000 from Italy under the *magister militum* Barbatio would head to Augst (*Augusta Rauracorum*) in Raetia. The idea was to catch the main Alamanni force in Alsace between the two Roman armies.

However large bands of Alamanni ignored the threat and invaded the rich Rhone valley, even trying to take the major regional town of Lyon. This bold move left them trapped in the interior of Gaul, with two Roman armies advancing to their rear. Julian, realising the Germans would try to escape north, despatched squadrons of cavalry to lie in ambush on the three main regional roads. These successfully intercepted and destroyed many of the returning bands of Alamanni. However, in Barbatio's sector the main body of Germans were allowed to pass through unmolested, these reaching the Rhine near Strasbourg where they set up camps on islands in the river. Julian was furious. He immediately headed north and assaulted one of the islands, wiping out the German camp there. The remaining Alamanni now retreated onto the eastern bank, abandoning their remaining island camps and much of the loot they had dragged across the length of Gaul.

Julian now set about rebuilding the fortress at Saverne (*Tres Tabernae*) that had been destroyed by the Germans. This key base sat astride the vital Metz (*Mediomatrici*) to Strasbourg trunk road, the site also commanding the heights overlooking the Rhine valley there. Barbatio meanwhile led his force into an ambush by a strong Alamanni force that had re-crossed the river. His vanguard fled in disarray and the *magister militum* panicked. He ordered his army into a hasty retreat, closely pursued by the Germans. He then completely lost his nerve and headed south across the Alps, aiming to winter in northern Italy. This was despite it being the middle of the campaigning season, leaving Julian to face the entire Alamanni force alone and sabotaging the pincer strategy.

Chnodomar, now free to roam northern Gaul again, targeted Julian's refortification of Saverne. He ordered a mass mobilisation of all the confederation's member tribes that gathered at Strasbourg. With other Germans soon joining, this gave him a large army of around 35,000, including all the other Alamanni kings. He then provoked Julian into action by sending him an ultimatum to evacuate Alsace immediately or be wiped out.

The Caesar's safer option here was to ignore Chnodomar's challenge and keep his troops in their fortified bases until Constantius sent reinforcements. However, he now doubted these would come given Barbatio's earlier performance. In effect he had now become the trapped force rather than the Alamanni. He therefore resolved to fight Chnodomar alone, with the backing of Florentius, the *vicarius* of Galliae who was keen to get his provinces there back under his control.

Julian set out at dawn on a hot August day, leading his army of around 13,000 to within sight of Chnodomar's fortified camp near Strasbourg. He then gave a speech to the men, suggesting they camp overnight and engage the Alamanni the following day when fresh. The troops would have none of it though, demanding immediate action. The Caesar consented and they advanced on the Germans.

Chnodomar now deployed his large army from its camp, choosing to face Julian on a gently sloping hill a few miles from the Rhine where the fields were partly ripe with wheat. The western edge of the site was defined by the Metz-Strasbourg Roman highway, on the far side of which was broken and wooded terrain impassable to Julian's cavalry. The Alamanni left wing was directly commanded by Chnodomar and his own guard cavalry, among whom he scattered lightly armed infantry concealed among the standing wheat. The German right wing sat on the highway, while in the rough terrain beyond the road a further substantial force was hidden in ambush. This wing was commanded by Chnodomar's nephew Serapio. The centre, where the majority of the Alamanni stood atop the crest of the hill, was divided up into various tribes under

their own kings (five major and ten minor such leaders are listed as present by the primary sources).

Julian positioned his infantry in two lines, these widely spaced apart and up to 16 ranks deep (spearmen for the most part, with archers at the rear). The second line would be deployed to exploit any successes, or to counter any enemy breakthroughs on the flanks or to their front.

The front line included troops from four legions, by now differently named from those of the Principate. These were the *Moesiaci, Pannoniaci, Iovani* and *Herculiani,* numbering 4,000 in total. Either side in the same line were deployed units of *auxilia palatina,* including the *Petulantes, Heruli, Cornuti* and *Brachiati,* numbering 2,000 it total. In the rear line was another legion, the *Primani,* numbering 1,000, together with more *auxilia palatina* troops from the *Celtae, Batavi* and *Regae* units, these totalling 2,000 men. On his left flank Julian deployed 2,000 more auxiliaries under Severus across the Metz–Strasbourg road, while on his right he deployed his cavalry including the heavily armoured cataphracts. Julian positioned himself between the two lines of foot.

As soon as the two armies were drawn up the German warriors demanded that Chnodomar and his guards should dismount and lead the Alamanni foot from the centre, which he did. Julian then opened the engagement by sending his horse archers forward to harass the densely packed German warriors to his front. He next ordered his right-wing shock cavalry forward, led by the cataphracts, who charged the German horse. As they entered the wheat fields these were ambushed by the German light troops hiding there, and when the German cavalry counter-charged the Roman horse broke. In their headlong flight they almost hit the Roman right-wing infantry in the first line, but these held their ground and the cavalry were rallied behind the foot by Julian himself.

The Germans, seeing the Roman cavalry on their left run, now charged en masse. Led by Chnodomar and the other Alamanni kings, they repeatedly crashed into the Roman front line of foot. The well-trained legionaries and *auxilia palatina* met each wave in the same way, the spearmen throwing clouds of javelins and darts (see Chapter 5) before setting their spears and shields to meet the Alamanni warriors, bowmen at their rear showering arrows over their heads into the German ranks. Finally, though the pressure told, a wedge of Alamanni led by a number of kings punching through the first Roman line, thousands of Germans pouring through the gap. However, the units either side held firm, and Julian now led the legionaries of the Primani forward from the second line to contain the breach. The move was successful, and the Germans were pushed back. Now exhausted and suffering severe losses, the Alamanni were pushed back, particularly on the wings of the battle line (on the extreme Roman left Severus has already forced the Germans from the field). Pushed into a denser and denser mass, unable to wield their weapons, the Alamanni finally broke and fled the field, many cut down by the pursuing Roman cavalry. A large number tried to swim across the Rhine but many drowned, weighed down by armour or hit by Roman missiles. Around 8,000 perished on the battlefield, and many more in the river. Julian lost just over 200, making this a great victory for the Caesar. Chnodomar was later captured, dying in Rome from disease a 'barbarian' prisoner.

This battle shows the field army legionaries and *auxilia palatina* of the late Dominate at the height of their powers. Once again discipline was a key to their success, with the first line of foot standing firm firstly when the Roman right-wing cavalry broke, and then when the same line was pierced by repeated German attacks. Once that occurred, the second line also remained steady, advancing to plug the gap and ensuring ultimate victory. Just as with the legions of the Principate, the élan of these later Roman warriors won the day.

Guerrilla Warfare

Finally, here I show how the legionaries and *auxilia* of Rome defeated opponents who specifically avoided a meeting engagement through the use of guerrilla tactics, a common occurrence in the Principate and Dominate.

Roman military might had such a fearsome reputation that often their opponents chose not to stand up to them in a set-piece battle but instead engaged them in guerrilla warfare. For example, as detailed above, such asymmetrical conflict was a key feature of the Severan campaigns of AD 209 and AD 210 in Scotland, offering an intriguing glimpse of how the Roman military countered this style of conflict. Both of these campaigns were grim for all of the protagonists. The weather was worse than usual, even in the far north of the islands of Britain, and the terrain proved particularly difficult for the Romans fighting the Maeatae and Caledonian confederations. These proved a desperate opponent, with their guerrilla tactics telling '... against the Romans and prolonged the war' according to Herodian (3.14). They were clearly far better suited to a life of living rough in their indigenous terrain when required, with Herodian adding that they dispensed with breast plates and helmets 'which would impede their movement through the marshes.'

These references illustrate the guerrilla warfare used by the native British opposition and it is perhaps useful to look elsewhere chronologically and geographically for analogies to see how the legionaries would have responded. The Roman military was well experienced to fighting such campaigns, particularly in Britain given the asymmetry when comparing their own forces to those of the natives (not the case against the Parthians and later Sassanid Persians in the east for example). This would also have been the case for Severus in North Africa earlier in his reign when he engaged the Garamantes tribe there who were similarly symmetrically disadvantaged against the Romans, and this previous campaign would certainly have made an impression on the emperor, the lessons learned later being deployed in Scotland.

Roman military textbooks detail how to conduct such a specialist style of warfare, for example former British 1st-century AD warrior governor Frontinus (1.6.3) explaining in his *Strategemata* how to deal with ambushes using classical world examples:

> When Iphicrates was leading his army in Thrace in a long file on account of the nature of the terrain, and the report was

brought to him that the enemy planned to attack his rear-guard, he ordered some cohorts to withdraw to both flanks and halt, while the rest were to quicken their pace and flee. But from the complete line as it passed by, he kept back all the choicest soldiers. Thus, when the enemy were busy with promiscuous pillaging, and in fact were already exhausted, while his own men were refreshed and drawn up in order, he attacked and routed the foe and stripped them of their booty.

What seems clear from these primary sources is that, despite the difficulties pinning down their opponents (who were clearly fighting for survival in the case of Severus in Scotland), the Romans always adapted to the tactics being used against them. Such adaption to the circumstances was one of the great characteristics of the Roman military,

relying on their sophisticated organization, training, élan and well-organised supply system to eventually give them an advantage in all kinds of warfare, including against an opponent who avoided confrontation. In particular, the legionaries would destroy the local economy employing slash and burn tactics to deprive the natives of their homes and food. In the AD 210 campaign in Scotland this reached its peak with Severus's order to kill all the natives the legionaries and *auxilia* came across. Thus, while things were grim for the Romans in these campaigns, they overcame the adversity and ensured that the discomfort felt by all levels of native northern British society (whose local economy was destroyed in the first year of campaigning) was far more brutal.

Julian the Apostate, victor of the battle of Strasbourg in AD 357 when Caesar in the western Empire. (Livius.org/Jona Lendering)

CHAPTER 7 †
NON-CONFLICT ROLES OF THE ROMAN MILITARY

A *beneficiarii* seconded from the legions to serve on the staff of a provincial governor or *procurator*, helping administer the Empire. Note his writing tablet. (Graham Sumner)

The legionaries, and later *auxilia* and naval *milites* of Rome, were not just warriors. They were also administrators, policemen, fire fighters, helped run agriculture and industry, and were outstanding engineers and builders. In this chapter I consider them in all of these roles, with a particular focus on engineering and construction.

Administration

The main political force in the Roman Republic and later the Empire was the state. This was intricately involved in every economic activity, usually geared to supporting its own continuance and infrastructure. In both Republic and Empire, it was a patrician institution with responsibilities including political, economic and social roles that were often related. To carry these out, in an age before a civil service, nationalised industries and a free market economy able to fund major capital expenditure projects, the Roman state turned to the only tool at its disposal, namely the military. This was the largest institution within the Republic and Empire, and it was in this capacity that the Roman military was the central instrument used to ensure the smooth running of the Roman system of government.

Such administrative activities would have been a key function for the military in a given province, in both Republic and Empire. This was because, as set out in Chapter 3, even when combining the governor and later *procurator*'s staffs together, there were only 80 or less senior officials to run the province. As administrators the military would have been at their most visible in a newly conquered territory where they exercised very wide powers. These included the ability to carry out summary justice and to impose restrictions on the movement of the native population. It is at this early stage of occupation that we also see the legionaries in particular overtly operating as administrators for the first time in the new land. This was in their capacity as skilled military land surveyors, able to

quickly survey the new territory. This allowed a rapid assessment of its likely contribution to the state treasury.

In the late Republic and Principate phase of Empire, legionaries of all ranks could then be seconded to the governor's own *officium consularis*, the main body used to govern a province. As set out in Chapter 3 these were called *beneficiarii consularis* and helped bolster his staff given the limited number of civilians at his disposal for such roles. Governors also often deployed such *beneficiarii* to command the operation of way stations on the major trunk routes of the Empire. Here they acted as the governor's local representative, fulfilling a variety of roles including the enforcement of tax collection, escorting officials and controlling traffic.

The *beneficiarii* were also employed more broadly in administrative roles across the provinces by governors. We have a number of very specific examples in the historical record and epigraphy, for example in Britain. These include the cavalry prefect Titus Haterius Nepos who is detailed carrying out a census in Annandale in Dumfries and Galloway around AD 117. Other examples include centurions such as T. Floridius Natalis of the *legio VI Victrix* performing the role of regional administrator at Ribchester, and C. Severius Emeritus of *legio II Augusta* who performed a similar role in Bath. In such roles they ensured the efficient operation of the state's administrative system.

The legions of the late Republic and Empire also included their own administrative specialists in addition to the *beneficiarii* seconded to the

(previous pages)
Stacks of voussoir arches in the Colosseum, Rome. Built by the Roman military for the Flavian emperors.

governor's staff. Such clerical legionaries were drawn from the ranks and performed roles within the legions that included keeping grain store records and managing the financial accounts of the troops. Called *immunes librarii*, they can be found across the Empire, for example Septimius Licinius of the *legio II Parthica* who set up a commemoration to a daughter in Albano, Italy, and Marcus Uplius Firminus who similarly set up an inscription in Torda in modern Romania (*Potaissa*).

Policing

Legionaries were also used in a policing capacity in the late Republic and Empire. This is most evident in the east. Here, the legions were often located near major urban centres such as Alexandria. For example, in the Principate phase of Empire, the two-legion garrison of Egypt was based at the legionary fortress of *Nikopolis*, close to the provincial capital. Meanwhile, the *Classis Alexandrina* was based in

the city itself. Given their size, such cities often experienced turbulent unrest and the military presence there was frequently deployed to restore order with violent force.

Elsewhere in the Principate phase of Empire, for example in Britain, we also see the proximity of the military to a civilian population reflected in the context of policing. A prime example is the Cripplegate *vexillation*-size fort in London, built during the reign of Hadrian as a response (it has recently been argued) to some kind of insurrection. Another example presents in northern Italy where Emperor Tiberius sent a cohort of legionaries to deal with an unspecified scandalous incident in the town of Pollentia. The troops surrounded the town and imprisoned most of the adult population who were then given life sentences in prison. Meanwhile a praetorian cohort was similarly used by Nero to stamp out insurrection in Pozzuoli (Puteoli) in Campania in AD 58. The military was also of course the force deployed to deal with slave revolts.

Tiberius for example dispatched a force to deal with such an incident in southern Italy in AD 24.

It was also the norm for legionaries to carry out other types of policing role in addition to using brute force to keep the late Republic and Empire's peace. Whether reporting to the governor or local magistracy, we have direct evidence for these military personnel being so deployed. For example, a document from Egypt dated AD 207 details a centurion named Aurelius Julius Marcellinus being contacted by a woman called Aurelia Tisais who claimed her father and brother had been murdered on a hunting trip. Another document, dated AD 193, has a centurion called Ammonius Paternus being contacted by a man known as Syros with regard to the abuse of tax collection.

In all of these roles the legionaries bolstered the regular urban gendarmerie. In the cities and towns of the Empire these were called *cohorts urbanae*, of which Rome had six cohorts, and *vigiles urbani* (city watchmen).

Firefighting

Firefighting was another public function of the late republican and Principate legionary, again usually in the context of deployment in the urban environment. Prime examples were the two cohorts permanently stationed at Ostia to guard against fire at the key port facilities there. This was an essential function for the warriors given the vital grain supply to Rome that transited from merchant ship to River Tiber there. Again, the legionaries bolstered other firefighting resources, particularly the *vigiles urbani*.

The Colosseum, where naval *milites* from the *Classis Misinensis* operated the *vela* sail awnings.

A typical Principate *muli mariani* (Marius' mule), as the legionaries were nicknamed given the load they carried when on campaign. This veteran is carrying his entire kit. (Graham Sumner)

The Military and the Games

The *milites* of the regional fleets were also deployed in a very specific civilian context to facilitate the smooth running of the games in the arenas of the Empire, particularly around the Mediterranean and in the east. This is with regard to their use in operating the *vela* (sail awnings) in arenas such as the Colosseum in Rome, which provided vital shade against the hot sun. Detachments from the Italian *Classis Ravennate* and *Classis Misinensis* were permanently stationed in Rome for this purpose, clearly a prestige appointment for these naval *milite*s. Such a role may occasionally have been slightly less savoury however, with Commodus known to have called on these sailors to punish the crowd on occasion, emphasising that even when deployed within a civilian context the military were still 'other' when compared to the rest of society.

Agriculture and Industry

Roman troops of all kinds also played a key role in agricultural and industrial enterprises in the late Republic and Empire. Their experience of both is detailed here.

In the first they needed to be fed, both when in camp and on campaign. Even in the case of the former, considerable effort was needed to supply the garrisoned troops. To that end the land around each permanent fortification was turned over to providing the supplies needed to feed the troops. This was a substantial task considering the large size of many Roman military formations. The troops ate two set meals per day, the *prandium* (breakfast) and the *cena* (evening meal), with the staple diet being that set out in Chapter 2.

It should be noted here that when considering the permanent garrisons of the Roman military, we are not just talking about the troops themselves. The legionaries and other troop types did not live in isolation but were always part of their own wider community. Many civilians lived alongside them, through both choice and obligation. When the military were stationed in their permanent bases such civilians (up to 200,000 by some calculations in Britain for example) most often resided in the surrounding *vicus* (settlements) (or *canabae* in the context of a legionary fortress). These featured all of the trades and supporting activities needed to

The town walls of the Roman civitates capital at Caerwent (*Venta Silurum*), with a bastion in view. All built by *legio II Augusta*.

A section of the town wall at Caerwent, showing how it was constructed with well-worked facing stone on the outside and a rubble core.

maintain the regional military presence, including those engaged in agriculture. It is therefore likely that even if the troops were directly engaged in agriculture to provide their own subsistence (at the very least through its management), they would have been part of this wider community.

However, it was when on campaign that the Roman military machine really swung into action in terms of subsistence, it being crucial to ensure the troops were sustained well enough to be at their martial best. Provisioning was carried out through three types of base – supply bases provisioned by the provincial governor (for example South Shields, Cramond and Carpow in the context of the Severan campaigns in Scotland), operational bases and tactical bases. The latter were often the marching camps described in Chapter 2, and it was not uncommon for those not slighted after their initial use to be converted into supply depots, often becoming permanent fortifications in this capacity. Meals were taken in the marching camps again in the morning and evening, though with the latter taking priority given the usual necessity for an early start. The legionaries and their supporting troops were required on campaign to carry three

days' worth of rations whose nature depended on the location of the campaign, with the supplies requisitioned from the surrounding populace/ countryside when the supply chain was stretched. The principal difference when on campaign to the diet in garrison seems to have been a switch in the use of the grain ration, from making bread to making the *bucellatum* (army biscuit).

Meanwhile, in addition to engaging in agriculture for their own subsistence, the Roman state also deployed the legionaries and other supporting troops to run agriculture imperial estates in the Principate and Dominate phases of Empire (land owned specifically by the emperor). These were particularly extensive in the east where they tracked crown land previously owned by earlier Hellenistic rulers. However, one of the better examples showing military involvement in the running of agricultural imperial estates is actually in Britain. This is Stonea in the Fens in East Anglia where there is evidence that after the Boudiccan revolt the region remained comparatively under-developed given the depopulation and economic turbulence after the rebellion (see Chapter 6). The state was therefore keen to use the military here to set things on a satisfactory course, especially given much of the land (some poor quality) would have needed careful management to bring it up to an acceptable standard for profitable agriculture. The military then remained throughout the occupation, with evidence of such a presence including military belt fittings and silver and gilt crossbow-type brooches (the latter late Roman and often associated with the military).

Turning to industry, a responsibility particularly associated with the Roman military was managing *metalla* enterprises. This is a catch all Roman term for any form of extractive industry, for example quarrying and mining. In the late Republic and Empire such activity was often on an epic scale. Given their importance to the economy, the state repeatedly turned to the military to ensure continuity of the supply of mined and quarried material from these enterprises.

In the south-east of Britain there are two overt examples of the military running such *metalla* during the Principate phase of Empire. These were in upper Medway Valley and the Weald in the south-east of the province. The former featured an intensive ragstone quarrying industry where five enormous quarries upriver of the tidal reach provided much of the building stone for the region (particularly London) from around AD 50 through to the middle of the 3rd century AD. It has recently been argued that given the scale involved the military would certainly have played a role here. Meanwhile, with regard to the Weald, this was the location of a widespread iron manufacturing industry making use of regionally mined iron ore, with the larger manufactories being located near the coast. This industry provided much of the iron needed for the Roman military in Britain for the same period of time as the nearby ragstone quarrying industry, with the state presence here the *Classis Britannica*.

Engineering and Construction

Perhaps the best-known non-conflict role of the Roman legionaries and their supporting troops was engineering and construction. The output of this expertise is evident across the Empire, whether in the form of the Roman road network, canals and canalised rivers, bridges, aqueducts, fortifications, public buildings or the wider built environment. Such projects were facilitated by the military both at a grass roots level by individual soldiers, and also by specialists. Both are considered here, with a focus specifically on the late republican and principate legionary.

The legionaries themselves were skilled engineers in their own right, with building and engineering playing an enormous part of their working life. To enable the warriors to fulfill such a roll, in addition to their panoply of fighting equipment, each legionary carried the engineering equipment detailed in Chapter 2.

When larger construction projects were undertaken by the legionaries it was common for manpower to be drawn from a variety of different units, for example the *vexillationes* from *legio II Augusta, legio VI Victrix* and *legio XX Valeria*

Roman military engineering deep in a mountain stream valley on the Sorrentine Peninsula. The *Aqua Augusta* provided water to aqueducts supplying water to all of the urban centres in the Roman Bay of Naples. (Author in view)

Victrix who all participated in the construction of Hadrian's Wall. Here, each legion was responsible for a specific stretch of wall construction. Such work entailed backbreaking hard physical labour, and a further example provides insight here through experimental archaeology. This is with regard to road building, a common task for the legionary. Work by the Royal School of Military Engineering in the UK has highlighted the sheer physicality of the work involved. They found it would have taken 40 man-hours to build 100m of roadway over grass, 450 over heathland and 600 through forest.

The legions of the later Republic and Principate also included specialist pioneer military engineers, and a large number of specialist craftsman, engineers and administrators (see above) attached to larger units, these including highly experienced surveyors, architects and builders. The pioneers fulfilled the same role as their counterparts in subsequent military formations throughout history. When on the march through enemy territory, these troops were tasked with forging ahead of the marching column to clear the path of the advance and, as the day's march neared its end, prepare for the construction of the marching camp. The legionaries then joined in the work as they arrived.

However, it is the specialist legionaries who are of most interest here. Each legion contained a very wide range of artisan skills and crafts. The primary sources say these includex ditch diggers, farriers, pilots, master builders, shipwrights, ballista makers, glaziers, arrow makers, bow makers, smiths, coppersmiths, helmet makers, wagon makers, foot-tile makers, water engineers, swordcutlers, trumpet makers, horn makers, plumbers, blacksmiths, masons, woodcutters, limeburners, charcoal burners, butchers, huntsmen, sacrificial animal keepers, grooms and tanners. All such specialist legionaries were dubbed *immunes* – soldiers exempted from general duties because of their skills.

Additionally, specialist military personnel in the

Legionary barrack blocks as they would have appeared at the Roman legionary fortress in York. (Graham Sumner)

legions also included *agrimensores* (land surveyors), *libratores* (land levelers) and *mensores* (quantity measurers). Further, in the case of the military building aqueducts, an *aqualegus* (aqueduct inspector) would participate. These legionaries were the supreme surveyors of the ancient world, putting the stamp of Rome in a very physical way everywhere they went. Highly skilled professionals, they used a number of tools, instruments, and techniques to plan the settlements, farmland, courses for roads and aqueducts and fortifications that were an everyday part of the experience of living within the Roman Empire.

The legionary expertise in surveying was an amalgam of the experience gained or acquired as the Republic, and later the Principate, expanded and integrated new cultures. Whether building roads of epic scale or creating new stone-built planned settlements, the legionary *agrimensores, libratores* and *mensores* used a panoply of advanced technical equipment that ensured the quality and accuracy of the work. This included:

- The *decempeda*, a graduated measuring rod of 10 Roman feet with iron or bronze caps at either end. This was the principal tool of the surveyor.
- The *groma*, a vertical staff with a tapered end. This featured at the top horizontal cross-pieces mounted at right angles onto a bracket. Each had a plumb line with bob attached hanging vertically from each end, the tool being used to survey straight lines and right angles.
- The *chorobates*, a Roman spirit level featuring a long wooden frame with vertical legs, plumb bobs, a water level in a channel carved in the top and sightlines to assist finding the true horizontal.
- The *dioptra*, a circular table fixed to a tripod calibrated with angles, originally invented in Greece. This was the forerunner of modern surveying equipment, used when even greater accuracy was required than that provided by the *chorobates*, or when a gradient was too steep to use the *groma*.
- The *libra*, a further means of measuring

gradients, thought to be a set of scales with a sighting tube.

- The *hodometer*, an advanced tool for measuring distance. This consisted of a small cart which the surveyor would push along featuring a one-toothed gear which was attached to the cart wheel, this engaging another gear featuring 399 short teeth and one longer tooth. Once the cart had travelled a distance of one Roman mile the long tooth pushed a pebble into a bowl, allowing the surveyor to count the distance travelled at the end of each day of surveying a new route.

The output of these specialist legionaries in terms of engineering and construction are too numerous to detail here, so I will choose one example to show all such specialists at their working best. This is with regard to the legionary fortress that played such a key role in the life of the legionary. I use that at York to provide specific detail.

York was a Roman founding, owing its existence to the Roman conquest campaigns following the AD 43 invasion. Our protagonist here is the Cerialis we last saw in disgrace following the Boudiccan revolt. By AD 71 he was back in imperial favour following his recent putting down of the Batavian Revolt of Julius Civilis in the Rhine Delta. As a reward he was made the governor of Britannia, tasked by Emperor Vespasian with securing the north from the local Brigantes tribe, the erstwhile Roman allies last mentioned in Chapter 2.

The primary sources say that Cerialis immediately headed north upon arrival, in the first instance ordering the veteran *legio IX Hispana* (with whom he had been disgraced in AD 60/61) out of its legionary fortress at Lincoln into Yorkshire where the troops constructed a new fortress on the northern bank at the point where they crossed the River Ouse. This was a particularly defensible position as the spot chosen was where the tributary River Foss runs into the Ouse, providing riverine protection on two flanks. It was here that the legionary *agrimensores, libratores* and *mensores* laid out the plan of the new fortress, using their

The Multangular Tower, a later Roman fortification at the legionary fortress in York, at that time the home of *legio VI Victrix*.

The south-western stone-built wall of the legionary fortress at York, built by *legio VI Victrix*.

decempedae, gromae, chorobates, dioptra, librae and *hodometers*.

Once the site had been surveyed the construction specialists got to work. Here the master builders managed an operation featuring a wide range of their *immunes* colleagues, including masons, woodcutters, limeburners, charcoal burners, plumbers, blacksmiths, ditch diggers, roof-tile makers, water engineers and glaziers. Raw muscle was provided by the non-specialist legionaries in the legion, the *auxilia* and the local population. The legionaries, specialists and otherwise, used a wide variety of equipment in the primary construction phase. At the most basic these included:

- Ropes, made in a variety of different ways to create elasticity, allowing them to be used not only for binding and pulling but also as a spring to conserve energy.
- Pulleys, used to gear force.
- Winches, mounted either horizontally or vertically. In the case of the former they could be utilised by turning the outward spokes of a horizontally positioned wheel using men or oxen. For the vertically mounted types of winch men only were used (though certainly not legionaries) to tread on the inside of the vertically positioned wheel.

The application of these basic units in various combinations allowed the creation of the wide variety of machinery used by the legionaries and others for construction projects. Such machinery included cranes and hoists to lift heavy materials to great heights, scaffolding, mills of all sizes to ground the raw materials to make mortar, trusses of ceramics or wood, and pile drivers to drive stakes and piles into the ground.

One good example of such technology is the tread wheel crane (called the *Polyspaston* by the Romans) that used the vertically mounted winch gearing detailed above. Of wooden construction, this crane was human powered by individuals actually inside the tread wheel, with the ropes attached to a pulley system that turned onto a spindle through the rotation of the wheel, allowing the crane to hoist or lower very heavy loads. A fine example of such a crane is depicted on a tomb near the Porta Maggiore in Rome. This substantial lifting device is shown actually being built. Meanwhile, if the load needing to be lifted was actually larger than the capacity of the treadwheel crane, a wooden lifting tower was built featuring a rectangular trestle designed such that the material needing to be lifted could be carried upright through the middle of the structure using human- or animal-powered capstans on the ground around the tower.

Back to York, in short order the fortress was completed. It was now that the other legionary immunes came into their own as they set up their operations to help facilitate the running of the legion. These included the farriers, pilots, shipwrights, ballista makers, arrow makers, bow makers, smiths, coppersmiths, helmet makers, wagon makers, swordcutlers, trumpet makers, horn makers, butchers, huntsmen, sacrificial animal keepers, grooms and tanners. *Legio IX Hispana* was soon at home and would stay until the early 2nd century AD when it was replaced by the *legio VI Victrix* in AD 122. An associated *canabae* also developed opposite the new legionary fortress on the south bank of the river.

The original fortress on the site in York was classically playing-card shape and very large, enclosing an area of over 20 ha and able to easily host the 5,000 or so men of the resident legion. Its original defences were a ditch and 3m high turf/clay rampart topped by a palisade, together with wood-built towers and gates. From around AD 150 however the whole was replaced by a stone-built structure with a tile bonding layer, this a common design visible across the Empire as far afield as the fortifications in London, Richborough, Rome and Constantinople. As the occupation progressed the defences increased in sophistication, ultimately featuring a string of defensive towers or bastions such as the Multangular tower visible today next to the modern Yorkshire Museum in what would have been the south-west corner of the fortress.

As with all legionary fortresses, that at York had three uses:

- To provide accommodation for the men and equipment of its resident legion.
- To protect the legion if their base was attacked. The sophistication of the defences were designed from the outset to discourage such an eventuality.
- To act as a base for the legion and other military units to initially suppress and then conquer its enemies.

Inside the fortress at York, in all its iterations, was a grid pattern of streets and buildings, showing the sophistication of the surveying and construction expertise of the legionaries who originally built the site. The four corners were positioned at the points of the compass, facing north, south, east and west, hence the playing-card shape. The principal streets within the fortress were called the *via principalis* (main street) and the *via praetoria*. The four *portae* (gates) to the fortress gave access to the main roads and still correlate with the modern entrances to the city. One gave access to Ermine Street, the great northern road linking York with London, while another gave access to Dere Street, the road north into Scotland.

At the centre of the fortress, dividing the *via praetoria* and with the *via principalis* passing across its front, was the parade ground featuring the *principia* (headquarters) building which housed the senior base commander and his staff. On one side of this parade ground, perpendicular to the *principia* itself, stood an associated basilica (great aisled hall). The scale of the latter, certainly from the time of Septimius Severus's arrival when he made the town his imperial capital, was immense given the size of the single column recovered in 1969 during excavations of the structure. At 68m long, 32m wide and 23m high, this basilica would have stood just short of the modern height of today's York Minster. Such a size for the rebuilt basilica (the *principia* itself would similarly have been restyled at the time of Severus's stay) would certainly reflect the use of the legionary fortress and its extensive *canabae* as the imperial capital while Severus prepared for his assault in the north.

From the *principia* the legion at York was administered and its religious ceremonies performed, while it was from the *tribunal* (podium) at one end of the adjacent basilica that the commanding officer (and later Severus as emperor) would have addressed his troops and received visiting dignitaries. Meanwhile, in the *principia* itself a row of rooms would have served as offices, with the central one being the *aedes* that was the legionary shrine and the spiritual heart of the fortress. It was here that the legionary standards were kept. The *aedes* also had a more practical function in that beneath its floor sat a vault in which was kept the legionary pay chest. There is no doubt that, even before any Severan expansion, the *principia* with its grand basilica at the legionary fortress in York would have been astonishing to the people of the area, a true statement of the power of Rome in the furthest dark north-west of the Empire. From the time of Severus, it would have been even grander.

Other buildings in close proximity to the *principa* included the *praetorium*, the commanding officer's house that was built in the same manner as a fine town house, this being used by him for business as well as domestic purposes. Meanwhile, also around the central parade ground (and again next to the principia to provide ease of access) was the building that housed the legionary supply

officer. The rest of the fortress interior was packed out with a wide variety of buildings and structures, some stone built and some wooden, set out in a regularised pattern such that any incumbent in the fortress would know as a matter of fact where every amenity was. Such buildings included a large number of barracks to house the troops, granaries to feed them, workshops to manufacture and maintain all of their equipment, a hospital and a bathhouse. The latter was a very important feature of the Roman cultural experience and served to remind many of the troops of their Mediterranean roots, at least early in the occupation. One can imagine how popular the bathhouse, with its piping hot steam rooms, would have been in the heart of a northern British winter to the legionaries of *legio IX Hispana* and later *legio VI Victrix*. The actual legionary bathhouse at York was located in the southern corner of the fortress during excavations in 1972 which uncovered an associated Roman sewer, this helping identify that it occupied an area of 9,100m².

A mystery surrounds one final key building associated with the Roman legionary fortress in York. This is its missing amphitheatre. These iconic Roman structures are often found in close proximity to fortifications of some kind. Examples in Britain include the fine amphitheatres at the legionary fortresses at Caerleon and Chester, and that at the *vexillation* fort at Cripplegate in London. However, one has yet to be found in York, although experts believe its remains are there but obscured by the modern built environment.

One can see from the above description of this complex fortification in York that the legionaries played the key role at every step of its construction and use. These elite warriors were thus the reason it was built, the means by which it was constructed, its inhabitants and ultimately its defenders, providing a superb example of the legionary as an engineer and builder.

(*opposite*)
Painted wall plaster from the *praetorium* of the legionary fortress in York, now on display in situ beneath the modern York Minster.

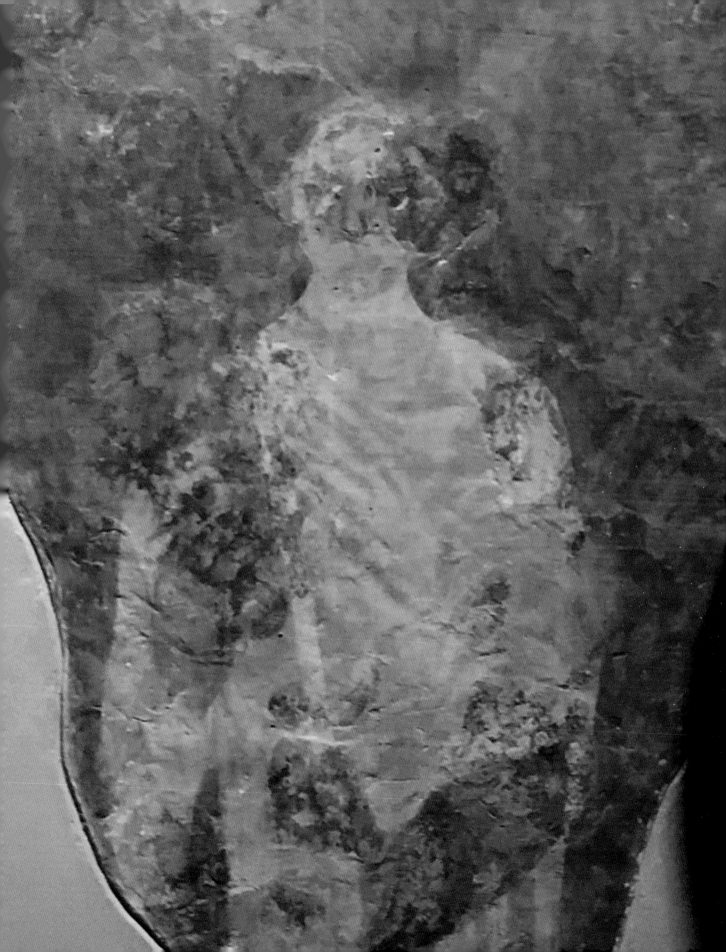

CHAPTER 8 ✝
ALLIES AND ENEMIES OF ROME

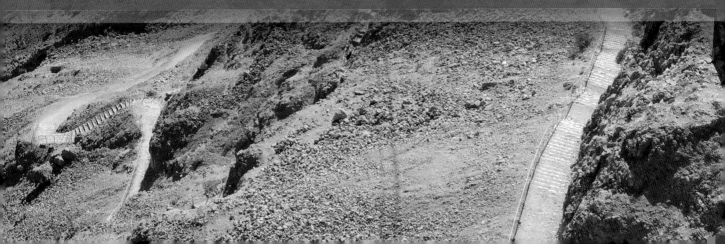

The ruins of the Roman
citadel at Histria, in the
Dobrogea region of modern
Romania.
(Getty Images)

Throughout this book the various allies and enemies of the Roman Republic and Empire have been referenced in the context of the Roman military establishment, and also the various campaigns and battles it fought. To provide further context, in this chapter I set out in detail the key allies and enemies at more length. For ease of access I do this geographically rather than chronologically, moving generally from west to east.

The Britons

The military system of the native Britons fought first by Caesar, and later by the Empire in its initial campaigns of conquest when creating the province of Britannia, and later in the far north in its various attempts to conquer or pacify the tribes there, remained the same for most of Rome's presence in the islands.

By the 1st century BC, the main island of Britain, in which Rome later carved its province, featured a dense network of tribes who were often at war with each other. Beginning in modern Kent and heading roughly clockwise, these included the Cantiaci, the Trinovantes to their north in eastern Essex, the Catuvellauni in western Essex through to Oxfordshire, the Atrebates in the Thames Valley, and the Regni and Belgae on the south coast. In the south-west were the Durotriges and Dumnonii, with the Dubonni and Cornovii to their north reaching into the Welsh Marches. Into Wales proper were the Silures, Demetae, Ordovices and Deceangli ranging south to north, with the Brigantes in the north of modern England, the Carvetii in the north-west, the Parissi north of the Humber, Coritani south of the Humber and Iceni in modern north Norfolk.

Heading into modern Scotland, the scene of so much campaigning during the Roman occupation of the south, the tribes there included the Votadini in the eastern Scottish Borders, the Selgovae in the central Borders, the Novantae in the western Borders, the Dumnonii around the Clyde, and the Epidii in the Mull of Kyntire. Then above the Clyde on the west coast, going south to north, the Creones, the Carnonacae and (at the far north-western tip of Scotland) the Caereni. On the east coast around the River Tay were the Venicones, and above them in Aberdeenshire, the Vacomagi and Taexali. Broadly, throughout the Grampians, were located the Caledonii, then around the Moray Firth, again going south to north, the Decantae, Lugi, Smertae and finally the Cornacii. As detailed in earlier chapters, many of these tribes had coalesced into two huge confederations by the end of the 2nd century AD, the Maeatae either side of the Clyde–Forth line, and above them the Caledonians. Late in the Roman occupation of Britain the Picts then came to dominate the far north of Scotland down into the Midland Valley. Additionally, the Romans also interacted with the various Scots Irish peoples of modern Ireland across the Irish Sea.

As experienced by Julius Caesar in his two incursions in 55 BC and 54 BC, Aulus Plautius in the AD 43 Claudian invasion and Gaius Suetonius Paulinus against Boudicca, native British armies featured a chariot-riding aristocracy, skirmishing cavalry riding ponies, short spear-armed line-of-battle warriors, and sling- or javelin-armed skirmishing foot troops.

In terms of army size, given few native British troops were professional warriors, various sized gatherings are reported in contemporary history. For example, when Cassivellaunus, likely the tribal leader of the Catuvellauni, fought Caesar he fielded 4,000 chariots at one stage, having sent the rest of his forces home. However, given he was

(*previous pages*)
The defender's view at Masada of the Roman siege works and marching camps. (Steve Tibble)

Roman *equites* practising
to fight the many enemies
of the Empire. (Graham
Sumner)

the leader of all resistance to Caesar in the south-east of Britain, it has been estimated he could have led up to 80,000 men. Meanwhile, as set out above, Boudicca could have led a force of 230,000, including 100,000 warriors in her incendiary insurrection. However, at the other end of the scale the Caledonians who fought Agricola at Mons Graupius in AD 83 only numbered 30,000 and were easily defeated by the Roman *auxilia* alone.

The elite troops in native British armies were the chariot-riding nobility, these reported in many engagements through to the 5th century AD (the latter in the context of the Scots Irish and Picts). They were most popular among the tribes in the south-east and east of the main island of Britain but were used throughout the British Isles given the status they bestowed on the chariot rider. Native British chariots featured two ponies harnessed with a yoke and breaststraps to a draft pole, a wooden fighting platform with wicker sides, and two wheels on a centrally mounted axle. They featured two crewmembers, these being an unarmed driver and the noble. The latter carried a Gallic shield that was either oval, oval with the upper and lower ends removed or round with a central boss. All were of plank construction. The noble also wore various kinds of Gallic helmet and a chainmail hauberk. He was armed with javelins and the long iron Gallic slashing sword. Caesar, Dio and Tacitus all describe these native chariots in action, all reporting how manoeuvrable they were and saying the Britons deliberately rode them across the front of an enemy battle line which they showered with javelins and insults. The noble then often jumped down to fight on foot, leading his own war band.

Meanwhile, British cavalry were much lighter than their Gallic counterparts described later. They acted in a supporting role to the chariots. Specifically, they skirmished with javelins, attacked flanks and pursued routers. When used in conjunction with the chariots they proved a particular nuisance for Caesar in his two incursions to Britain.

By far the biggest component of native British armies were their line-of-battle spearmen. These were mostly farmers who were called up in a mass levy when needed, they armed in a similar manner to their Gallic neighbours. The main defensive equipment was the Gallic shield, or a simpler wicker and hide design. Few wore helmets and fewer any form of armour. The main weapon was a light spear or javelin, with some troops also armed with the long Gallic slashing sword or a dagger. In Britain these warriors formed a spear wall if required, usually in a strong defensive position as with those opposing Plautius in his river crossing battle in Kent in AD 43, and the Caledonians deploying on the steep slopes of Mons Graupius in AD 83. However, the preferred tactic was the use of natural terrain to ambush their opponents, often as part of a guerilla campaign. The Maeatae and Caledonian confederations fighting Septimius Severus in AD 209 and AD 210 provide a good example of this.

In Britain the favoured missile weapon used by skirmishers was the sling, particularly in the south-west. The Durotriges and Dumnonii tribes who fought Vespasian are a good example of this. Javelin armed skirmishers are also reported, though no bowmen.

The only major change in the nature of the opponents the Romans fought in Britain came in the form of the Picts who appear from the later 3rd century AD, gradually taking over the territory in the north of Scotland. Picts are first mentioned in contemporary history by the writer Eumenius in AD 297, the name referencing their propensity for body tattoos and painting themselves in woad. They were not a single tribe, but rather a confederation, as with the earlier Maeatae and Caledonians. Their armies continued to use light chariots and skirmishing light cavalry, but many of their infantry were differentially armed when compared to their predecessors. The most obvious change was a switch to a different shield design over time, these made of hide stretched across two crossed sticks held together at the juncture. Many are depicted in Pictish artwork, usually carvings on stone monuments, and are shown as small square or round designs. Axes also feature as side arms on the carvings, as do bowmen.

The Attacotti, a people who frequently fought with the Picts, are worth a final mention. Of possible Scots Irish descent, these fierce warriors are mentioned by late Roman historians such as Ammianus Marcellinus in campaigns such as the Great Conspiracy in AD 367, when a coordinated campaign by Picts, Attecotti, Scots Irish and Germanic raiders almost overwhelmed the diocese (see Chapter 5 for detail). The Attecotti were particularly noted for their ferocious charge when trying to break an enemy battle line. The Romans were so impressed with the Attacotti that they recruited them en masse into bespoke *auxilia* units after the comes Theodosius defeated the Great Conspiracy, with four units detailed in the *Notitia Dignitatum*. These were most likely *auxilia palatina* units.

The Gauls

The Romans fought the Gauls on numerous occasions, including those residing in Cisalpine

Gaul in the north of Italy who sacked Rome in 390 BC, and their Galatian cousins in central Anatolia as the Romans conquered the eastern Mediterranean. However, it is through Julius Caesar and his Gallic conquests that we know most about their military systems, and I focus on this period here.

Caesar fought one of the most sanguineous conflicts in Roman history when he conquered Gaul between 58 and 52 BC, this including his two incursions to Britain. He himself boasted that one million Gauls were killed and another million enslaved as he carved out the new Roman territories there, with Caesar having to create many new legions to achieve this.

In 58 BC, looking to his north from his new province of Transalpine Gaul along the Mediterranean coast, Caesar would have seen five broad tribal groupings in Gaul and beyond. These were Gallia Aquitania in the south-west, Armorica in the west, Gallia Celtica in central Gaul, Gallia Belgica to its north, and then Germania across the River Rhine. In his campaigns to conquer Gaul he fought many of the huge tribal confederations across this vast territory, including the Helvetii in 58 BC, Belgae in 57 BC, Veneti in 56 BC and then various large scale revolts in conquered territories, these culminating in the Great Revolt under Vercingetorix in 52 BC (see Chapter 6).

Caesar's Gallic opponents proved fearsome warriors. Broadly their military system was similar to that of the Britons across the English Channel and North Sea. This included a chariot-riding aristocracy, and line-of-battle infantry armed with short spears and long slashing swords. Their infantry formations were more likely to take on the Romans in open battle than the Britons. However, the major difference was with regard to Gallic cavalry who were heavily armed and armoured and charged to contact rather than skirmish. I therefore concentrate on these here.

Gallic cavalry gradually replaced their chariotry over time, though some of the latter were still in use during Caesar's campaigns in Gaul. As with the chariots, the cavalry largely comprised the Gallic nobility, paying high prices to buy powerful horses that became prized possessions. These gave them a distinct advantage against contemporary mounted opponents. They carried substantial shields similar in design to Gallic foot troops, though had a much higher proportion equipped with iron or bronze helmet and armour, the latter usually chainmail. For weaponry short spears and javelins were carried, with most also equipped with the long Gallic slashing sword. Cavalry swords were often of much better quality than those of the infantry.

Gallic cavalry were well trained and could perform a variety of manoeuvres on the battlefield. Their most common attack was to advance on the enemy line of battle at speed, stopping just short and unleashing a shower of javelins. If this disordered their opponents, they then drew their swords and charged home. If not, the missile attack was repeated.

Gallic cavalry were well known in the ancient world for a particularly brutal habit, namely head hunting. The 1st-century BC historian Diodorus provides context here, saying (5.29.4–5):

The Gauls cut off the heads of their enemies slain in battle and fasten them about the necks of their horses. They hand over the blood-stained spoils to their attendants to carry off as booty, while striking up a paean over them and singing a hymn of victory. They nail up the heads on their houses, just as hunters do when they have killed certain wild beasts. They embalm in cedar oil the heads of their most distinguished enemies and keep them carefully in a chest. These they display, with pride, to strangers, declaring that one of their ancestors, or his father, or the man himself, refused the offer of a large sum of money for this head. They say that some of them boast that they refused the weight of the head in gold.

Writing shortly afterwards, the Greek geographer, philosopher and historian Strabo (4.4.5) echoes these views, adding that Roman travellers in Gaul had seen many such heads, so many in fact that eventually they got used to the sight. Today, most of the evidence of this practice comes from hillfort sites, particularly in boundary ditches and next to gateways where many of the crania found display weapon injuries. It is unclear if these were placed there deliberately or were the casually discarded heads of decapitated lower-class warriors.

One point to note here, based on contemporary

sources and particularly sculpture and epigraphy, is that this practice of head hunting for trophy heads found its way into the regular Roman army once Augustus created his auxiliary cavalry units at the beginning of the Principate. The vector of cultural transmission was clearly the Gauls used in late republican armies as mercenaries. By way of the example, when Caesar won the final victory over his Pompeian rivals at Munda in Spain in 45 BC some of his troops erected a palisade on which they displayed the severed heads of slain opponents to intimidate any surviving Pompeains who had fled within the town walls of Munda.

By the time of the Empire auxiliary cavalry themselves are depicted in sculpture brandishing severed heads. Four prime examples include those on the Great Trajanic Frieze detailed in Chapter 4 reused on the Arch of Constatine. On one panel spanning two of the slabs three auxiliaries stand with right arms raised presenting the heads of Dacians to Trajan. The style of their armour and shields indicates they are cavalry. Meanwhile another auxiliary, this time mounted, reaches down with his left hand to grasp the hair of a Dacian, his right hand holding a *spatha* ready to decapitate his opponent. Next, on Trajan's Column one of the helical friezes shows the severed heads of two Dacians impaled on poles next to two auxiliary cavalrymen as nearby legionaries build a fort. Moving on, a gruesome scene is depicted on the Bridgeness Slab, the easternmost distance slab along the Antonine Wall which records the building of '4652' paces of the then northern frontier by legionaries of the Caerleon-based *legio II Augusta*, the original now in the National Museum of Scotland in Edinburgh. The inscription on the slab is flanked by scenes of victory, on the left showing an auxiliary cavalryman riding down four natives. One has been decapitated, with his headless body slumped forward in a seated position while his head falls to the ground. Finally, on the Column of Marcus Aurelius one of the helical friezes (scene LXVI) shows the seated emperor listening to an advisor while two auxiliaries to his left distract him by holding up severed German heads.

Meanwhile, Roman military tombstones also show head-hunting practices openly professed by members of auxiliary cavalry units while based in Britain. A good example is provided by the late 1st-century AD memorial to Aurelius Lucius in Chester. This shows his groom holding up a severed head. Meanwhile, a tombstone dated to between AD 75 and AD 120 from Lancaster shows Insus, a citizen of the Treviri and trooper with the *Ala Augusta*, grasping the head of a decapitated enemy.

Isolated skulls found on Romano-British sites have also been identified as possible trophies. Skull fragments in Flavian pits at the fort at Newstead are also thought to be discarded military trophies, while the skull of a young male found in the fort ditch at Vindolanda has sword wounds to the head and has also been interpreted as a trophy. Further, at Colchester six skulls, mostly young males and with some showing trauma associated with decapitation, were found in the town ditch and have also been identified as trophies. Finally, it has recently been argued that the hundreds of severed heads found in the upper reaches of the Walbrook Valley in London dating to the AD 120s or early AD 130s are those of the victims of a mass beheading event after some kind of insurrection in the provincial capital.

The Germans and Goths

In considering the Germans and Goths who appear so frequently in this work, I first comment on terminology. In this book the words German and Goth are frequently used, confusingly perhaps given that the Goths themselves were of German descent. Both words are problematic given they infer a tribal identity that in reality did not exist. While each grouping may have often shared the same blood and cultural practices, the tribes within more often fought themselves than the Romans, and indeed later in the Empire provided many of the troops and military leaders in the Dominate Roman army. Even the term tribe itself is problematic given many were confederations of various regional groupings. While acknowledging these issues, I retain the use of the words here for ease of reference, especially given they were terms well understood by the Romans.

The Germanic peoples of continental northern

Europe were a major opponent of the later Roman Republic and Empire and were identified by the Romans themselves as a distinct ethnic group when compared to their southerly Gallic neighbours. The Germans originated in the westward Indo-European migrations from the Pontic-Eurasian steppe and by 3,300 BC had split off from the main migratory group to head north-west towards the southern coastline of the Baltic Sea. They are often referred to as Teutonic, Suebian or Gothic in antiquarian literature.

Writing at the end of the early 1st century AD, Strabo (7.1.2/3) provides contemporary insight into how the Romans viewed the Germans, saying:

Now the parts beyond the Rhenus [Rhine], immediately after the country of the Gauls, slope towards the east and are occupied by the Germans, who, though they vary slightly from the Celtic stock in that they are wilder, taller, and have yellower hair, are in all other respects similar, for in build, habits, and modes of life they are such as I have said the Gauls are. And I also think that it was for this reason that the Romans assigned to them the name Germani, as though they wished to indicate thereby that they were 'genuine' Gauls, for in the language of the Romans Germani means genuine.

The last point above, referencing the Germans as 'genuine' Gauls, is most likely a literary device by Strabo reflecting what he believed was their superior martial prowess following the conquest of Gaul by Caesar in the 50s BC and the ease with which the Gallic provinces were later incorporated into the Empire.

The Germanic tribes known to the Romans originated in homelands in southern Scandinavia and the far north of Germany where they had been settled for over 2,000 years following the earlier Indo-European migrations. The later republican Romans described four broad Germanic groupings, the first being the Ingaevones. These comprised the Cimbri, Teutones and Chauci tribes. These were based in the Jutland peninsula, Frisia and northern Saxony. Another early Germanic grouping was the Irimones, these situated further to the east between the Oder and Elbe rivers. A third grouping was called the Istvaeones, later located on the Rhine and around the Weser. The final group was called the Herminones, comprising the Suebi (from whom the Marcomanni descended, see below, as well as the Quadi, Semnones and Lombards), Chatti and Herunduri tribes, these later dominating the Elbe region. All four of these early terms for the large tribal collectives gradually fell out of use as individual tribes came to be known to the Romans.

Once the German tribes began their migrations south from their original southern Scandinavian and north German homelands, they carved out new territories between the Rhine and the Pripet Marshes in modern Belarus. There they slowly consolidated until they eventually coalesced into the huge confederations which caused so much trouble to the later Roman Empire, particularly after the Hunnic expansions westward from the Central Asian steppe drove them increasingly against the Roman *limes* along the Rhine and Danube. By then six major confederations had emerged, these being the western Visigoths, eastern Ostrogoths, Vandals, Burgundians, Langobards and Franks, all later playing a key role in the fall of the Roman Empire in the west.

The early German armies faced by the Romans, for example in the Cimbrian Wars, were very similar to their Gallic counterparts though lacked chariots. The cavalry in these armies also fought in much the same way as the Gauls, though the horses tended to be smaller. However, a particular innovation of early German armies was the deployment of light troops among the ranks of their own cavalry. Armed with javelins and shields, these swarmed around the flanks of opposing troops, hamstringing their mounts if they were cavalry.

Early German infantry formations often fought in a wedge formation rather than as a standard shield wall. Most warriors wore little armour though often carried a shield, usually square in design. Their principal weapons were javelins that they carried in quantity, aiming to shower an opposing formation with volleys prior to contact. A common type was called the *framea*, which featured a narrow blade and long socket. Some German tribes also deployed troops armed with long thrusting spears in their front ranks, for example the Cherusci and the Batavians. The main side arm was the long dagger, for example the Saxon *Seax*, though a few warriors also carried a sword if they could afford it.

Later German armies evolved from these early troop types into formations often very different, based on regional circumstances. For example, the Ostrogoths had a much higher proportion of cavalry given their close proximity to the Sarmatians and the Turkic steppe tribes. These mounted warriors often wore armour and helmet and carried a large round shield. The main weapon was the light spear, of which a number were carried, and a long sword. Their preferred tactic was an impetuous charge to contact. Most foot troops of later Ostrogoth armies were bowmen. Meanwhile, the Vandals who eventually settled in North Africa after a long migration had an even higher percentage of cavalry in their armies who fought in the same way.

By way of contrast, Visigothic armies featured mostly foot troops still fighting in the same manner as their early German predecessors. However, several confederations were well known to the Romans for their use of specific weapon types. The included the *francisca* (throwing axe) and *angon* (armour-piercing javelin) used by the Franks, the latter detailed in Chapter 5, and the *bebrae* (heavy throwing spear) used by the Marcomanni.

German troops of all periods were known for their blood chilling war cry called the *barritus*. This started in a low voice and rose to a high-pitched chilling scream. Many Roman units later adopted this in the Dominate phase of Empire when large numbers of Germans were recruited into the legions and auxiliary units, and German leaders came to dominate the Roman officer class.

The Spaniards

The Romans first came across Spanish warriors when they fought as mercenaries in Carthaginian armies. They later fought a series of wars in the Iberian Peninsula when creating their early provinces of Hispania Citerior and Hispania Ulterior. The final conflicts there were the Cantabrian Wars fought by Augustus to conquer the far north of the Peninsula from 27 BC to 14 BC.

Several peoples inhabited pre-conquest Spain but, excepting the coastal Punic and Greek colonies, most fought in a similar fashion. The principal groupings were:

- The Celtibarians, four tribes who occupied central Spain. This was an amalgam culture that evolved after a large group of Meseta Celts migrating from Gaul merged with Iberian natives living there. They often served as mercenaries in other Spanish armies.
- The Iberians in the eastern and southern coastal region. Here cultural exchange with their Punic and Greek colonial neighbours is evident, though not in their military formations.
- The Lusitanians in the region of modern Portugal.

Spanish armies were rarely more than 40,000 strong. Around 15% were cavalry, these a heavier type who were broadly similar to those of their Gallic neighbours (though carrying a small round shield called a *caetra*), and a lighter skirmishing type using javelins. The latter were particularly noted for fighting in a formation called the Cantabrian Circle. Here, a group of horsemen formed a single-file rotating circle, each man throwing his javelin at the closest point to the enemy battle line. The effect was a continual stream of javelins hitting the enemy formation in close proximity to each other, thus providing a very dense concentration of firepower.

Meanwhile two types of foot troops featured, *scutarii* (line-of-battle infantry) who charged to contact using a variety of throwing weapons, and *caetrati* (skirmishers, named after their shield). Celtibarian *scutarii* were particularly known for their fierce charge, while Lusitanian armies had the highest proportion of *caetrati*.

The Romans were highly impressed by their Spanish opponents and adopted a number of their weapons as their own, most notably the *gladius Hispaniensis*.

BRITAIN

54/55 BC

GERMANIA

54 BC

55 BC

57 BC

53 BC

ATLANTIC
OCEAN

GAUL

52 BC

58 BC

56 BC

ITALY

Alesia
(Clermont-Ferrand)
52 BC

Corsica

Rome

Ilerda
49 BC

Sardinia

SPAIN

Munda
45 BC

AFRICA

NUMIDIA

MAURITANIA

Thapsus
46 BC

0   400 Miles

0   400 Kilometers

The Samnites

Of all Rome's enemies when conquering the Italian Peninsula, the Samnites proved the most troublesome in the long run. The Samnites were the largest and most powerful of the Oscan-speaking peoples and resided in the highlands of south-central Italy. They comprised four tribes who early on formed a league, the tribes being the Pentri, Caudini, Hirpini and Caraceni.

When on campaign Samnite armies fought under an annually elected general. The army was organised into *legiones* that may have been much larger than their Roman equivalent given the elite Linen Legion had – at least at one stage – 16,000 men. Armies of up to 70,000 are recorded, 10% of whom were cavalry.

Samnite mounted troops fought with a short spear and javelin and often never participated in battle given their small numbers. However, Samnite line-of-battle infantry were often well equipped and were easily able to stand up to their Roman counterparts, often winning. A variety of helmet types were worn, including the Etrusco-Corinthian, Attic and Montefortino types favoured by the Romans, while for a shield various types were used including those similar to the Roman *scutum* (the Samnites may actually have been the vector by which the Romans came to use the design) and the Greek *aspis*. For body armour the Samnites wore triple disc, disc and square bronze pectorals covering their heart and upper chest that were held in place with leather straps. They fought with short spears and javelins and many carried swords such as the *kopis*.

The Numidians

Numidia, an ancient kingdom in modern Algeria and Tunisia, was initially divided between the Massylii federation in the east and Masaesyli federation in the west. After the Second Punic War Massinissa, the king of the Massylii, defeated Syphax of the Masaesyli and unified the whole region into one kingdom.

The Romans first came across Numidian warriors when they served as mercenaries and allies in Carthaginian armies, and they were so impressed they were soon recruited into Roman armies. Rome fought two specific wars against them, the Jugurthine War at the end of the 2nd century BC, and then when fighting the rebel leader Tacfarinas at the beginning of the 1st century AD. They also participated in the Roman civil wars in the 1st century BC, with for example King Juba I as an ally of Pompey, while his neighbour Bogud of Mauretania was allied to Julius Caesar.

Numidian armies were famed for their skirmishing light cavalry armed with javelins. These were much sort after as mercenaries, and later once Numidia had been incorporated into the Empire formed the basis of the Principate *symmachiarii* (javelin-armed mounted skirmisher). The Numidians also occasionally used war elephants of the African forest type, and in the later 1st century BC often re-equipped their foot warriors in panoply similar to that worn by contemporary Roman legionaries.

The Carthaginians

Carthage was a Phoenician colony on the North African coast near modern Tunis. From here it came to dominate the western Mediterranean, building a trading Empire that was to prove the Roman Republic's most troublesome enemy. Rome fought three major wars against Carthage, including the Second Punic War when Hannibal's campaigns in Italy humbled the Roman legions time and again. The name Punic derives from the Roman name for the Carthaginians, the *poeni*.

Given the Carthaginian Empire, which included colonies in Spain, Sicily and Sarbinia, was largely one of maritime commerce, its armies largely consisted of mercenaries. Generals were elected, building out their armies around a core of Carthaginian troops. These could include chariots and later elephants, the latter again of the African forest type. A civic cavalry could also be levied from wealthier citizens, these often armoured and fighting with a short spear and sword. When necessary a levy of citizen foot troops could also be raised, and in large numbers as at the battle of Bagradas River in 255 BC in Tunisia during the

First Punic War when 12,000 fought alongside 4,000 native horse. Some of these spearmen became highly experienced, as with those who fought with Hannibal in Italy. They were armed with a long thrusting spears, often armoured, and carried substantial round and oval shields. They deployed in dense phalanxes.

Meanwhile key Carthaginian mercenaries included Numidians in large numbers, Spaniards (Celtibarians were particularly favoured), Gauls, various Italian peoples and Balearic slingers.

The Dacians

The Dacians were an Indo-European people who lived in the Carpathian Mountains and to the west of the Black Sea. The Dacian kingdom reached its maximum size under its King Burebista who ruled from 82 BC to 44 BC, after which it began to disintegrate. Roman advances in the Balkans and later the incorporation of Moesia as a Roman province by Augustus led to conflict between the Dacians and the Romans.

In the first instance this was in the reign of Domitian when in AD 86 they attacked some Roman troops, this leading to an inconclusive campaign against them. Trajan then fought his two famous campaigns against them in AD 101–102 and AD 105–106, these well recorded on his column in the Forum of Trajan in Rome. Large parts of Dacian territory were then incorporated into the new Roman province of Dacia.

Riverine galleys of the River Danube during Trajan's conquest of Dacia on the base of Trajan's Column.

Trajan's Column in
Rome, the centrepiece
of the Forum of Trajan,
celebrating his conquest of
Dacia.

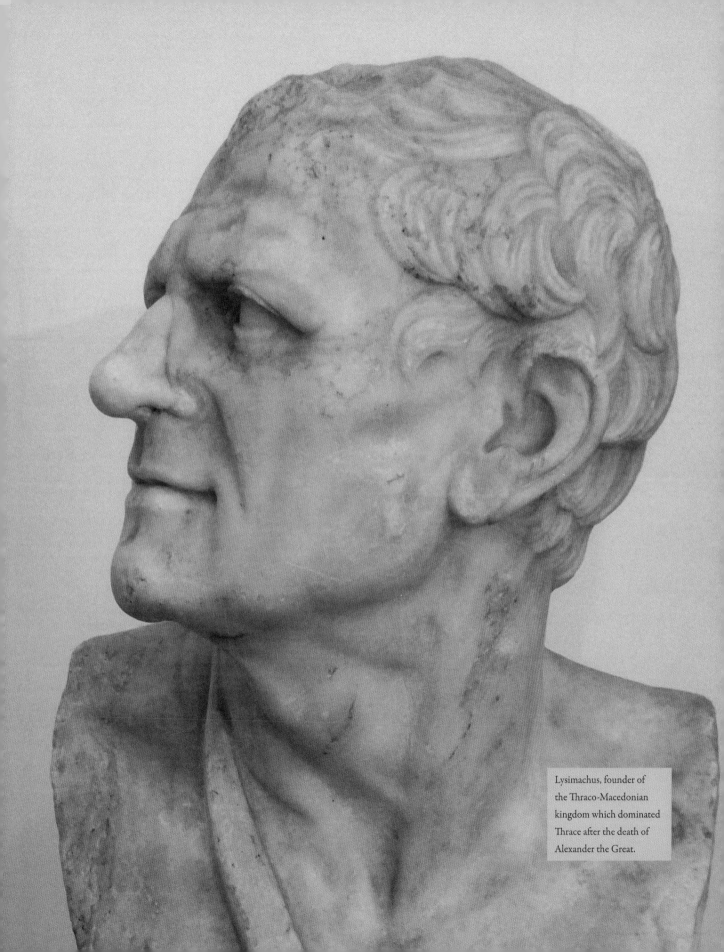

Lysimachus, founder of the Thraco-Macedonian kingdom which dominated Thrace after the death of Alexander the Great.

Trophies from Trajan's Dacian Wars displayed on the base of Trajan's Column in Rome. Sarmatian banded leather armour and Dacian shields.

Dacian armies showed influences from their Gallic, Thracian and Sarmatian neighbours. Given their mountainous homeland Dacian armies were largely comprised of infantry, relying on allies including the Sarmatians if they needed a larger mounted component. Many of the foot carried the vicious looking *falx* (two-handed chopping weapon) with its large downward curved blade, introduced to Dacian armies through their Bastarnae neighbours. Meanwhile other foot troops carried short spears and javelins. All relied on a fierce charge to contact to defeat the enemy battle line, the Dacians proving a very tough opponent for the Romans.

The Hellenistic Kingdoms

Rome fought a variety of wars against Hellenistic opponents, including the four Macedonian Wars, the Roman–Seleucid War, three Mithridatic wars and Caesar's Alexandrian war. Given the importance of these conflicts as the power of republican Rome grew, I consider their armies at length here.

The strategy and tactics used by the Hellenistic kingdoms against Rome in the eastern Mediterranean were firmly rooted in a bespoke military tradition very different to that of the Republic. Thus, one can see a common thread in the armies of Macedon, the Seleucid Empire, the Pontic Empire, Ptolemaic Egypt and the other successor states. As a general rule, such armies became more eclectic in their composition the further east their origins, but still retained a Hellenistic core.

Strategically, conflict in the Hellenistic military tradition initially remained largely seasonal and amateur. This was despite considerable military development and innovation from the Peloponnesian War in the 5th century BC onwards. The only real exceptions were Philip II and Alexander the Great who as the leaders of the Macedonian army were renowned for their ability to wage war all year round, often campaigning in harvest time and winter to ensure strategic surprise and the ability to pursue a beaten army vigorously.

However, after the death of Alexander and the ending of the first phase of the Wars of the Successors, seasonal campaigning became the norm once more. It was to remain so through to the end of the period, with strategic objectives equally limited and focused. Examples include:

- Antiochus III's campaign in 220 BC to recover his provinces on the eastern Iranian plateau from the usurping rebel satrap Molon.
- The never-ending push and shove in the Levant between the Seleucid and Ptolemaic kingdoms during six successive Syrian Wars.
- Macedon's increasingly desperate struggle for survival against growing Roman interest in the Balkans during the Four Macedonian Wars.

Far more research has been done into Hellenistic military theory at a tactical level. This remained heavily focused on the use of the phalanx. In a modern context the term refers to any dense

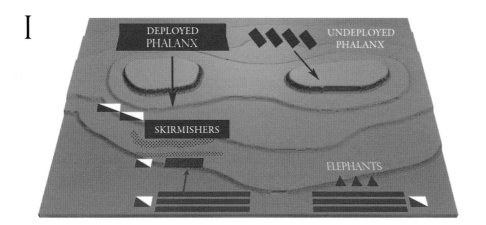

I

DEPLOYED PHALANX

UNDEPLOYED PHALANX

SKIRMISHERS

ELEPHANTS

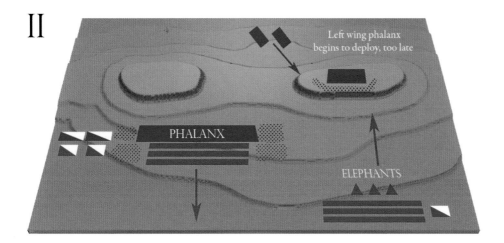

II

Left wing phalanx begins to deploy, too late

PHALANX

ELEPHANTS

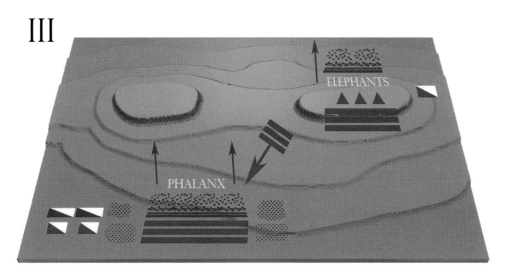

III

ELEPHANTS

PHALANX

The battle of Cynoscephalae in 197 BC where the Roman general Flamininus crushed the army of Philip V to win the Second Macedonian War. (Nigel Emsen)

BRITONS

GERMANS

ILLYRIANS

GAULS

IBERIANS

Massilia

Ancona

Trasimene

Rome

Cannae

Capua

Taras

Saguntum

Carthago Nova

Tingis

Hippo

Carthage

Syracuse

Zama

NUMIDIANS

Leptis

| 0 | (km) | 500 |
| 0 | (mi) | 300 |

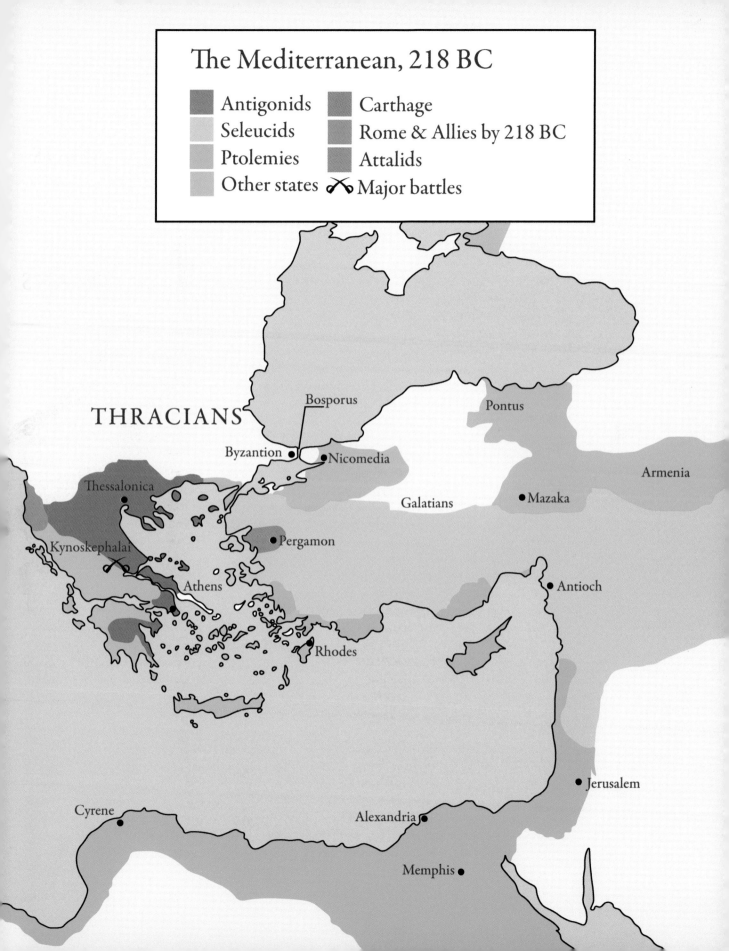

The Mediterranean, 218 BC

Antigonids
Seleucids
Ptolemies
Other states
Carthage
Rome & Allies by 218 BC
Attalids
Major battles

THRACIANS

Bosporus
Byzantion
Nicomedia
Pontus
Armenia
Thessalonica
Galatians
Mazaka
Kynoskephalai
Pergamon
Athens
Antioch
Rhodes
Jerusalem
Cyrene
Alexandria
Memphis

formation of infantry, but within the Hellenistic military tradition it refers specifically to organised and deep formations of spearmen and, later, pikemen.

The original Greek phalanx formation developed after 700 BC and played a key role in the early armies of Rome, and those of many of her enemies, all as detailed in Chapter 1. It was soon being used by leading city-states including Corinth, Sparta and Argos. The formation comprised the heavy infantry hoplite and had its origins in two developments, one economic and one political.

First, the re-opening of trade routes after the Greek 'Dark Age'. This led to the renewed establishment of colonies, for example in Italy, Anatolia and the Aegean Islands, increasing prosperity and thus the number of men within a city state able to afford the full panoply of hoplite armour and weaponry. At this early stage such equipment was principally – if affordable – bronze body armour and helmet, the *aspis* and the long thrusting spear.

Second, the actual emergence of the polis, the self-sufficient autonomous state. This bound citizens more closely together within their communities than previously. Given the first duty of the polis was to defend itself in time of war, this was the catalyst to organise the now more numerous fully armed hoplites into what became the classic Greek hoplite phalanx.

As detailed in Chapter 2, in the context of the Tullian Etrusco-Roman phalanx, in such a formation the front-rank troops fought with their long spears held in an overarm thrusting position, covered by the interlocking *aspis*. Those at the rear added their weight to the formation, replacing those falling in battle at the front. In normal circumstances, when two hoplite phalanxes fought, they would head directly for each other, break into a run for the last few metres, then shove and stab each other until one line broke. Warfare using such phalanxes tended to feature the best troops deploying on the right-hand side. This often caused the line of battle to wheel right to left.

In terms of hoplite equipment, the most essential item was the *aspis*, a shallow bowl between 80cm and 100cm wide. This was a wooden design

covered completely with bronze, featuring a double grip made from a metal or leather strap across the centre through which the left arm was inserted, and a leather grip on the outer rim. The other key item of protection was the helmet, this evolving over time into a variety of popular designs. These ranged in complexity from those termed Pilos, a simple bronze conical cap, to Thracian. The latter had long cheek guards meeting at the chin and a peak at the front that extended around the side, protecting the eyes and ears.

For armour, by the Hellenistic period only elite hoplites and officers wore the bronze (and even more rarely iron) muscled cuirass that had replaced earlier bronze types. The most common type of body armour, if worn at all, was made from layers of linen glued together to form a stiff shirt up to 5cm in thickness. Such a corselet covered the torso, with a skirt of the same material hanging from the bottom split into *pteryges* to allow ease of movement. Bronze or iron plates and scales could also be added to protect vital areas. Finally, the better-off hoplite would also wear iron or bronze greaves sprung onto their calves to protect the knee and lower leg.

In terms of weaponry, hoplites were principally armed with a 1.5m to 2.5m long thrusting spear. This was usually made of ash, with a leaf-shaped iron head and a bronze butt-spike. The spear was complemented by a sword, either a leaf-shaped iron blade some 60cm in length or the vicious-looking *kopis* often used in early Roman armies.

Each polis used the hoplite phalanx in differing ways. Sparta, the most militaristic, treated its entire male citizen population as lifelong conscripts forbidden from any other work except soldiering. Even Athens required all males between to 17 and 59 to serve in times of war. Others had elite units within their wider hoplite formations, for example Thebes with its *heiros lochos* (Sacred Band) of 300 paired warriors. This played a prominent role at the battle of Leuctra in 371 BC but was annihilated at the battle of Chaeronea in 338 BC when fighting Philip II of Macedon.

The depth of the hoplite phalanx was a matter of city state preference and tactical expediency. Thucydides (*The Peloponnesian War*, V.68) says the Spartan phalanx at the first battle of battle of Mantinea in 418 BC, when they and their allies defeated Argos, Athens and their allies, was eight deep. This was also the standard depth for Athenian phalanxes, though other states such as Thebes often deployed their phalanxes much deeper, for example 25 deep at the battle of Delium against the Athenians in 424 BC and 50 deep on the right flank at the battle of Leuctra in 371 BC, the latter against a Spartan phalanx 12 deep. In this context the dense formation of infantrymen became a tactical battering ram to smash its way through the Spartan left flank. Though an excessive example, this does illustrate a trend for ever deepening hoplite phalanxes.

Leuctra also illustrates the increasing use of tactical innovation in phalanx warfare, with the Thebans deploying obliquely and withholding their centre and left flank while using their extra-deep right to such great effect. This tactic of attacking with a strong wing, most often the right as set out above, while refusing another was one which was readily adopted by Alexander and continued to be a major tactical feature on the battlefield throughout the Hellenistic period.

In terms of unit organisation, hoplites formed up with a frontage and depth of some 90cm per man, with each hoplite's right side protected by the neighbouring projecting shield. All of the above various depths detailed were created by multiples of four-men deep, though there is little evidence of any particular sophistication here outside of the Spartan army. However, in the case of the latter we have much detail thanks to Xenophon and his *Constitution of the Lacedaemonians*, dating to the beginning of the 4th century BC. This most organised of hoplite phalanxes was divided into six morai, each commanded by a senior officer called a polemarch. Below him were various officers of decreasing seniority, starting with four lochagai, then eight pentecosters and finally 16 *enomotarch*s, the latter commanding a platoon-sized *enomotia* of 36 men. These were divided into three files of 12, the *enomotarch* commanding the right-hand file with his *ouragos* (second-in-command) at the rear of the same file. The idea here was to ensure that every Spartan unit, no matter how small, had

its own commander. The much less complicated Athenian system from the same period featured 10 regiments called *taxeis* of variable size, one drawn from each of the tribes of Athens and commanded by a *taxiarch*.

Hoplite phalanx tactics continued to develop over time. This was largely in the context of new tactical threats, for example light troops. In the first instance, in the early 4th century BC century the Athenian general Iphicrates is credited with reforming the panoply of his light troops to allow them to stand in the line of battle alongside traditional hoplites, while still retaining their ability to engage with other light troops. This created a 'light hoplite', with such troops armed with a leather-faced round shield slightly smaller than its bronze-faced *aspis* counterpart, a lighter quilted cuirass instead of the stiff layered leather cuirass, and a longer spear. Troops armed in such a way were first used in the Corinthian War from 395 BC to 387 BC.

The next major tactical innovation begins with the accession to the Macedonian throne of Philip II. As part of his wider military reforms he further developed the concept of the deep phalanx and adopted the lighter panoply associated with the Iphicratean-style hoplite – smaller shield, lighter armour – but with an even longer spear which now became the *sarissa*, a pike used two-handed.

Specifically on equipment, the Macedonian phalangite shield was a rimless, slightly concaved 60cm-diameter bronze design hung on the left shoulder and held in place with an arm grip for the left arm and a strap around the neck – both hands were needed to wield the pike. The armour of the Hellenistic pikeman was similar to that of the later classical hoplite, with front rank troops the most likely to wear armour. This was most often the linen variety, again sometimes reinforced with bronze or iron plates or scales. Very late in the Hellenistic period contact with the Galatians and Rome also saw the introduction of the mail shirt.

The helmet of the pike phalangite was again similar to those of later hoplites, with the advanced Thracian type dominating for front rankers. The traditional Macedonian broad-rimmed *kausia* hat was worn when on the march. Front rank troops were also the most likely to wear leg greaves.

Aside from the shield, it was the *sarissa* that most clearly differentiated the Macedonian pikeman from the hoplite. Between 4.5m and 5.5m long when first introduced, this had grown to 7.3m by the time the Romans fought the Macedonians. The pike was usually made from ash, with *sarissa* fittings from a tomb in Vergina in northern Greece indicating the shaft was made in two pieces, with an 17cm-long iron tubular sleeve locking them together. As with the hoplite spear, the pike featured a leaf-shaped iron blade and a butt-spike secured with hot pitch. The latter was significantly heavier than that used on hoplite spears given the role it had in helping balance the weapon as the pike was held using as handgrip towards the rear. Again, as with the hoplite, the pikeman also carried a sword, usually either the leaf-shaped iron blade or the *kopis*.

We know much more about the organisation of the Macedonian pike phalanx than the Greek hoplite phalanx due to the Tactica military manual of Asklepiodotos. Dating to the 1st century BC, this may actually be a reproduced long-lost work by Posidonius of whom Asklepiodotos was a pupil. The latter was a sophist and historian who Plutarch (*Life of Aemilius*, 19) says was a contemporary of the Macedonian King Perseus and who described the crucial battle of Pydna. Asclepiodotos's work is particularly useful given its focus not only on the phalanx but also other ancillary arms such as cavalry, light infantry and elephants. The work was heavily utilised in later Roman military manuals.

The Tactica and later manuals indicate the Macedonian pike phalanx was a step-change in complexity compared to earlier classical Greek examples, featuring three densities of formation. These were:

- Open order, with a frontage and depth per man of 1.8m and with no special name. This was the natural formation when deploying or manoeuvring.
- *Pyknosis*, with a frontage and depth half of that above and the usual battle formation.
- *Synaspismos*, the locked shields formation with a frontage and depth half of that used

for *pyknosis*. This was a purely defensive formation, used for example against Darius III's scythed chariots at the battle of Gaugamela in 331 BC.

The original *sarissa*-armed phalanxes of Philip II were formed in files 10 deep, known as *dekas*. However, as the Hellenistic Age progressed the usual file depth increased to 16, with the basic unit formed 16 wide, resulting in a unit of 256 men. This was known as the speria, broken into two taxis in better-trained formations. The Macedonian phalanxes that faced Rome in the Macedonian Wars featured four such speiriai which were formed into a *chiliarchia* of around 1,000 men, commanded by a *chiliarch* or *hegemon*. Four *chiliarchia* were then formed into 4,000 men-strong *strategiai* commanded by a *strategos*. While the standard deployment of this phalanx was 16 deep as set out above, the formation was flexible enough to deploy shallower or deeper. Thus, at the battle of Issos in 333 BC Alexander deployed the phalanx eight deep to maximise his frontage, while at the battle of Magnesia in 190 BC Antiochus III deployed his pikes 32 deep, as did Philip V at the battle of Cynoscephalae in 197 BC.

Within the phalanx of a given army, different units had different standings based on their seniority. For example, the senior regiment of the Antigonid phalanx was the *peltastoi* who had a lighter panoply and shorter *sarissa* than their counterparts elsewhere in the phalanx. Within their ranks sat the ultimate elite among the foot troops of the army, the *agema* guard. Meanwhile, the main body of the phalanx was called the *chalkaspides*, the ratio between the senior troops and main phalanx at the battle of Sellasia in 222 BC being 3,000 (including the *agema*) to 10,000. This breakdown of elite and line phalangites was common across all Hellenistic armies, though the units sometimes had different names. For example, the guard phalangites in the Seleucid armies retained the *argyraspists* (silver shields) name of the early Successor armies. Polybius (*The Rise of the Roman Empire*, 5.79.4) says these were specifically armed 'in the Macedonian manner.'

When deployed for combat the Macedonian

pike phalanx featured the front five ranks with pikes held level at the waist to provide an impenetrable hedge of spear points. Those in the rear ranks then added their weight to the phalanx during the charge, replacing fallen comrades at the front just as with the earlier Greek phalanx. These rear rank troopers, with their hedge of raised pikes, also broke up the impact of missiles fired at the phalanx. It is this Macedonian pike phalanx that led Polybius to comment on its imperviousness if tackled frontally in good conditions, saying (*The Rise of the Roman Empire*, 18.28–32):

> ... so long as the phalanx retains its characteristic form and strength nothing can withstand its charge or resist it face to face ... we can easily picture the nature and the tremendous power of a charge by the whole phalanx, when it advances 16 deep with levelled pikes.

Traditional hoplite infantry did continue in use into the later Hellenistic period, with Greek mercenaries equipped as such being a common feature in such armies. Gradual change to the pike-armed phalangite was the norm however, with Sparta for example switching from the former to the latter in its battle line by 208 BC.

One further innovation of the Hellenistic period was the appearance of a third principal line-of-battle troop type from the 3rd century BC, who formed the core of many of the armies faced by the Romans in the eastern Mediterranean. Called *thureophoroi*, these were named after their oval *thureos*, a development of the Gallic infantry shield. This was smaller and less substantial than the *aspis* but, like the Iphicratean shield, more flexible. Armed with a long thrusting spear and javelins, but unarmoured except for a helmet, these were initially light troops who were equipped for close combat in a secondary role. However, given their ubiquity in contemporary epigraphy and artwork, they seem to have eventually become a standard line of battle troop type, fighting alongside pike phalangite. They were also ideally equipped for garrison duties. In some armies *thureophoroi* were used as a transitional stage between the traditional hoplite and the pike armed phalangite, for example Boeotia which switched from hoplite to

thureophoroi by 270 BC and then on to the pike by 245 BC.

A further development of the *thureophoroi* was an armoured variant known as the *thorakitai* (cuirassier), wearing a light version of the Gallic chainmail shirt. These are mentioned by Polybius in the Achaian and Seleucid armies (*Rise of the Roman Empire*, 15.5 and 10.29.6) and were used to bolster the staying power of the less well-armoured *thureophoroi*.

Later Hellenistic armies also featured line-of-battle troops armed and equipped as 'Romans', as with the Numidians. This followed initial contact with the growing Republic to the west, especially in the Macedonian and Seleucid–Roman Wars. They first appear in the Seleucid army from the time of Antiochus IV in the famous Parade of Daphnae. Here, 5,000 of the *argyraspides* were armed and equipped as Romans with heavy throwing javelins, stabbing swords and chainmail shirts. This amounted to 50% of the guard troops. Similar 'Romanised' troops appear in the Ptolemaic armies around the same time.

A final component of Hellenistic armies in their lines of battle were mercenaries hired from across the geography of the then known world, ranging from Illyrians and Thracians from the Balkans, the fierce Galatians in central Anatolia and Indians from the sub-continent there. Such troops types usually fought in their native styles.

A key issue faced by all armies fighting in the Hellenistic military tradition as the Hellenistic Age progressed was the increasing difficulty in raising skilled foot troops for the line of battle, particularly phalangites. This had more of an impact on Macedon than the other Hellenistic kingdoms. There, it was arguably a lack of manpower rather than inferiority in military technique that sealed Macedon's fate. In 334 BC when Alexander crossed into Asia, Macedon could mobilise some 24,000 phalangites. However, by the time of the Cynoscephalae campaign in 197 BC Macedon could raise only 16,000 phalangites (plus 2,000 *peltastoi*, see below), and this by conscripting 16-year-olds and retired veterans. This total had risen to a phalanx of 21,000 by the time of Perseus's Third Macedonian War, but only through an emergency socio-economic policy of requiring native Macedonian's to beget more children.

One of the reasons for this evident decline in the number of trained phalangites was the vast geography of the Hellenistic world. The world the Successors inherited from Alexander after his death in Bablyon in 323 BC spread from the western Balkans to India, with his active troops, military settler veterans, mercenaries and allies spread across this huge global landscape. The biggest concentrations were in Babylonia, where the Royal army was based, and the Macedonian homeland. Once his Empire began its break up these troops were more or less locked in place unless their leader suffered a major defeat – as with Eumene's *argyraspides* – or for some reason mercenaries were unable to be paid. The overall effect was to dilute this core feature of armies fighting in the Macedonian manner across all the territories of the Hellenistic world.

A number of methods were used to compensate. At first veteran troops were often 'run on' for as long as possible, with again Eumene's *argyraspides* a good example. At the same time native troops from the conquered territories were recruited and trained to fight in the Hellenistic military tradition, for example the Persians equipped as phalangites under Alexander. Later, both Antigonus *Monophthalmus* and Eumenes used similar *pantodapoi* phalangites in their conflict, while the Ptolemies used native Egyptians trained as phalangites from the time of Ptolemy IV Philopator.

Later, a further way of shoring up the battle line was to increase the use of *thureophoroi, thorakitai* and indigenously armed mercenaries. Further, the decreasing size of the core phalanx led to new tactical innovations. These included interspersing light troops between units of the battle line, as with Pyrrhus of Epirus in his Italian campaigns. Cavalry and elephants were similarly deployed, as by Antiochus III at the battle of Magnesia in 190 BC. Allies also troops played an increasing role in Hellenistic armies, for example Pyrrhus's Oscans and Italiotes.

Meanwhile light troops formed a significant component of armies fighting in the Hellenistic military tradition, particularly in the east. These are recorded in use in Greek armies as early as the Persian invasion of Greece in 490 BC. Later, Athens is recorded as deploying 800 archers at the battle of Plataea in 479 BC during Xerxes' subsequent invasion.

Such troops can be categorised into two specific types, *peltastoi* and *psiloi*. The former were the better equipped, using javelins and named after their distinctive crescent-shaped wicker shields. Such better-equipped light troops were more suitable for close combat than the *psiloi*. They were often used in ambushes and to drive away enemy skirmishers.

Meanwhile *psiloi* is a catch all term for all other Hellenistic light infantry, these armed with javelins, bows, slings and, in *extremis*, anything that came to hand. For the armies of Macedon the javelin was the most important, these deployed in loose formations up to eight deep. Such skirmishers were used for scouting and controlling rough ground, while in battle they were deployed ahead the main battle line, phalanx or otherwise, to open the engagement. Once hand-to-hand combat was imminent, they then withdrew behind the battle line. They were also used to control flanks and the rear, while a further tactic was their use supporting mounted troops, including elephants. Some nations had an association with particular *psiloi* specialisations, for example Cretan archers and Rhodian slingers, both thought by contemporaries to be superior to others using the same weapon.

Turning to cavalry fighting in the Hellenistic military tradition, these were an inferior component of classical Greek armies, excepting in the *poleis* in Thessaly. However, their use was on the increase by the 4th century BC when innovators such as Thebes began using mounted troops in association with light infantry to pin one or both of their opponent's flanks.

The rise to dominance of Macedon under Philip II saw mounted troops take on a much more important role by the mid-4th century BC. Here, cavalry equipped as lance-armed shock troops were used to break through a weak point in the enemy battle line once pinned by the phalanx. Such tactics reached their zenith under Alexander who perfected this co-operation between the various arms of his army.

The importance of cavalry in Hellenistic armies was most manifest in the east where a few battles were actually cavalry only affairs. The most notable example was in 208 BC at the Arios River in western Afghanistan when Antiochus III defeated the Bactrian-Greek King Euthydemus I.

However, as the Hellenistic Age progressed the importance of cavalry in Hellenistic armies, particularly in the west, diminished. In the first instance this was manifest in tactics and equipment. Cavalry in many Greek armies at the beginning of the Hellenistic age was based on the *ilai* of 128 commanded by an *ilarchai*. Each *ile* was ideally 16 wide and eight deep, with a frontage of 90cm per mount. Specialist formations included a rhomboid type used by the *poleis* in Thessaly where the *ilarchai* took point nearest the enemy. A further development was the Macedonian wedge of lancers. This half-rhomboid formation, adopted by Philip II from the Scythians and Thracians, was used with telling effect by Alexander and his successors on many occasions.

For weaponry, the standard Macedonian cavalryman at the beginning of the period was armed with the *xyston* (lance). This gave rise to their name, *xystophoroi*. For a side arm they fielded the same range of swords as the infantry. In terms of armour they again had access to the same options as the infantry, though with a higher percentage wearing all-metal cuirasses. All such armour was adapted for mounted use. Helmets were also worn by all, with the Boeotian design featuring an open face the most popular.

However, by the time Macedon faced the growing might of Rome, Hellenistic line-of-battle cavalry had diminished to a skirmishing force using light spears and javelins. These only engaged enemy cavalry in hand-to-hand combat when necessary. Such a change in role is often associated with the introduction of the large cavalry shield in the 3rd century BC. This followed Pyrrhus's campaigns in Italy where he was suitably impressed by their use. The Galatian invasion of Greece in 279 BC was another catalyst. The advent of these shields made using the long *xyston* problematic for cavalry using the saddle technology of the day.

The diminishing capability of the Hellenistic cavalryman was also matched by a decrease in their size as a percentage of the army. A key factor here was the need for mounted military settlers to have larger estates than their infantry equivalents. This was fine while Alexander and his immediate successors were gathering larger and larger tracts of land through imperial expansion. However, once such opportunities became less common as the Hellenistic world began its geographic regression from the mid-3rd century BC, the ability of rulers to parcel out such land reduced significantly. This led to an overall reduction in available mounted troops, particularly those fighting in the Hellenistic tradition. This can be seen with Philip V's 'conscription' decree, found in the *Kassandreia* and other *diagrammata* (ordinance) documents. These recorded emergency efforts to expand his cavalry force in the context of the Second Macedonian War. However, it failed as he could only field 2,000 mounted troops against the Romans. After even more aggressive recruitment methods, his son Perseus could still only field 3,000 in the Third Macedonian War.

The diminishing role for cavalry continued through to the end of the Hellenistic period. They remained strongest in the east where innovations such as the cataphract emerged in the armies of the Seleucid Empire and the Bactrian-Greek kingdom following contact with the Parthians. Troops equipped in this way, featuring fully armoured horse and rider fighting in deep formations with long thrusting spears, originated among the Dahae and Massagetae central Asiatic steppe peoples, then becoming a key feature of Parthian armies as detailed later. In the eastern kingdoms *xystophoroi* also remained in use for longer, and it was also more common to see cavalry armed in their native styles, for example Persians and Indians.

Light cavalry specifically used for skirmishing and scouting were also a key component of Hellenistic armies. Again, like their foot equivalents, specialist types emerged, armed mainly with javelins and bows. Such troops were more common in the east. Meanwhile, in the west a particular light cavalry troop type emerged in the 3rd century BC whose name became synonymous with skirmishing javelin-armed cavalry at the time. These were the Tarantines, named after Taras (modern Taranto) in south-eastern Italy.

Finally, I come to the most glamorous components of Hellenistic armies, namely elephants, camels and scythed chariots. The former made a huge impression on contemporary Hellenistic audiences from the time of Alexander's anabasis. This was initially at the battle of Gaugamela in 331 BC when Darius II used 15 Indian elephants. Later, in India proper, they became a common opponent. As detailed in Chapter 2, these animals made such an impression on Alexander that when he returned from India be bought 200 back with him. They then became a common feature in Hellenistic armies from the Successors Wars onwards, sparking an arms race amongst the protagonists to have the biggest elephant corps.

Two different elephant types were used in Hellenistic armies. The first was the Indian variety first encountered by Alexander. The Macedonian elephant corps was created using such beasts bought back from Alexander's eastern campaigns. These were distributed throughout the early Successor kingdoms after his death, with those remaining in Macedonian service lasting until mid-way through the reign of Antigonus *Gonatus* (277 BC to 239 BC). The Seleucid Empire and those further east were more fortunate, proximity to India allowing frequent resupply of the beasts.

Meanwhile the second type was the smaller African forest elephant used by Ptolemaic Egypt, detailed earlier in republican Roman, Numidian and Carthaginian service. These were sourced from the Horn of Africa after the Ptolemies were cut off from supplies of Indian elephants by the Syrian Wars.

The importance of the various Hellenistic elephant corps is reflected in the specific title given to the official in charge of their use, the *elephantarchos*. This was a key figure in early Hellenistic royal courts. Hellenistic elephants were equipped for war in different ways, depending on their size and training. In addition to the mahout who controlled the animal, their vast bulk and tusks were potent weapons in their own right. To this was added a fighting crew, either sitting astride the animal's back or in bespoke towers. The latter were an innovation that appeared by the time of battle of Paraitacene in 317 BC when Antigonus *Monophthalmus* fought Eumenes. Troops deployed in either way were armed with a variety of weapons, ranging from pikes used to stab downwards, to bows and javelins.

In battle, while elephants could be kept in reserve, they were most frequently deployed line abreast across the front of the main line of battle – centre, flanks or both. They were particularly useful against cavalry given the horses' natural dislike of their sound and smell, unless specifically trained to counter this. Other tactics were also used, for example the deployment of some of Antiochus III's elephants at the battle of Magnesia in 190 BC between units of his phalanx. Elephants were also sometimes deployed with a 'guard' of light troops to screen them from missile-equipped enemy troops given their vulnerability to being hamstrung, even when wearing banded leg armour. Elephants are also naturally nervous and were targeted in a variety of ways to make them panic. If this happened, they became as much a threat to their own side as their opponents. Some went to extreme lengths here, for example the use of squealing pigs by the Romans against Pyrrhus and the Megarans against Antigonus *Gonatus*. In the latter example, as an added flourish, the Greeks covered their pigs with tar and set them alight. The Romans also allegedly fielded 300 'anti-elephant wagons' against Pyrrhus at the battle of Asculum in 379 BC. These were of the larger four-wheel variety and featured poles fitted with mobile horizontal beams that were equipped with large blades, tridents and grapnels wrapped in pitch-daubed tow that was then set alight. They were initially successful in slowing an Epirote breakthrough of the Roman battle line led by his elephants but were then overwhelmed by light infantry.

When deployed and commanded well, elephants could be very effective. In one engagement, that of the Seleucid king Antiochus I against the Galatians in 273 BC in Asia Minor, a swift victory followed an elephant charge that broke the Galatian chariots and cavalry. It became known as the 'Elephant Victory'.

Next, camels were also a feature in some Hellenistic armies. These were usually the single-humped Arabian variety rather than their two-humped Bactrian counterpart. The latter were most often used as transport animals to carry baggage. Arabian camels were certainly a feature of Seleucid armies which made use of Bedouin camel riders, fielded in large numbers at the battle of Magnesia. Tactically they were utilised in a similar manner to cavalry, with the added advantage that horses were scared of their sound and smell in similar way to elephants.

Finally, scythed chariots were the ultimate classical world wonder weapon. Drawn by four armoured horses and featuring a single armoured driver, scythed chariots had razor-sharp metal blades attached to their wheel axle-ends, yoke and shaft, the latter projecting forward of the horses. Alexander first encountered them at the battle of Gaugamela where a charge of 200 opened the battle. They were later used in Hellenistic armies by the Seleucid Empire and the Pontic kingdom and were also deployed by the Galatians. Scythed chariots were more of a terror weapon than a real threat, usually failing. This happened at Gaugamela, and also at Magnesia when deployed by Antiochus III. On both occasions their presence was countered by light missile-armed troops. At Magnesia they were actually driven back into their own troops and contributed significantly to the Seleucid defeat.

The Thracians

The Thracians were a variety of tribes living in the north-western Balkans who were renowned for their martial prowess. They were often employed as mercenaries in the armies of the eastern Mediterranean and later Rome. From the 4th century BC, the Odrysians were the most powerful tribe, though the region came under Hellenistic control from the time of Alexander the Great. After his death in 323 BC the Successor general Lysimachus carved out a kingdom of his own here which lasted through to his death in 281

BC at the battle of Corupedium. The region was then the subject of Galatian raiding as they passed through on their way to Anatolia, with one group setting up the Kingdom of Tylis in the south-east of the region. There they remained, predating the surrounding area, until a newly resurgent Odrysian kingdom defeated them around 200 BC. The Odrysians then became the dominant Thracian tribe again, though in the early 1st century BC the region attracted the interest of the Romans for the first time as the Republic began to expand its influence in the eastern Mediterranean. Then in 72 BC Marcus Terentius Varro Lucullus became the first Roman leader to campaign against the Thracians, specifically the Getae group of tribes, in the context of the Third Mithridatic War. The Romans remained in the region, but in 62 BC a coalition of Scythians, Bastarnae, Getae, and Greek colonists defeated the Roman consul Gaius Antonius Hybrida at the battle of Histria. However, once Octavian became the final surviving warlord of the late republican civil wars, he determined to subjugate the entire Balkan Peninsula once and for all. As a pretext he used an incursion of the Bastarnae across the Danube to campaign there, putting Marcus Licinius Crassus in charge of the campaign. In 29 BC Crassus defeated the Bastarnae with the help of the Getic prince Rholes who became the dominant political force in the region. Then, in 16 BC the Sarmatians invaded Getic territory and were driven back by Roman troops. The Getae then became a Roman vassal state under the Thracian King Rhoemetalces I. Next, in AD 6 Augustus founded the province of Moesia, this incorporating much of the Thracian territory south of the Danube. The Getae Thracian tribes to the north of the river continued their own tribal autonomy outside the Roman Empire. Later, after an anti-Roman Revolt, any remaining Thracian territory south of the Danube was annexed into the new province of Thracia in AD 46 after the death of the last Thracian King Rhoemetalces III.

Lowland Thracian armies could field up to 40% of their total as mounted warriors, many of these equipped in a similar way to their Greek counterparts and fighting with short spears and javelins. Others were light cavalry skirmishers equipped with javelins and bows. However, it was the Thracian *peltastoi* who were most sought after as mercenaries, particularly when equipped with the *rhomphaia*, the two-handed cutting polearm.

The Huns

The Huns proved the most difficult opponent faced by the Dominate Roman military, ravaging large sections of both the eastern and western Empire in the later 4th and 5th centuries AD. Further, as they expanded from their central Asian homelands, they drove the various German and Gothic confederations to the north of the Rhine and Danube hard against, and then through, the Roman frontiers there.

A nomadic confederation of mounted tribesmen, they most likely originated from the eastern edge of the Altai Mountains and the Caspian Sea, in roughly the region of modern Kazakhstan. They are first mentioned in contemporary sources in AD 91 living in the region around the Caspian Sea, at that time simply being one of the many tribes of interest to the Empire there.

However, by the later 4th century AD the Hunnic westward migration became a major problem for the Romans, with, for example, their territories in Thrace and Syria overrun. This threat became existential under Attila who ruled the Hunnic confederation from AD 434 to AD 453 and who raided deep into the western and eastern Empires. He was finally defeated by the western *magister militum* Flavius Aetius at the battle of the Catalaunian Plains in AD 451. Then, after Attila's death in AD 453 his sons fought each other for supremacy, squandering their resources, with the empire Attila built finally falling apart by AD 469.

Hunnic armies, especially later when fighting the Dominate Empire, were conglomerates of Hunnic horsemen and groups of the various subject peoples they conquered. The latter included Alans, Goths, Franks, Burgundians and Thuringians. Hunnic warriors were largely light cavalry horsemen, with a very few (usually nobles) equipped with armour and lance as well as the bow.

Unlike many contemporaries, Hunnic light cavalry often fought at close quarters, also carrying short spears and swords. The Hunnic bow was of the powerful composite type and, at around 140cm long, large for its day.

The Sarmatians

The Sarmatians were a series of peoples of Iranian origin who migrated from the Central Asian steppe between the 6th and 4th century BC. They eventually settled in the region of modern southern European Russia and in the Balkans east of the Dacians and north the Danube. Closely related to the Scythians, they were noted for their high standards of horsemanship. By the early 4th century BC, the Sarmatians held control of most of the land between the Ural Mountains and the Don River. From there they crossed the Don, conquered the Scythians and replaced them as the dominant force in the Pontic Steppe. The Romans first encountered the Sarmatians when the latter invaded Moesia Inferior during Nero's reign in the 1st century AD. They then fought alongside the Dacians as allies when Trajan carried out his two campaigns of conquest there in the early 2nd century AD, and next were allies of the various German tribes fighting Rome during the Marcomannic Wars in the later 2nd century AD. By that time the Romans had begun to adopt Sarmatian equipment and tactics and they now also frequently recruited into the Roman military as auxiliaries. Their territory was finally overrun by the Huns when the latter passed through their lands in the AD 370s.

The principal Sarmatian tribes included the Siracae, Iazyges and Rhoxalani. The vast majority of troops in their armies were mounted lancers, these carrying a 3.5m *kontos* (lance). This was held two-handed, braced across the thighs, allowing them to charge to contact at breakneck speed, even against disciplined foot. Many were also armed with a bow. Those who wore armour were clad in coats of horn scales or chainmail, as depicted on the base of Trajan's Column.

The Armenians

Armenia was originally a satrapy of the Achaemenid Persian Empire. Only superficially affected by Alexander the Great's conquests, it became a semi-autonomous region within the sphere of influence of the Seleucid Empire. Then, after the defeat of the Seleucids at the battle of Magnesia in 188 BC, Artaxias I founded a dynasty there in his name, unifying its various territories and enlarging what became the Armenian kingdom. It then reached the zenith of its power during the reign of Tigranes the Great from 95 BC to 55 BC, briefly becoming the most powerful state in the Roman east, controlling both Mesopotamia and Syria as the Seleucid Empire began its final collapse. However, Tigranes made a fatal error in siding with Mithridates VI of Pontus in the Third Mithridatic War, earning the enmity of Rome. Defeated at the battle of Tigranocerta by Lucius Licinius Lucullus, he later fought and lost to Gnaeus Pompey, then finally submitting to Rome. From that time Armenia, sometimes independent and sometimes not, became a buffer between Rome in the west and the Parthians and later Sassanid Persians in the east.

The Armenian army was heavily influenced by the Parthians and later Sassanid Persians. It featured fully armoured cataphract cavalry, mounted bowmen and loose formation foot armed with short spears, javelins or bows. Tigranes also trained some foot to fight as a poor-quality Hellenistic phalanx, and others as imitation Roman legionaries.

Sarmatian chainmail armour and *draco* on the base of Trajan's Column.

(*above*)
The Arch of Septimius Severus in the *Forum Romanum*, built to celebrate his victories over the Parthians and their eastern allies.

(*right*)
Caracalla with a Parthian captive on the Arch of Septimius Severus in Rome.

The Parthians

On a one-for-one basis, the Parthians were the only real near-symmetrical threat faced by the republican and Principate Romans until the arrival of the Sassanid Persians. They were originally a Saka tribe called the Parni, its ruler Arsaces I giving the ruling dynasty its name. They invaded the region later called Parthia in northern Iran in the 3rd century BC. This bought them into conflict with the Graeco-Bactrian kingdom which they quickly defeated, then turning their attention to the Seleucid Empire and invading Media and Mesopotamia under Mithridates I in the mid-2nd century BC. From there they gradually fought their way westwards, playing a major role in bringing the Seleucid Empire down and eventually coming into conflict with the Romans and Armenians. In the first instance they resoundingly defeated the triumvir Crassus at the battle of Carrhae in 53 BC, and then raided the Roman east in 40 BC and 39 BC, before losing to a Roman force under Publius Ventidius Bassus at the battle of Cyrrhestica. Over the next 250 years the Romans and Parthians then regularly raided each other's territory. For the Romans Trajan and Septimius Severus were particularly successful, both sacking the Parthian capital at Ctesiphon, with Trajan also creating his short-lived provinces of Assyria and Mesopotamia out of Parthian territory in the early 1st century AD. The dynasty ended when Ardashir I overthrew Artabanus IV, the last Parthian king, and established the Sassanid Persian Empire in AD 224.

As detailed in Chapter 4, the Parthian army featured an interesting combination of extremes. These were fully armoured noble cataphract lancers and lightly armoured skirmishing horse archers famous for their 'Parthian Shot'. The ratio in Parthian armies was usually around 10% armoured shock cavalry, using the *kontos*, and 90% horse archers using a powerful composite bow.

The Sassanid Persians

The Sassanid Persian Empire was founded by its first King Ardashir I when, as the ruler of Parthian satrapy of Persis, he usurped against Artabanus V, the last Parthian king. The Sassanids proved to be a true symmetrical threat against the late Principate and Dominate Roman Empire in the east, and later the Byzantine Empire.

Once in power Ardashir consolidated central control of his newly won territory, defeating several early local rebellions. Then, to win the political backing of the old Parthian aristocracy, he invaded the Roman east in AD 230, penetrating deep into Roman-controlled Mesopotamia and Syria. He then demanded the Romans give back all their former Achaemenid Persian territories, including those in Anatolia. The Romans, caught off guard, tried to negotiate but this proved fruitless and so Emperor Severus Alexander launched a campaign against Ardashir I in AD 232, finally repulsing him. However, taking advantage of the chaos in Rome at the beginning of the 'Crisis of the 3rd Century', Ardashir attacked again in 238. After his death his son Shapur I continued the war through to AD 240, capturing several cities in Mesopotamia and

Syria, these including Carrhae and Nisibis.

After this conflict ended, Shapur I turned his attention to the east, conquering Bactria and the western part of the Kushan kingdom. War then resumed in the west when he was defeated by the Romans under the Gordian III at the battle of Rhesaina in AD 243. The Roman emperor then campaigned down the Euphrates valley, but was defeated by Shapur I at battle of Meshike in AD 244. Gordian III lost his life either in or after the battle and his successor Philip I the Arab signed a peace treaty with Shapur and withdrew. However, this was not to last and in AD 253 the war resumed when Shapur I used a Roman intervention in Armenia to again attack. He conquered Armenia, killed its king and then defeated a 60,000 strong Roman army at the battle of Barbalissos. This left Syria open to a full Sassanid invasion in which he sacked Antioch on the Orontes, the provincial capital. It was also at this time the Persians captured the fortified frontier-trading town of Dura-Europos.

Roman attempts to counterattack between AD 258 and AD 260 then ended in spectacular failure when Emperor Valerian was captured at Edessa by Shapur I. The Persians then advanced through Cappadocia deep into Anatolia but were finally defeated by a hastily gathered Roman force there. Shapur I was later ejected from Roman territory by their ally, King Odaenathus of Palmyra.

Next the Romans took the offensive in AD 283 under Emperor Carus, campaigning down the Euphrates valley and sacking the Sassanian capital Ctesiphon. Then in AD 296 Emperor Galerius was defeated at Narseh near Callinicium, but in AD 298 he again took the offensive and won successive victories. The Romans then sacked Ctesiphon again, after which they inflicted a severe peace treaty on the Persians. This caused unrest to spread throughout the Persian Empire, this finally supressed by Sharpur II when he became emperor in AD 309. In AD 337, part way through his long reign, he then attacked the eastern Roman Empire again which led to a series of drawn-out conflicts in which nine major battles were fought. These came to an end when Julian the Apostate was killed while withdrawing from a failed invasion of Persia. An

unfavourable peace for Rome followed, after which the Persians turned their attention to the east where they subdued the remaining part of the Kushan kingdom. After Shapur II's death in AD 379 the Persians consolidated their Empire, with a long peace with Rome only interrupted by two conflicts in AD 421 and AD 440. In this period, they also defeated repeated invasions by the Huns, though in AD 483 Sassanid Emperor Peroz I was killed when trying to drive out another Hunnic incursion. From that point, after the collapse of the Western Roman Empire, the Sassanid Persians became a principal opponent of the Byzantine Empire.

Sassanid Persian armies were largely comprised of mounted warriors. Line-of-battle cavalry were called Asvaran, these initially equipped in the same way as the lance-armed cataphracts of their Parthian forebears. Over time these changed into armoured mounted horse archers, they also carrying light spears and fine quality long swords. Again, as with their Parthian predecessors they also fielded large numbers of unarmoured skirmishing horse archers. To these they also added war elephants sourced in India, while most of their foot troops comprised a levy of poor-quality spearmen.

The Jewish Revolts

The Romans fought three Jewish rebellions in the 1st and 2nd centuries AD, each testing the Empire's military capability to its extreme limit. The First 'Great' Jewish Revolt broke out in AD 66. It originated with local protests against religious intolerance and then escalated into anti-taxations protests. Soon Roman citizens in Judaea were being attacked, with the Empire responding by plundering the Second Temple in Jerusalem and executing 6,000 Jewish captives. This prompted a full rebellion, with the Roman garrison being overrun, the Roman officials in Jerusalem then fleeing. The Roman commander in Syria, Cestius Gallus, then led an army featuring *legio XII Fulminata* and large numbers of auxiliary units into Judaea to put the rebellion down. However, this was ambushed and defeated by Jewish rebels at the battle of Beth Horon, with 6,000 Romans killed and the legionary *aquila* lost.

This event shocked the Roman world and

Emperor Nero responded by putting together a large army with four legions, auxiliary units and regional allied troops. He appointed soon-to-be Emperor Vespasian as its commander, the veteran of the Claudian conquests of Britain then appointing his son Titus (also a future emperor) as its commander. In AD 67 he invaded Galilee, in the first instance targeting the regional Jewish strongholds there. However, Vespasian soon returned to Rome when news of Nero's death reached him in AD 69 and it was Titus who finally besieged Jerusalem in AD 70. By this time the city was packed with thousands of rebels who had fled the Roman predations in Galilee. These were now deployed to defend the city's three impressive wall circuits. The first two were breached within the first three weeks of the siege. However, a stubborn stand prevented the Romans from breaking through Jerusalem's third and thickest wall, with it taking a further three months to finally force a breach. This resulted in a massacre of Jewish warriors and the burning of the Second Temple there, the latter's treasures carried to Rome where they formed the centrepiece of Titus's triumph (this recorded on his arch in the *Forum Romanum*). Following the fall of Jerusalem *legio X Fretensis* then carried out a regional mopping up operation, finally capturing the Jewish stronghold of Masada in AD 73/74.

The Second Jewish Revolt (the Kitos War) broke out in the context of Trajan's invasion of Parthia from AD 114. Here, the ever-restless emperor decided to tackle Rome's 'eastern question' head on as he sought more martial glory after his Dacian Wars. Some have argued that his motivations here were actually economic following his annexation of the key desert trading centre of Petra and creation of the province of Arabia Petraea, after which he built an extensive road network in the east called the *Via Traiana Nova* which stretched from Busra al-Sham (*Bostra*) in Syria to Aqaba (Aila) on the Red Sea coast. This meant that the only trading route to import spices and silk from India outside of Roman control was the Parthian port city of Charax Spasinu on the Persian Gulf. Capturing this would give the Roman's a monopoly in this lucrative trade.

As so often when the Romans campaigned in

(*opposite*)
The Arch of Titus in the *Forum Romanum*. It was built to celebrate Titus and his father Vespasian's defeat of the First 'Great' Jewish Revolt. The Arch of Septimius Severus is in view in the rear.

The enormous mole built
by the Romans as they
besieged Masada.
(Steve Tibble)

the east, Armenia to the south of the Caucasus Mountains was the first focus of their attention. Trajan had already shown an interest in the region when reports arrived saying that Sarmatians were arriving on the kingdom's northern borders in large numbers. The Romans feared this would turn into a flood of migrants who would destabilise their eastern provinces and resolved to use Armenia as a barrier. Trajan began planning the annexation of the kingdom, but the Parthian King Osroes I moved first, placing his nephew Exederes, the son of a favourite brother, on the Armenian throne. Trajan promptly declared war, keen to avoid the humiliation of being outmanoeuvred politically by the Parthians. This gave Osroes pause for thought, and he offered to remove Exederes and replace him with another nephew called Parthamasiris. Though Trajan rejected his offer, the Parthian king followed through his suggested plan anyway, hoping it would still placate the Romans. It didn't, and it is unclear why he expected Trajan to respond positively to yet another royal Parthian nephew being placed on the Armenian throne. By now all of the Roman plans were in place and Trajan invaded Armenia in late AD 114. He quickly defeated the Armenian forces sent to confront him, together with their Parthian allies, and then killed Parthamasiris before following through on his plan to annexe Armenia as a Roman province.

Next, in AD 115 Trajan then invaded northern Mesopotamia which he quickly overran, annexing this as another new province which he called Assyria. This secured Trajan's northern flank and rear, allowing him to campaign far down the Tigris and Euphrates valleys. Here he used these vast rivers to transport much of his force, including a large siege train. The latter allowed him to quickly capture and sack Ctesiphon, before next sailing further downriver all the way to the Persian Gulf where he famously bathed in the warm waters there. To mark his success, he then founded a third Roman province in the region that he called Mesopotamia, before following in the footsteps of Alexander the Great back to Babylon where he overwintered. Writing 250 years later, Eutropius (8.5) says that he then ordered a fleet to be built in the Red Sea with which he intended to 'lay waste' to the western coastline of India.

However, this was not to be. As ever with the Romans in the east, total victory proved elusive, and later in AD 115 major revolts broke out in the region. This included the Second Jewish Revolt in Judaea, which led to the Jewish populations in Aegyptus (especially in Alexandria), the twin senatorial province of Cyrenaica et Creta to its east, Cyprus, and also Assyria and Mesopotamia to rebel. The latter province was particularly badly hit given the large number of Jewish exiles and refugees living there following the Roman defeat of the First Jewish Revolt. Insurrections also broke out in the latter two new provinces among Parthian remnant populations where some of the wealthy former Hellenistic cities had been used to a large degree of autonomy under their former Parthian rulers. Soon Roman military resources were stretched to the limit.

The second revolt proved even more sanguineous than the first given its much wider geographic spread. It was so serious that it threatened to undo Rome's political settlement along the south-eastern shores of the Mediterranean. At first, with Trajan in Babylon, the rebels were able to massacre many Roman garrisons, officials and citizens across the region. The Romans, used to running their provinces with a light touch, always responded brutally against rebelling populations, and Trajan decided to make a specific example of the Jewish insurrectionists, slaughtering huge numbers of them. This was on such a scale that he was forced to repopulate areas now devoid of their original populations with Roman citizens to avoid good quality agricultural land falling out of use.

The rebellion was eventually put down by the Roman general Lusius Quietus whose *nomen*, in corrupted form, later gave the war its contemporary name as the Kitos War. As the conflict came to an end, he eventually chased down the Jewish leader Lukuas to Judaea where he then sentenced to death in absentia his two deputies, the brothers Julian and Pappus. They had taken refuge in the Judaean city of Lydda along with a huge number of surviving rebels and refugees. The Romans promptly put this under close siege, eventually capturing it after a vicious assault. Most of the captives were executed including the two brothers, bringing the rebellion to an end in AD 117.

However, it is the Third 'bar Kokhba' Jewish Revolt that proved the most problematic for Rome. This rebellion was named after its leader Simon bar Kokhba, a mysterious figure whose actual family name we may not know given bar Kokhba seems to be an epithet meaning 'son of a star' in Aramaic. This rebellion was even more serious than either of its predecessors given that, for the first time, the various Jewish communities in the region closely coordinated their campaigning against the Romans. Led by the charismatic bar Kokhba, who many declared was a heroic messiah who would restore a united Kingdom of Israel, the Romans were soon on the back foot, with many garrisons once more being put to the sword.

In its initial stages the bar Kokhba revolt was surprisingly successful, with one contemporary report saying it resulted in the destruction of an entire Roman legion. The rebels may also have actually recaptured the city of Jerusalem and were certainly able to secure much of the province of Judaea under their control given they eventually announced the actual creation of the Kingdom of Israel.

However, the Romans soon regrouped. Gathering resources from across the Empire, they deployed a massive army featuring six full legions, *vexillationes* from six others, and a large number of mounted and foot auxiliary units to settle matters with the Jewish rebels across the region once and for all. Once in theatre they adopted a scorched-earth strategy that ultimately extirpated most of the rebels, laying waste to much of the Judaea. In the final phase of the conflict bar Kokhba fled to his last surviving fortress, which was located at Betar, near modern day Battir. The Romans promptly besieged him there, capturing it after a lengthy siege. All inside perished, either in the final assault or in the ensuing massacre of those captured, excepting one lone rebel who escaped. Among the dead was bar Kokhba himself.

Roman punishment for Judaea and the Jewish rebels was particularly harsh, even by their own extreme standards when stamping out a revolt. Judean society had already been shattered by 70 years of on-off civil war, with a large proportion of the population killed, dead through starvation, enslaved or exiled (note the resettlement needed after the Second Jewish Revolt detailed above). Now Hadrian permanently changed the nature of the province, renaming it Syria Palaestina and turning Jerusalem into a pagan city that he renamed *Aelia Capitolina*. In so doing he set in train a process designed to deliberately erase Jewish history, executing many surviving Jewish religious leaders and scholars, and banning the Torah and the use of the Jewish calendar. Any surviving Jews were banned from living within sight of newly styled *Aelia Capitolina*, with Eusebius quoting Ariston of Pella in describing the impact of this (*Ecclesiastical History*, 4.6.4):

> Thus when the city came to be bereft of the nation of the Jews, and its ancient inhabitants had completely perished, it was colonised by foreigners, and the Roman city which afterwards arose changed its name, and in honour of the reigning Emperor Aelius Hadrian was called Aelia.
>
> Given the severe dislocation caused by the three failed Jewish Revolts, only small Jewish communities remained in former Judaea, and the demography of the renamed province now shifted in favour of the non-Jewish population. From this point the remaining centres of Jewish cultural and religious life were all to be found outside of the province, particularly in Babylonia, with other minor communities scattered around the Mediterranean.

The majority of Jewish troops fighting in the revolts were irregular infantry deployed in loose formation. Most were unarmoured excepting a shield when these were available, armed with short spears, javelins and side arms including swords and long curved knives. However, in each revolt the rebels made use of captured Roman equipment, including artillery. Though they did stand up to the Romans in open battle, they preferred ambushes and guerrilla campaigns. Jewish troops proved particularly difficult for the Romans to defeat in sieges where they defended fanatically, on two occasions choosing suicide rather than surrender.

The Blemmye

The Blemmye were a nomadic tribal people whose kingdom existed from around 600 BC through to the 6th century AD in Nubia. They proved a particular nuisance to Roman Egypt, often raiding the upper Nile region of the province and later diocese.

As detailed in Chapter 3, although they were not a particularly sophisticated opponent in terms of their tactics and technology, the size of their armies often proved problematic for *legio II Traiana Fortis* deployed there. The Romans countered the threat with a series of fortifications and watchtowers built to protect the rich agricultural land in the Nile Valley.

Most Blemmye and Nobatae warriors were unarmoured bowmen who often rode mules and donkeys, making their armies highly manoeuvrable. They also occasionally used war elephants of the African forest variety.

(*opposite*)
Relief images of the Sassanid Persian kings Shapur II and either Shapur III or Ardashir III, Taq-e Bostan, Iran. Dated to around AD 383.
(Livius.org/Jona Lendering)

Conclusion

In this extensive review of the Roman military establishment in both Republic and Empire we have seen Roman warriors of all kinds up close and personal. In the first instance they were brutally efficient soldiers, imbued for much of the history of the Republic and Empire with a deep sense of martial valor.

Always ready to serve the Republic and later emperor across the whole geographical diversity of Roman controlled territory, the legionaries and later auxiliaries were the tip of the Roman military spear during the early years of republican and imperial expansion, and later the bulwark upon which the various peoples attacking Roman territory crashed, they always eager to denude the later Empire of its wealth and stability. The image of these Roman warriors has come down to us through the epigraphic and sculptural record, and more recently through archaeological data, to become a fixed point in the modern world's appreciation of the world of Rome. A prime example is the classic Principate legionary wearing his *lorica segmentata*, 'imperial' Gallic helmet, *scutum*, and with *gladius* in hand.

Yet we have also seen in this book that the Roman legionaries and later *auxilia* were so much more. In the first instance we have come to appreciate their human face, looking at how they were recruited, their terms of service, what they ate, how they campaigned, and how they fought. We have also seen the legionaries and *auxilia* carrying out a myriad of non-conflict related tasks, always the first port of call for the Roman state when called on to perform a duty. Such tasks, as I have detailed, ranged from administering the Empire, policing it both without and within, being a fire fighter, helping run the games, running agriculture and industry, and engineering and construction. In this latter role we see across the entirety of the later Republic and Empire the fruits of the skill of the Roman soldiery as engineers, for example with the many roads and buildings which still exist today.

Finally, we have considered the legionaries and later *auxilia* as part of the wider Roman republican and imperial military system, often fighting alongside naval *milites*, mercenaries and allies. Further, as we have seen, their martial spirit and expertise was to far outlast the decline of the Empire in the west, if only in the form of Byzantine *skutatoi*, and our appreciation of the Roman world to this very day. The Roman military machine was often preeminent in its own time, and still defines the Roman Republic and empire in our modern world today.

(*opposite*)
A Principate legionary practising to receive a shock cavalry attack. This became increasingly important after the Romans fought the Sarmatians and later mounted Goths. (Graham Sumner)

Acknowledgements

I would like to thank those who have helped make this appreciation of the Roman military possible. Firstly, as always, Professor Andrew Lambert of the War Studies Department at KCL, Dr Andrew Gardner at UCL's Institute of Archaeology and Dr Steve Willis at the University of Kent. All continue to encourage my research on the Roman military. Next, my publisher Ruth Sheppard at Casemate. Also, Professor Sir Barry Cunliffe of the School of Archaeology at Oxford University, and Professor Martin Millett at the Faculty of Classics, Cambridge University. Next, my patient proofreader and lovely wife Sara, and my dad John Elliott and friend Francis Tusa, both companions in my various escapades to research this book. As with all of my literary work, all have contributed greatly and freely, enabling this work on the Romans at war to reach fruition. Finally, I would like to thank my family, especially my tolerant wife Sara once again and children Alex (also a student of military history) and Lizzie.

Thank you all.
Dr Simon Elliott
April 2020

Select Bibliography

Ancient Sources

Apuleius, *The Golden Ass*, 2008. Walsh, P. G., Oxford: Oxford World Classics.

Marcus Aurelius, *Meditations*, 1964. Staniforth, M., London: Penguin.

Julius Caesar, *The Conquest of Gaul*, 1951. Handford, S. A., London: Penguin.

Marcus Cato, *De Agri Cultura*, 1934. Ash, H. B. and Hooper, W. D., Harvard: Loeb Classical Library.

Cassius Dio, *Roman History*, 1925. Cary, E., Harvard: Loeb Classical Library.

Diodorus Siculus, *Library of History*, Volume 3, 1939. Oldfather, C. H., Harvard: Loeb Classical Library.

Eusebius, *Ecclesiastical History: Complete and Unabridged*, 2011. Crusé, C. F., Seaside, Oregon: Merchant Books.

Flavius Eutropius, *Historiae Romanae Breviarium*, 1993. Bird, H. W., Liverpool: Liverpool University Press.

Quintus Horatius Flaccus (Horace), *The Complete 'Odes' and 'Epodes'*, 2008. West, D., Oxford: Oxford Paperbacks.

Gaius, *Institutiones*, 1946. De Zulueta, F., Oxford: Oxford University Press.

Historia Augusta, Life of Pertinax, 1921. Maggie, D., Harvard: Loeb Classical Library.

Sextus Julius Frontinus, *Strategemata*, 1969. Bennett, C. E., Portsmouth, New Hampshire: Heinemann.

Herodian, *History of the Roman Empire*, 1989. Whittaker, C. R., Harvard: Loeb Classical Library.

Homer, *The Iliad*, 1950. Rieu, E.V., London: Penguin.

Justinian, *The Digest of Justinian*, 1997. Watson, A., Philadelphia: University of Pennsylvania.

Livy, *The History of Rome*, 1989. Foster, B. O., Cambridge, MA: Harvard University Press/Loeb Classical Library.

Pausanias, *Guide Greece: Central Greece*, 1979. Levi, P., London: Penguin.

Pliny the Elder, *Natural History*, 1940. Rackham, H., Harvard: Harvard University Press.

Pliny the Younger, *Epistularum Libri Decem*, 1963. Mynors, R. A. B., Oxford: Oxford Classical Texts – Clarendon Press.

Plutarch, *Lives of the Noble Greeks and Romans*, 2013. Clough, A. H., Oxford. Benediction Classics.

Polybius, *The Rise of the Roman Empire*, 1979. Scott-Kilvert, I., London: Penguin.

Quintilian, *Institutes of Oratory*, 2015. Selby Watson, J., Scotts Valley, California: Create Space Independent Publishing Platform.

Suetonius, *The Twelve Caesars*, 1957. Graves, R., London: Penguin.

Cornelius Tacitus, *The Agricola*, 1970. Mattingly, H., London: Penguin.

Cornelius Tacitus, *The Annals*, 2003. Grant, M., London: Penguin.

Cornelius Tacitus, *The Histories*, 2008. Fyfe, W. H., Oxford: Oxford Paperbacks.

Strabo, *The Geography,* 2014. Roler, D. W., Cambridge: Cambridge University Press.

Aurelius Victor, *De Caesaribus*, 1994. Bird, H. W., Liverpool: Liverpool University Press.

Zosimus, *New History,* 1982. Ridley, R.T., Leiden: Brill.

Modern Sources

Avery, A. 2007. *The Story of York*. Pickering: Blackthorn Press.

Barker, P. 1981. *The Armies and Enemies of Imperial Rome*. Cambridge: Wargames Research Group.

de la Bédoyère, G. 2017. *Praetorian: The Rise and Fall of Rome's Imperial Bodyguard*. New Haven: Yale University Press.

de la Bédoyère, G. 2017. The Emperors' Fatal Servants. *History Today,* March 2017, Issue, 58–62.

Bentley, P. 1984. A Recently Identified Valley in the City. *London Archaeologist*, V.5 Number 1, 13–16.

Bidwell, P. 2007. *Roman Forts in Britain*. Stroud: Tempus.

Birley, A. R. 1981. *The Fasti of Roman Britain*. Oxford: Clarendon Press.

Birley, A. R. 1993. *Marcus Aurelius: A Biography.* London: Routledge.

Birley, A. R. 1999. *Septimius Severus: The African Emperor*. London: Routledge.

Birley, A. R. 2005. *The Roman Government of Britain*. Oxford: Oxford University Press.

Birley, A. R. 2007. The Frontier Zone in Britain: Hadrian to Caracalla. In: de Blois, L. and Lo Cascio, E. eds. *The Impact of the Roman Army (200 BC–AD 476).* Leiden: Brill, 355–370.

Bishop, M. C. 2016. *The Gladius*. Oxford: Osprey Publishing Ltd.

Bishop, M. C. *Lucius Verus and the Roman Defence of the East*. Barnsley: Pen & Sword.

Bonner, S. 2014 *Education in Ancient Rome*. London: Routledge.

Bradley, K. 1998. *Slavery and Society at Rome*. Cambridge: Cambridge University Press.

Breeze, D. J. 2000. *Roman Scotland*. London: Batsford Ltd/ Historic Scotland.

Burgess, R. W. 1993. Principes cum Tyrannis: Two Studies on the Kaisergeschichte and Its Tradition. *The Classical Quarterly*, V.43, 491–500.

Connolly, P. 1988. *Greece and Rome at War*. London: Macdonald & Co (Publishers) Ltd.

Cornell, T. J. 1993. The End of Roman Imperial Expansion. In: Rich, J. and Shipley, G. eds. *War and Society in the Roman World*. London: Routledge, 139–170.

Cornell, T. J. and Matthews, J. 1982. *Atlas of the Roman World*. Oxford: Phaidon Press Ltd.

Cowan, R. 2002. *Aspects of the Roman Field Army: The Praetorian Guard, Legio II Parthica and legionary vexillations – PhD Thesis*. Unpublished: University of Glasgow.

Cowan, R. 2003a. *Roman Legionary, 58 BC–AD 69*. Oxford: Osprey Publishing.

Cowan, R. 2003b. *Imperial Roman Legionary, AD 16–284*. Oxford: Osprey Publishing.

Cowan, R. 2007. *Roman Battle Tactics 109 BC–AD 313*. Oxford: Osprey Publishing.

Cowan, R. 2015. *Roman Legionary AD 284–337*. Oxford: Osprey Publishing.

Cunliffe, B. 1988. *Greeks, Romans and Barbarians. Spheres of Interaction*. London: Batsford Ltd.

D'Amato, R. and Sumner, G. 2009. *Arms and Armour of the Imperial Roman Soldier*. Barnsley: Frontline Books.

D'Amato, R. 2009. *Imperial Roman Naval Forces 31 BC–AD 500*. Oxford: Osprey Publishing.

D'Amato, R. 2016. *Roman Army Units in the Western Provinces* (1). Oxford: Osprey Publishing.

D'Amato, R. 2018. *Roman Heavy Cavalry* (1). Oxford: Osprey Publishing.

Elliott, P. 2014. *Legions in Crisis*. Stroud: Fonthill Media ltd.

Elliott, S. 2016. *Sea Eagles of Empire: The Classis Britannica and the Battles for Britain*. Stroud: The History Press.

Elliott, S. 2017. *Empire State: How the Roman Military Built an Empire*. Oxford: Oxbow Books.

Elliott, S. 2018. *Septimius Severus in Scotland: The Northern Campaigns of the First Hammer of the Scots*. Barnsley: Greenhill Books.

Elliott, S. 2018. *Roman Legionaries*. Oxford: Casemate Publishers.

Elliott, S. 2019. *Julius Caesar: Rome's Greatest Warlord*. Oxford: Casemate Publishers.

Ellis Jones, J. 2012. *The Maritime Landscape of Roman Britain*. Oxford: BAR/Archaeological and Historical Associates Ltd.

Erdkamp, P. ed. 2013. *The Cambridge Companion to Ancient Rome*. Cambridge: Cambridge University Press.

Frere, S. 1974. *Britannia: A History of Roman Britain* (3rd edn). London: Routledge.

Golvin, J. C. 2003. *Ancient Cities Brought to Life*. Ludlow: Thalamus Publishing.

Goldsworthy, A. 2000. *Roman Warfare*. London: Cassell.

Goldsworthy, A. 2003. *The Complete Roman Army*. London: Thames and Hudson.

Graafstaal, E. 2018. What Happened in the Summer of AD 122. Hadrian on the British Frontier Archaeology, Epigraphy and Historical Agency. *Britannia*, V.48, 76–111.

Heather, P. 2009. *Empires and Barbarians*. New York: Macmillan.

Heather, P. 2018. *Rome Resurgent*. Oxford. Oxford University Press.

Hekster, O. 2002. *Commodus: An Emperor at the Crossroads*. Leiden: Brill.

Henig, M. The victory gem from Lullingstone Roman villa. *Journal of the British Archaeological Association,* 160 (2007), 1–7.

Herrmann-Otto, Elizabeth. 2013. Slaves and Freedmen. In: Erdkamp, P. eds. *The Cambridge Companion to Ancient Rome*. Cambridge: Cambridge University Press, 60–76.

Hingley, R. 1982. Roman Britain: The structure of Roman imperialism and the consequences of imperialism on the development of a peripheral province. In: Miles, D. ed. *The Romano-British Countryside: Studies in Rural Settlement and Economy*. Oxford: BAR/Archaeological and Historical Associates Ltd, 17–52.

Hingley, R. 2005. *Globalizing Roman Culture – Unity, Diversity and Empire*. London: Routledge.

Hingley, R. 2018. *Londinium: A Biography*. London: Bloomsbury Academic.

Holland, T. 2019. *Dominion*. London: Little, Brown.

Hornblower, S. and Spawforth, A. 1996. *The Oxford Classical Dictionary*. Oxford: Oxford University Press.

James, S. 2011. *Rome and the Sword*. London: Thames and Hudson.

Jones, B. and Mattingly, D. 1990. *An Atlas of Roman Britain*. Oxford: Oxbow Books.

Kamm, A. 2011. *The Last Frontier: The Roman Invasions of Scotland*. Glasgow: Tempus.

Kean, R. M. and Frey, O. 2005. *The Complete Chronicle of the Emperors of Rome*. Ludlow: Thalamus Publishing.

Keppie, L. 2015. *The Legacy of Rome: Scotland's Roman Remains*. Edinburgh: Berlin.

Kiley, K. F. 2012. *The Uniforms of the Roman World*. Wigston: Lorenz Books.

Kolb, A. 2001. The Cursus Publicus. In: Adams, C. and Laurence, R. eds. *Travel and Geography in the Roman Empire*. London: Routledge, 95–106.

Kulikowski, M. 2016. *Imperial Triumph: The Roman World from Hadrian to Constantine*. London: Profile Books.

Lambert, M. 2010. *Christians and Pagans*. New Haven: Yale University Press.

Le Bohec, Y. 2000. *The Imperial Roman Army*. London: Routledge.

Levick, B. 2007. *Julia Domna: Syrian Empress*. London: Routledge.

Matyszak, P. 2009. *Roman Conquests: Macedonia and Greece*. Barnsley: Pen & Sword.

Mattingly, D. 2006. *An Imperial Possession, Britain in the Roman Empire*. London: Penguin.

Mattingly, D. 2011. *Imperialism, Power and Identity – Experiencing the Roman Empire*. Princeton: Princeton University Press.

McHugh, J. S. 2015. *Commodus: God and Gladiator*. Barnsley: Pen & Sword.

McLynn, F. 2010. *Marcus Aurelius: Warrior, Philosopher, Emperor*. New York: Vintage.

Millett, M. 1990a. *The Romanization of Britain*. Cambridge: Cambridge University Press.

Millett, M. 1995. *Roman Britain*. London: Batsford.

Moorhead, S. and Stuttard, D. 2012. *The Romans Who Shaped Britain*. London: Thames and Hudson.

Mouritsen, H. 2015. *The Freedmen of the Roman World*. Cambridge. Cambridge University Press.

Oleson, J. P. 2009. *The Oxford Handbook of Engineering and Technology in the Classical World*. Oxford: Oxford University Press.

Ottaway, P. 2013. *Roman Yorkshire*. Pickering: Blackthorn Press.

Parfitt, K. 2013. Folkestone During the Roman Period. In: Coulson, I. ed. Folkestone to 1500, *A Town Unearthed*. Canterbury: Canterbury Archaeological Trust, 31–54.

Parker, A. 2019. *The Archaeology of Roman York*. Stroud: Amberley Books.

Parker, P. 2009. *The Empire Stops Here*. London: Jonathan Cape.

Pausche, D. 2009. Unreliable Narration. *Historia Augusta,* V. 8, 115–135.

Perring, D. 2017. London's Hadrianic War. *Britannia*, V.41, 127–147.

Pitassi, M. 2012. *The Roman Navy*. Barnsley: Seaforth.

Pollard, N. and Berry, J. 2012. *The Complete Roman Legions*. London: Thames & Hudson.

Potter, D. 2004. *The Roman Empire at Bay, AD 180–395*. London: Routledge.

Potter, D. 2009. *Rome in the Ancient World: From Romulus to Justinian*. London: Thames & Hudson.

Reid, R. 2016. Bullets, Ballistas and Burnswark: A Roman Assault on a Hillfort in Scotland. *Current Archaeology,* Issue 316, V.27, 20–26.

Rodgers, N. and Dodge, H. 2009. *The History and Conquests of Ancient Rome*. London: Hermes House.

Rubin, Z. 1980. *Civil-War Propaganda and Historiography*. Leuven: Peeters.

Salway, P. 1981. *Roman Britain*. Oxford: Oxford University Press.

Scarre, C. 1995. *The Penguin Historical Atlas of Ancient Rome*. London: Penguin.

Scarre, C. 1995. *Chronicle of the Roman Emperors: The Reign-by-Reign Record of the Rulers of Imperial Rome.* London: Thames and Hudson.

Schmitz, M. and Sumner, G. *Roman Conquests: The Danube Frontier*. Barnsley: Pen & Sword.

Southern, P. 2001. *The Roman Empire from Severus to Constantine*. London: Routledge.

Southern, P. 2013. *Roman Britain*. Stroud: Amberley Publishing.

Starr, C. G. 1941. *The Roman Imperial Navy 31 BC–AD 324*. New York: Cornell University Press.

Toner, J. 2015. *The Day Commodus Killed a Rhino: Understanding the Roman Games*. Baltimore: John Hopkins University Press.

Wilcox, P. 1986. *Rome's Enemies (3): Parthians and Sassanid Persians*. Oxford: Osprey Publishing.

Wilkes, J. J. 2005. Provinces and Frontiers. In: Bowman. A. K., Garnsey, P. and Cameron, A. eds. *The Cambridge Ancient History Vol. XII, The Crisis of Empire, AD 193–337*. Cambridge: Cambridge University Press, 212–268.

Windrow, M. and McBride, A. 1996. *Imperial Rome at War*. Hong Kong: Concord Publications.

Index

Cerialis, Quintus Petillius, governor, 216, 241
Chauci, 202, 205, 256
Chester, 87, 165
Cirencester, 87
cives Romani, 2
civitas capital, 18, 87
Classis Britannica, 10–11, 14, 87, 153–157, 164, 175, 177, 207, 210, 220, 239
Classis Flavia Moesica, 98, 153, 204
Classis Flavia Pannonica, 198, 153, 203
Classis Germanica, 95, 153, 203
Classis Misenensis, 153, 155, 234
Claudian invasion, 194–200
Claudius, emperor, 10, 13, 65, 87, 99, 104, 115, 154, 156, 158, 165, 187, 193, 196, 198, 200
Cloaca Maxima, 115
cohors IV Gallorum, 151
cohortes urbanae, 115
coloniae, 10, 18, 134, 205
Column of Marcus Aurelius, 140–142, 145, 199–202, 204, 255
Comitatenses, 15–16, 18, 163–164, 168–174, 226
comitatius praesentalis, 18, 168
Commodus, emperor, 12, 13, 16, 85, 111, 189, 206, 220, 237
Conference of Lucca, 8
Consilium Principis, 18, 84
constitutio Antoniniana, 98
contos, 19, 148, 149, 202
Corbridge, 87, 207
Corsica, 5, 36, 98
Costoboci, 203
Crisis of the Third Century, 3, 14, 19, 83, 85, 100, 117, 163, 171, 175, 279
Ctesiphon, 206, 279, 282

cuneus, 19, 138
cura annonae, 19, 38
Curial class, 2, 19
cursus honorum, 3, 83, 167
Cyrenaica, 5, 104

Dacia, 12, 19, 85, 97–98, 103, 114, 140, 155, 173, 201, 203–205, 222, 255, 260, 264, 267, 281
Danube, River, 85–86, 95, 97, 120, 122, 163, 168–169, 187, 201–206, 221–222, 256, 260, 275–276
Dere Street, 87, 90, 207, 210, 245
Diocletian, emperor, 3, 14, 19, 21, 83, 87, 97–98, 117, 120, 131, 163–167, 171
Diocletianic reformation, 119
Dominate, 1, 3, 14, 19, 55, 62, 83, 85, 98, 117–118, 120, 122, 161–168
Domitian, emperor, 85, 114
Domna, Julia, 84, 111, 206
Dura-Europos, 142, 279

Ebro, River, 74
Elbe, River, 256
Epirus, 5, 36, 99
Equestrian class, 2
equites cataphractarii, 19, 149, 150
equites clibanarii, 19, 175
equites contariorum, 19, 149, 166
equites dalmatae, 19, 175
equites illyriciani, 19, 148
equites mauri, 19, 175
equites sagittarii, 19, 148, 175
equites scutarii, 19, 175
equites singulares Augusti, 19, 157, 168

equites, 15, 19, 53, 56, 148, 102, 148, 175
evocatii Augusti, 19, 157
Exe, River, 216
Exeter, 87, 216
expeditio felicissima Britannica, 163, 206
expeditio Sarmatica, 205

fabricae, 19, 94, 173, 226
falx, 19, 139, 264
fiscus, 19, 84, 134, 137, 140, 159, 204, 207
foederates, 20, 122, 164, 169, 172
Forum Romanum, 20, 27, 46, 105–106, 110, 114, 115, 159, 167, 223, 278, 281
Fosse Way, 87, 216
Furtius, king, 205

Gallia Lugdunensis, 94, 219
Gallic Empire, 14, 117
Garamantes tribe, 104, 228
Germania Inferior, 94–95, 154, 165, 205, 221, 222
Germania Superior, 94–95, 202, 205, 222, 225
gladius Hispaniensis, 20, 58, 140, 257
Gracchus, Tiberius Sempronius, 38
Grampians, 11, 149, 251
greave, 52, 138
Greece, 36, 45–47, 60, 66–67, 78, 86, 98, 104, 203, 213
guerilla warfare, 253

Hadrian, emperor, 12–13, 83, 85, 99, 102–104, 115, 201, 206, 234, 284
Hadrian's Wall, 12–13, 83,